アドベンチャー

日本語 1

Adventures in Japanese 1
Textbook

Hiromi Peterson and Naomi Omizo

Illustrated by Michael Muronaka & Emiko Kaylor

Cheng & Tsui Company

2004 Edition

10 09 08 07 06 05 04 03   8 7 6 5 4 3 2 1

Published by

Cheng & Tsui Company
25 West Street
Boston, MA 02111-1213 USA
Fax (617) 426-3669
www.cheng-tsui.com
"Bringing Asia to the World"™

Printed in the U.S.A.

Adventures in Japanese Vol. 1 Textbook, 2004 Edition:
ISBN 0-88727-420-X (Paperback)
ISBN 0-88727-421-8 (Hardcover)

Companion textbooks, workbooks, hiragana/katakana workbooks, flashcards, and audio products
for this and other levels of the *Adventures in Japanese* series
are also available from the publisher.

ADVENTURES IN JAPANESE 1

CONTENTS

FOREWORD

As a recent author of an elementary Japanese textbook for college students, I am keenly aware of the difficulty of writing an elementary textbook. It is time-consuming, energy-consuming and creativity-consuming. Writing an elementary Japanese textbook for high school students must be much harder than writing the counterpart for college students, because it involves a host of age-adequate considerations peculiar to high school students.

Adventures in Japanese has been prepared by highly experienced and knowledgeable high school teachers of Japanese, Hiromi Peterson and Naomi Omizo, who know exactly what is teachable/learnable and what is not teachable/learnable for high school students. They know how to sustain the students' interest in the Japanese language and its culture by employing so many age-adequate, intriguing activities with a lot of fun illustrations. The grammar explanations and culture notes provide accurate and succinct pieces of information, and each communicative activity is well designed to assist the students in acquiring actual skills to use grammar and vocabulary in context. In short, *Adventures in Japanese* is an up-to-date high school Japanese textbook conceived and designed in a proficiency-based approach. It comes with a teacher's manual which is intended to help a novice high school teacher of Japanese teach Japanese in a pedagogically correct manner from day one.

I am pleased that at long last we have a high school textbook that is both learnable and teachable, and very importantly, enjoyable. I endorse *Adventures in Japanese* wholeheartedly.

Seiichi Makino
Professor of Japanese and Linguistics
Department of East Asian Studies
Princeton University

TO STUDENTS:

What is an ideal Japanese language high school textbook? Is it one from which you can enjoy learning Japanese? Is it one which encourages you to communicate successfully in the language? Is it one which opens doors for you to experience Japan, its people and its culture?

As teachers of Japanese, we have tried to design a text from which you will have fun learning, and one which will encourage you to continue your study of Japanese, a truly exciting and dynamic language!

While keeping your interests foremost in our minds, we have also incorporated the overall goals of our Japanese language curriculum into the writing of our text. These goals are:

1. to create a strong foundation of the Japanese language through the development of the four language skills: speaking, listening, reading and writing.
2. to strengthen, in particular, students' conversational skills.
3. to deepen students' understanding of the Japanese people and culture through the study of the language and the many aspects of Japanese culture.
4. to encourage a rediscovery of the students' own language and culture through the study of Japanese language and culture.
5. to encourage the growth of culturally sensitive, globally aware, responsible world citizens.

More concretely, these are areas which you can look forward to learning as you progress through Volume I of this textbook series.

Topics

Topics which appeal to students such as yourselves were selected. Situations which you are likely to encounter in your daily lives are used in this text. By the time you complete this text, you will have learned how to introduce yourself and others, identify and locate things, discuss your daily activities, describe things and people, talk about your family and your home, discuss school (subjects, grades, extra-curricular activities, friends and teachers), express your likes and dislikes as well as your strengths and weaknesses, speak about the highlights of your birthday, describe your physical ailments, and much more!

Tasks

Each lesson starts with two or three tasks which are the goals for the lesson. You are expected to converse in Japanese with another person in each of the situations. At the end of the semester, you will have an oral proficiency interview with your teacher based on these tasks.

Vocabulary

Vocabulary was also selected carefully. Basic vocabulary and vocabulary essential to discussing the topics listed above are taught. Many are vocabulary words which students in our previous classes have found important to know and have enjoyed using. Traditional Japanese expressions, i.e., "*Doomo sumimasen*" as well as those less commonly found in traditional basic texts but frequently used in daily Japanese conversations, i.e., "*Ganbatte!*" abound in this text. The optional vocabulary corner gives you additional vocabulary which you may want to use.

Grammar

We have organized the introduction of grammatical structures so that you will be able to systematically build from the very basic to the more complex. We have also made an extra effort to use previously learned structures throughout the text to provide opportunities for you to review them. On completing this text, you will have the grammatical capability of: 1) describing actions and things affirmatively and negatively in the present, future and past tenses; 2) ask and respond appropriately to questions; 3) form simple compound sentences; 4) make suggestions; 5) extend, accept, and decline invitations to do things; 6) make requests; 7) ask for and grant permission to do things; 8) express your wants and preferences; 9) discuss your plans; 10) use the complicated Japanese system of verbs of giving and receiving at a basic level, and much more! Finally, we have tried to avoid using complicated grammatical terminology and have kept our explanations simple.

Writing

At the end of level one, you will have learned to write and correctly use *hiragana* and *katakana*, two of the basic Japanese syllabaries. Your text provides romanization (English spellings of Japanese words) until Lesson 4. Thereafter, it is assumed that you will be able to read *hiragana*. *Katakana* is introduced after Lesson 8. Romanization is provided for *katakana* up to Lesson 10. In addition to *hiragana* and *katakana*, you will learn to write a few *kanji* (Chinese characters)! You will be expected to write the characters 月 (month) and 日 (day) when writing dates. You will also learn other *kanji* (1 ~ 10 and days of the week).

Culture

Culture cannot be detached from the teaching of language. We have thus included many cultural explanations. Lessons in culture can also be drawn from many of the illustrations. Your teacher will surely also share a wealth of other cultural anecdotes to enhance your understanding of the Japanese people. The Japanese Culture Corner gives you a chance to compare your culture and Japanese culture. You are encouraged to find answers by checking in books, talking to friends, or using the Internet.

Fun Corner

Japanese culture includes many crafts and games. This text introduces *origami* (a balloon, a box, a crane), songs (*The Elephant, Rain*), the making of rice balls and *mochi*, games (*karuta, gomokunarabe*), tongue twisters, and a Japanese folk tale (*Rolling Musubi*). Have fun!

Review Questions

After every even-numbered lesson, there is a list of about 30 commonly asked questions related to the topics covered. Ask your partner these questions in Japanese and your partner should answer you without looking at the textbook. Take turns. Pay attention to speed, intonation and pronunciation. This part is included in the review tape for listening practice. You may practice answering using the tape.

It is our hope that upon completing this volume, you will be able to communicate successfully at a very basic level, orally and in written form.

One piece of advice from your teachers: the key to success in the early years of foreign language study is frequent and regular exposure to the language. Take advantage of class time with your teacher, use your lab time effectively, and keep up with your work. Learn your material well, don't hesitate to try it out, and most of all, enjoy! And, as the Japanese say, "*Ganbatte!*"

ACKNOWLEDGMENTS

Adventures in Japanese was developed thanks to the efforts and contributions of many people at Punahou School and beyond. We gratefully express our appreciation to all who contributed in any way, even if we may have failed to mention them below.

First and foremost, a warm thanks to all of our students who have contributed directly and indirectly to the development of the text. They have provided us with a purpose, motivated us, taught us, given us ideas and suggestions, and encouraged us in many ways.

We acknowledge Professor Seiichi Makino of Princeton University, who has written the foreword, conducted workshops for us and offered us much support and encouragement throughout the project. We thank Professor Masako Himeno of the University of the Air in Japan for her guidance over many portions of the text and for her valuable suggestions and support. We express our gratitude to our illustrators, former Punahou student Michael Muronaka, former colleague Emiko Kaylor, and former student Mark Bailey. Our thanks are extended to present and former Japanese language colleagues at Punahou School who contributed to the writing of the text, to the creation of supplementary materials, or suggestions for improving the text: Junko Ady, Linda Fujikawa, Elaine Higuchi, Emiko Kaylor, Carin Lim, Emiko Lyovin, Naomi Okada, Carol Shimokawa, Michiko Sprester, Misako Steverson and Hiroko Vink-Kazama. We also acknowledge Janice Murabayashi, a former Social Studies colleague, for writing the questions on Japanese culture and Kathy Boswell, a former English colleague, for naming our text. Our gratitude is also extended to Miyoko Kamikawa, who assisted with the translation and interpretation of the *karuta* cards. We thank Wes Peterson for generously sharing his technological expertise and support throughout the project.

We also thank Carol Loose, Linda Palko, Martha Lanzas, and the staff at the Punahou Visual Production Center for their years of assistance with the compilation of the text.

We also recognize Mike Dahlquist, Celia Calvo and the staff at the Punahou ITV (Instructional Television) for their help in the production of many of the preliminary audio materials. We also thank the management and staff at Radio KZOO for the use of their studios and their assistance in the production of the final editions of the tape. In particular, we express our gratitude to Sharon Sakamoto and Harry Kubo at KZOO and Janet Irie and Daniel Hishikawa for production of the tapes. We extend our thanks to Mr. Takuroo Ichikawa for the use of the tape of his musical presentation. Our appreciation is also extended to faculty member Junko Ady for sharing her vocal talents for the songs on tape and to Amy Mitsuda, Music Department Chairperson at Punahou, for her piano accompaniment.

We thank all of the administrators at Punahou School for their support of our textbook effort.

Finally, we express our appreciation to our families for their unwavering support of our efforts in the development of *Adventures in Japanese*.

Hiromi Peterson and Naomi Hirano-Omizo

REFERENCES

Hello Japan. Tokyo: メイクフレンズ・フォー・ジャパン・キャンペーン事務局, 1994

犬棒かるた. Tokyo: オクノ株式会社

Japan: An Illustrated Encyclopedia. Tokyo: Kodansha Ltd., 1993

JTB's Illustrated Book Series. Tokyo: Nihon Kootsuukoosha Shuppan Jigyookyoku

Joya, Mock. *Things Japanese.* Tokyo: Tokyo News Service, 1960

Kawashima, Masaru. 漢字をおぼえる辞典: Obunsha 1975

Makino, Seiichi and Tsutsui, Michio. *A Dictionary of Basic Japanese Grammar.* The Japan Times

Sato, Esther and Sakihara, Jean. *Japanese Now*, Vol.1—4. Honolulu: University of Hawaii Press, 1982

Shokyu Nihongo Tokyo Gaikokugo Daigaku Fuzoku Nihongo Gakkoo.

Seki, Kiyo and Yoshiki, Hisako. *Nihongo Kantan.* Tokyo: Kenkyuusha

スクールカット図典学校生活編 & 家庭生活編. 東陽出版

Tohsaku, Yasu-Hiko. *Yookoso* New York McGraw-Hill, 1994

Young, John and Nakajima-Okano, Kimiko. *Learn Japanese: New College Text*, Vol.1—4.
　Honolulu: University of Hawaii Press, 1985

Until Japan came in contact with China, it had no writing system of its own. Japanese was a spoken language only. The Japanese adopted the Chinese writing system to express their spoken language in writing. The Chinese form of writing is called *kanji*, which literally means "Chinese characters." *Kanji* is now one of three systems the Japanese use to write their language. *Hiragana* and *katakana* are the two other systems. These are phonetic systems, whereas *kanji* is a system based on meaning rather than sound. However, both *hiragana* and *katakana* are derived from *kanji*. For example, to express the "ka" sound, the Japanese took the *kanji* 加 (also read "ka" in Chinese), and modified it to a more stylized form, か, which is the *hiragana* symbol "ka." *Katakana* also grew out of *kanji*, but it is a representation of a portion of a *kanji*. For example, for the same "ka" sound, カ was taken from the left portion of the *kanji* 加 and became the *katakana* alphabet カ.

The Japanese incorporated *kanji* into their language in several different ways. First of all, in most cases, the Chinese-assigned meaning of a *kanji* was not changed. That is, given a certain *kanji* (i.e., 山), both a Chinese-speaking person and a Japanese-speaking person will tell you that this character means "mountain." In addition to its meaning, the Japanese borrowed various Chinese sounds which the Chinese used to read *kanji*. Often, several sounds were borrowed for the same character, depending on when and where the sounds were borrowed. Chinese has many dialects and contact between Japan and China lasted hundreds of years, which resulted in many possible "borrowings." Any sound borrowed from the Chinese language is called the "on" reading of the *kanji*. Besides possibilities of having numerous "on" readings, most *kanji* also have at least one "kun" reading. The "kun" reading is the word which the Japanese used in their native language before their contact with China. For example, the "kun" reading of the kanji 山 is *yama*, which is the native Japanese word for "mountain." Its "on" readings are "san" or "zan," which are derived from the Chinese pronunciations of that character. "On" readings are now used in Japanese words as parts of *kanji* combinations which include the meaning of "mountain." For example, the word "kazan" contains the sound "zan," because the literal meaning of this word is "fire mountain" or "volcano." As a result, any one *kanji* in Japanese may have as many as six to seven readings!

Modern day Japanese sentences are composed of a combination of *kanji*, *hiragana* and *katakana*. Words which have strong semantic value, that is, nouns, verbs, adjectives and some adverbs, are written in *kanji*. Conjugated portions of verbs, adjectives or nouns (tenses, negations, etc.), particles, interjections, and most adverbs and other parts of sentences which do not convey the major message in the sentence are written in *hiragana*. *Katakana* is now used mainly to write words of foreign origin, or names of foreigners. It is also sometimes used as a device to call attention to certain words (i.e., in advertising, announcements, etc.). It is also sometimes used to write onomatopoetic expressions.

Presently, Japanese elementary school children learn about a thousand *kanji* characters besides *hiragana* and *katakana*. By the end of high school, students in Japan will have learned about 2,000 *kanji* characters. *Kanji* is continually changing. Some are simplified, new combinations are created, and others are dropped because of lack of usage. Although *kanji* may appear to be difficult and cumbersome, the Japanese find it a valuable part of their language.

ひらがな HIRAGANA

Hiragana are Japanese phonetic characters. There are 46 basic characters. *Hiragana* are written in square blocks. *Hiragana* strokes are not straight, but slightly curved. The reason is that *hiragana* were created by the Japanese during the Heian period (794 - 1192) from the cursive style of *kanji* (Chinese characters). It is important to follow the correct stroke order so you can write *hiragana* faster and in better form. Each stroke generally starts from left to right and/or from top to bottom. There are three ways to finish a stroke. A stroke may end as a blunt stop 一, a hook ↓, or a tail し. The way each stroke ends is obvious when *hiragana* is written with a brush, but it is not as obvious when written with a pen or a pencil. There are also several printing fonts, which may differ slightly in appearance.

	W	R	Y	M	H	N	T	S	K		
ん n	わ wa	ら ra	や ya	ま ma	は ha	な na	た ta	さ sa	か ka	あ a	← / a / line
		り ri		み mi	ひ hi	に ni	ち chi	し shi	き ki	い i	← / i / line
		る ru	ゆ yu	む mu	ふ hu/fu	ぬ nu	つ tsu	す su	く ku	う u	← / u / line
		れ re		め me	へ he	ね ne	て te	せ se	け ke	え e	← / e / line
	を o	ろ ro	よ yo	も mo	ほ ho	の no	と to	そ so	こ ko	お o	← / o / line

(Particle)

P	B	J	G
ぴゃ pya	びゃ bya	じゃ ja	ぎゃ gya
ぴゅ pyu	びゅ byu	じゅ ju	ぎゅ gyu
ぴょ pyo	びょ byo	じょ jo	ぎょ gyo

R	M	H	N	T/C	S	K	
りゃ rya	みゃ mya	ひゃ hya	にゃ nya	ちゃ cha	しゃ sha	きゃ kya	YA
りゅ ryu	みゅ myu	ひゅ hyu	にゅ nyu	ちゅ chu	しゅ shu	きゅ kyu	YU
りょ ryo	みょ myo	ひょ hyo	にょ nyo	ちょ cho	しょ sho	きょ kyo	YO

【 Japanese Writing Format 】

Japanese was originally written vertically on a page starting from right to left. Many Japanese books are still printed in this way. Therefore the front cover of a Japanese book opens from the opposite side of a Western book. Recently, Japanese is sometimes written horizontally as is English and books written this way open the same as Western books.

1. Vertically : Start from the right-hand column and read down, then return to the top of the next column on the left.

2. Horizontally: Read across from left to right, as in reading English.

$2\downarrow$ $1\downarrow$

ご	あ
ざ	り
い	が
ま	と
す	う

$1\rightarrow$

あ	り	が	と	う

$2\rightarrow$

ご	ざ	い	ま	す

【 Japanese Punctuation 】

1. まる MARU   。   Period: It is used always at the end of a sentence.

2. てん TEN   、   Comma: Unlike English, there is no definite rule for using commas. Japanese people use commas where they normally pause in speaking.

3. かっこ KAKKO   「」   Quotation marks

4. There is no question mark in Japanese.

5. Each punctuation mark occupies its own block.

Position of punctuation.

    1. Vertically

「
は
い
、
げ
ん
き
で
す
。
」

    2. Horizontally

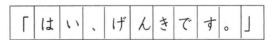

「	は	い	、	げ	ん	き	で	す	。	」

3

ひらがな

HIRAGANA STROKE ORDER

	W	R	Y	M	H	N	T	S	K		
ん N	わ	ら	や	ま	は	な	た	さ	か	あ	A
		り		み	ひ	に	ち	し	き	い	I
		る	ゆ	む	ふ	ぬ	つ	す	く	う	U
		れ		め	へ	ね	て	せ	け	え	E
	を O (Particle)	ろ	よ	も	ほ	の	と	そ	こ	お	O

By the end of this lesson, you will be able to communicate the information below in the given situations.

【１-1 タスク１】

You meet a Japanese exchange student for the first time. Greet and introduce yourself.

【１-1 タスク２】

You see Mr. Tanaka, your Japanese teacher, on Monday. It is morning and it is hot. Address him, greet him properly and ask how he is.

【１-1 タスク３】

You lead the customary opening greetings for your Japanese class. Jon is taking his time. Report that Ben is absent and Meagan is tardy.

1 か

【かいわ: Dialogue 】

はじめまして。　　　　　How do you do?
HAJIMEMASHITE.
わたしは　<u>ジョン</u>です。　I am <u>Jon</u>.
WATASHI WA <u>JON</u> DESU.
どうぞ　よろしく。　　　Nice to meet you.
DOOZO YOROSHIKU.

【たんご: Vocabulary】

1.はじめまして。	HAJIMEMASHITE.	How do you do?
2.わたし	WATASHI	I (used informally by anyone)
3.ぼく	BOKU	I (used by males)
4.は	WA	[particle marking the topic of the sentence]
5.です	DESU	am, is, are
6.どうぞ　よろしく。	DOOZO YOROSHIKU.	Nice to meet you. (DOOZO means "please."
		YOROSHIKU means "Please do me a favor.")

【 *オプショナルたんご: Optional Vocabulary】

1.*わたくし	*WATAKUSHI	I (used formally by anyone)

わたし　　　　　ぼく　　　　　*わたくし

WATASHI　　　　BOKU　　　　* WATAKUSHI

Used by anyone　Used by males　Used formally by anyone

【ぶんぽう : Grammar】

* optional

> A. Noun 1 は　Noun 2 です。　　Noun 1 = Noun 2.
>
> 　Noun 1 WA　Noun 2 DESU.　This pattern is used when one equates the first noun to the second.

1.わたしは　<u>やまもと</u>です。

　WATASHI WA <u>YAMAMOTO</u> DESU.

I am <u>Yamamoto</u>. (わたし WATASHI may be used by anyone.)

2.ぼくは　<u>ケンたなか</u>です。

　BOKU WA <u>KEN TANAKA</u> DESU.

I am <u>Ken Tanaka</u>. (ぼく BOKU is generally used by males only.)

3.*わたくしは　<u>スミス</u>です。

　WATAKUSHI WA <u>SUMISU</u> DESU.

I am <u>Smith</u>. (わたくし WATAKUSHI may be used by anyone in formal situations.)

【 ● ぶんかノート : Cultural Notes】

1. How to Bow

When Japanese people greet one another, it is common practice to bow. Japanese express the degree of respect they have for others by the depth of the bow and its frequency. Hugging and kissing, even among close family and friends, are not seen in Japan. When Japanese greet foreigners, they may shake hands. When the other person bows, one should also bow. Not acknowledging the other person is considered rude. When bowing, pay attention that your:

　a. eyes move downward with the bow. Do not attempt to make eye contact during a bow.

　b. feet are positioned together, facing forward.

　c. hands are placed relaxed but straight alongside your body if you are a male. Females lightly cross their hands at their fingertips in front of their body while bowing.

　d. body is not slouched or not turned away from the other person.

2. Male Speech and Female Speech

Japanese language has words used only by males and words used only by females.
わたし WATASHI is used by anyone, but ぼく BOKU is used only by males. If a female uses ぼく BOKU, she is considered "tomboyish."

3. Formal Speech and Informal Speech

Certain words in the Japanese language are used in formal situations and others in informal situations. わたくし WATAKUSHI is used formally in business situations or in public speaking. わたし WATASHI and ぼく BOKU are used in less formal daily situations.

4. Family Names and Given Names

In Japanese, family names precede given names, which is the opposite from English. This is because in Japan and much of Asia, the family is considered more important than the individual. In Japan, students are called by their family names at school. When foreigners visit Japan, given names are used among close friends, and family names are used in formal situations.

7

1 か

5. *Meishi*

めいし MEISHI are business cards. Japanese business people exchange them when they introduce themselves. めいし MEISHI include all the information needed for future business reference, such as one's personal name, company name, position in the company, address, telephone number, fax number, e-mail address, etc. Japanese handle the めいし MEISHI with respect. It is handed over with two hands and given so it faces the other person directly. Upon receiving one, the receiver reads the information on it carefully, then puts it in a めいしいれ MEISHI-IRE, a special case made for holding めいし MEISHI. めいし MEISHI are never placed in back pockets or any other location which would show disrespect to the other person.

 アクティビティー: Activities】

A. Class Work

Everyone introduces themselves with proper bows in class.

A. Five Japanese Vowels

/a/ あ is pronounced like *a* in f<u>a</u>ther.　　"ah"

/i/ い is pronounced like *i* in mach<u>i</u>ne.　"ee"

/u/ う is pronounced like *ue* in S<u>ue</u>.　　"oo"

/e/ え is pronounced like *e* in l<u>e</u>dge.　　"eh"

/o/ お is pronounced like *o* in <u>o</u>bey.　　"oh"

B. 46 Basic Japanese Syllables

Begin from the top of the right-hand column and read down, then go to the top of the next column on the left.

ん	わ	ら	や	ま	は	な	た	さ	か	あ	← / a / line
n	wa	ra	ya	ma	ha	na	ta	sa	ka	a	
		り		み	ひ	に	ち	し	き	い	← / i / line
		ri		mi	hi	ni	chi	shi	ki	i	
		る	ゆ	む	ふ	ぬ	つ	す	く	う	← / u / line
		ru	yu	mu	hu	nu	tsu	su	ku	u	
		れ		め	へ	ね	て	せ	け	え	← / e / line
		re		me	he	ne	te	se	ke	e	
	を	ろ	よ	も	ほ	の	と	そ	こ	お	← / o / line
	o	ro	yo	mo	ho	no	to	so	ko	o	

(Particle)

C. Other Syllables

ぱ	ば		だ	ざ	が
pa	ba		da	za	ga
ぴ	び		ぢ	じ	ぎ
pi	bi		ji	ji	gi
ぷ	ぶ		づ	ず	ぐ
pu	bu		zu	zu	gu
ぺ	べ		で	ぜ	げ
pe	be		de	ze	ge
ぽ	ぼ		ど	ぞ	ご
po	bo		do	zo	go

ぴゃ	びゃ	じゃ	ぎゃ	りゃ	みゃ	ひゃ	にゃ	ちゃ	しゃ	きゃ
pya	bya	ja	gya	rya	mya	hya	nya	cha	sha	kya
ぴゅ	びゅ	じゅ	ぎゅ	りゅ	みゅ	ひゅ	にゅ	ちゅ	しゅ	きゅ
pyu	byu	ju	gyu	ryu	myu	hyu	nyu	chu	shu	kyu
ぴょ	びょ	じょ	ぎょ	りょ	みょ	ひょ	にょ	ちょ	しょ	きょ
pyo	byo	jo	gyo	ryo	myo	hyo	nyo	cho	sho	kyo

9

D. **Equal Stress on Each Syllable**

Unlike English, emphasis on syllables tends to be uniform in Japanese. No one syllable should be accented more heavily than any of the other syllables in the word.

1. HI-RO-SHI-MA (Hiroshima)
ひろしま

2. O-KI-NA-WA (Okinawa)
おきなわ

3. O-SU-SHI (sushi)
おすし

4. SA-SHI-MI (raw fish)
さしみ

E. **Long Vowels**

If the same vowel appears twice in succession, it is pronounced as a prolonged sound. It is important to pronounce a long vowel carefully since a long vowel often changes a word's meaning.

1a. I̲E [I-E] (house)
いえ

1b. I̲IE [I-I-E] (no)
いいえ

2a. E̲ [E] (picture)
え

2b. E̲E [E-E] (yes)
ええ

3a. OJI̲SAN [O-JI-SA-N] (uncle)
おじさん

3b. OJI̲ISAN [O-JI-I-SA-N] (grandfather)
おじいさん

4a. OBA̲SAN [O-BA-SA-N] (aunt)
おばさん

4b. OBA̲ASAN [O-BA-A-SA-N] (grandmother)
おばあさん

5a. SHUJIN [SHU-JI-N] (husband)
しゅじん

5b. SHUUJIN [SHU-U-JI-N] (prisoner)
しゅうじん

F. /L/ and /R/ sounds

Japanese /ra/, /ri/, /ru/, /re/, /ro/ sounds are produced so that the initial "r" sounds somewhat like a combination of the English "l" and "r" sounds. Japanese people have difficulty distinguishing English "l" and "r" sounds.

1. RAJIO (radio)
ラジオ

2. REPOOTO (report)
レポート

3. RESUTORAN (restaurant)
レストラン

G. /N/ sound

This is a nasal sound. It does not occur at the beginning of words, but is found within or at the end of words. It is pronounced by exhaling through the nose.

1. HON (book)
ほん

2. MIKAN (orange)
みかん

3. ENPITSU (pencil)
えんぴつ

4. PAN (bread)
パン

5. SHINBUN (newspaper)
しんぶん

6. ZUBON (trousers)
ずぼん

1 か

H. /TSU/ sound

This is pronounced like "-ts" at the end of the word "cats." It is then lengthened with the /U/ sound. The /TSU/ sound may appear at any position in a word.

1. T<u>SU</u>KI (moon)
つき

2. MA<u>TSU</u> (pine tree)
まつ

3. KU<u>TSU</u> (shoes)
くつ

4. T<u>SU</u>KUE (desk)
つくえ

5. MA<u>TSU</u>RI (festival)
まつり

6. T<u>SU</u>RI (fishing)
つり

I. /FU/ sound

The English "f" is pronounced by blowing through the upper teeth resting on the lower lip. When pronouncing the Japanese /f/, however, there is no contact between the lip and teeth as one blows out. The Japanese /f/ sounds like a breathy "wh" sound.

1. <u>FU</u>NE (ship)
ふね

2. <u>FU</u>JISAN (Mt. Fuji)
ふじさん

3. <u>FU</u>E (flute)
ふえ

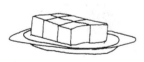

4. TOO<u>FU</u> (tofu)
とうふ

5. NAI<u>FU</u> (knife)
ナイフ

6. <u>FU</u>YU (winter)
ふゆ

J. Double Consonants /っ/

Double consonants such as "kk," "ss," "tt" or "pp" are pronounced with a slight pause between the first and second consonant sounds, as in "ba<u>d b</u>oy" or "har<u>d r</u>ock" in English.

1. KOPPU (cup)
コップ

2. BATTO (bat)
バット

3. ZASSHI (magazines)
ざっし

4. GAKKOO (school)
がっこう

5. ISSHO (together)
いっしょ

6. IPPAI (full)
いっぱい

K. Devoiced Vowels

Japanese vowels are usually voiced, but when the vowel /i/ or /u/ occurs between two consonants, the vowel is often not pronounced. The final /u/ in *desu* and *masu* is not pronounced.

1. HITO (person)
ひと

2. KUSURI (medicine)
くすり

3. SUSHI (sushi)
すし

4. GAKUSEI DESU. (He is a student.)
がくせいです。

5. IKIMASU. (I will go.)
いきます。

6. OHAYOO GOZAIMASU. (Good morning.)
おはよう　ございます。

1 か

L. **Pitch**

Pitch is important in Japanese pronunciation, as certain syllables in a word must be pronounced with a high or low pitch. The meaning of a word may differ depending on the pitch. See the examples below.

1a. HASHI (bridge)
はし　橋

1b. HASHI (chopsticks)
はし　箸

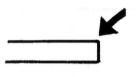

1c. HASHI (edge)
はし　端

2a. HEN (weird)
へん　変

2b. HEN (area)
へん　辺

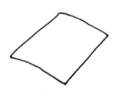

3a. KAMI (paper)
かみ　紙

3b. KAMI (God)
かみ　神

4a. AME (rain)
あめ　雨

4b. AME (candy)
あめ　飴

5a. IPPAI (one cupful)
いっぱい

5b. IPAI (full)
いっぱい

M. **Intonation**

Intonation is relatively flat in Japanese. For statements, the sentence ending is usually even.
Questions without か KA end in a rising intonation. (With a か KA, the intonation is not raised.)

1a. WAKARIMASU. (I understand.) ⇩
わかります。

1b. WAKARIMASU? (Do you understand?) ⇧
わかります？

2a. WATASHI. (Me.) ⇩
わたし。

2b. WATASHI? (Me?) ⇧
わたし？

【たんご: Vocabulary】

1.これ
   KORE
   this one
(Refers to something near the speaker.
Used only for things, <u>not for people</u>.)

【ぶんぽう: Grammar】

A. Noun 1 は　 Noun 2 です。 　　　Noun 1 = Noun 2.
Noun 1 WA　 Noun 2　DESU.　 This pattern is used when one equates the first noun to the second.

1. これは　 おです。　　　　　　　　This is <u>O</u>.
   KORE WA <u>O</u> DESU.

【 アクティビティー: Activities】

A. ひらがな PAIR WORK - Connection Game

Cut out the *hiragana* flash cards あA, いI, うU, えE, おO. Find a partner and put your cards
together with your partner's and shuffle the 10 cards. Lay the 10 cards face down on the desk. Take
turns flipping a card and finding the matching card. You say, "Kore wa あ desu." , "Kore wa い
desu." If the cards match, they are yours. If they don't match, it is your partner's turn.

1 か

【たんご: Vocabulary】

1. おはよう。
OHAYOO.
Good morning. (Informal)
Used among friends until late morning. It originally meant "it is early."

2. おはよう　ございます。
OHAYOO GOZAIMASU.
Good morning. (Formal)
Used formally until late morning. GOZAIMASU adds politeness.

3. こんにちは。
KONNICHI WA.
Hello. Hi.
Used from late morning to pre-dusk hours. It originally meant "today is."

4. さようなら。
SAYOONARA.
Good-bye.

5. やまだせんせい
YAMADA-SENSEI
Mr./Mrs./Ms./Dr. Yamada
SENSEI is attached to names of teachers, doctors, and statesmen to show respect. SENSEI can be used alone when addressing a person or as a word which means "teacher" or "mentor."

6. まりさん
MARI-SAN
Mari.
-SAN is a sufix attached to names. It is not attached to one's own name or one's own family members' names. -SAN may be used for both males and females. It is attached to both given and family names.

7. はい。
HAI.
Yes.
HAI may be used in response to roll call. It indicates acknowledgement that one is present.

【*オプショナルたんご: Optional Vocabulary】

1.*こんばんは。
*KONBAN WA.
Good evening.
Used from dusk through the night.
KONBAN means "tonight."

2.*じゃあね。
*JAA NE.
See you.
Informal expression used
among friends upon parting.
It originally meant "and then."

3.*ジョンくん
* JON-KUN
Jon. John.
-KUN is a suffix usually attached to
boys' names. It is used instead of
-SAN by superiors to refer to or address
persons of lower status.

【 ● ぶんかノート: Cultural Notes】

Polite Words

Japanese language has many words which show politeness. When you use them, you express your respect to the other person. For instance, in the morning you greet your friends with おはよう OHAYOO, but should greet your teacher with おはよう ございます OHAYOO GOZAIMASU. If you greet your teacher with おはよう OHAYOO, you show a lack of respect toward your teacher.

せんせい SENSEI itself is a word used to refer to teachers and doctors. By calling your teacher せんせい SENSEI, you show respect to your teacher. When using せんせい SENSEI with a teacher's name, せんせい SENSEI should follow, not precede the teacher's name, i. e., さいとう せんせい SAITO SENSEI.

Using ～さん -SAN after a person's first name or last name shows respect. You should never use さん SAN after your own name. When talking about your family members to outsiders, do not use さん SAN after your family members' names.

【 アクティビティー: Activities】

A. Pair Work

You meet your teacher. Address and greet him/her:
1. in the morning.   3. at night.
2. in the afternoon.   4. upon leaving.

B. Pair Work

You meet your friend. Address and greet him/her:
1. in the morning.   3. at night.
2. in the afternoon.   4. upon leaving.

C. Class Work   You take attendance.

1か

【たんご: Vocabulary】

1. はじめましょう。
HAJIMEMASHOO.
Let's begin.

2. きりつ。
KIRITSU.
Stand.
Used at ceremonies or in formal situations.

3. れい。
REI.
Bow.
Used at ceremonies or in formal situations.

4. ちゃくせき。
CHAKUSEKI.
Sit.
Used at ceremonies or in formal situations.

5. (お)やすみです。
(O)YASUMI DESU.
~ is absent.
The use of お O adds politeness. お O is not used when referring to your own absence.

6. ちこくです。
CHIKOKU DESU.
~ is tardy.
Refers to persons being late to class, meetings, etc.

7. はやく。
HAYAKU.
Hurry!

8. おわりましょう。
OWARIMASHOO.
Let's finish.

9. なに／なん
NANI / NAN
what?
The choice of NANI or NAN depends on the initial sound of the following word.

10. か
KA
?
Sentence-ending particle indicating a question.

【＊オプショナルたんご: Optional Vocabulary】

＊すみません。　おそく　なりました。
*SUMIMASEN. OSOKU NARIMASHITA.
I am sorry to be late. (lit. I am sorry. I have become late.)

【ぶんぽう: Grammar】

A. Obvious topics are omitted in Japanese.

Unlike English sentences which require a subject (i.e., he, she, they, it, we, I, etc.), in Japanese, subjects are frequently omitted, especially when the subject or topic is understood by both the listener and speaker. Such sentences are more natural in Japanese.

1. Teacher: 「ジョンさん。」　　　　　　　Jon.
       JON-SAN.

  Student: 「ちこくです。」　　　　　　　(He is) tardy.
       CHIKOKU DESU.

B. Noun 1 は　なんですか。　　　　　What is Noun 1?
  Noun 1 WA NAN DESU KA.

In Japanese, the word order of a question sentence is the same as for statements, except that か KA is attached to the end of the sentence.

1. Teacher: 「これは　なんですか。」　　What is this?
       KORE WA NAN DESU KA.

  Student: 「おです。」　　　　　　　　It is <u>O</u>.
       <u>O</u> DESU.

1 か

【 ● ぶんかノート : Cultural Notes】

How are the three types of Japanese characters—*kanji* (Chinese characters), *hiragana* and *katakana* — used?

Kanji (Chinese characters)	Hiragana	Katakana	
加	か	カ	— KA
安	あ	ア	— A
世	せ	セ	— SE

Kanjii are characters derived from the Chinese writing system. These characters are distinguished by their meanings. *Kanji* is used mainly to write nouns and the main portion of verbs and adjectives. Every *kanji* has multiple readings. There are two types of *kana* writing systems: *hiragana* and *katakana*. Both writing systems are phonetic, that is, each *hiragana* and *katakana* symbol represents a sound, much like the English alphabet. Both *hiragana* and *katakana* were developed from *kanji*. *Hiragana* is a stylized form of *kanji*; *katakana* represents portions of *kanji* characters. *Hiragana* is used for writing verb and adjective endings (i.e., portions which conjugate), particles, most adverbs and other verbs or nouns which are not commonly written in *kanji*. *Katakana* is now mainly used to write foreign loan words. Onomatopoetic expressions are also sometimes written in *katakana*. *Katakana* may also be used as attention-getting devices in ads, fliers, etc.

【 アクティビティー: Activities】

A. Class Work

   One student leads the class. Everyone else follows his/her instructions.
   1. This is the beginning of a <u>morning</u> Japanese class. Start the class with the traditional opening.
   2. This is the beginning of an <u>afternoon</u> Japanese class. Start the class with the traditional opening.
   3. This is the end of a Japanese class. Lead the closing. If a classmate does not stand quickly, tell that student to hurry.

B. Class Work

   Take attendance and then report to the teacher who is absent and who is tardy.

C. ひらがな Pair Work

   Cut out the *hiragana* flash cards and ask your partner what they are.

【たんご: Vocabulary】

1. Numbers

1 いち ICHI	2 に NI	3 さん SAN	4 し, よん, （よ-） SHI, YON, (YO-)	5 ご GO
6 ろく ROKU	7 しち, なな SHICHI, NANA	8 はち HACHI	9 く, きゅう KU, KYUU	10 じゅう JUU

2.

すみません。もう　いちど　おねがいします。
SUMIMASEN. MOO ICHIDO ONEGAISHIMASU.
   Excuse me.   One more time please. (Please repeat it.)
もう MOO means more, いちど ICHIDO means one time,
おねがいします ONEGAISHIMASU is commonly used when one asks a
favor of someone.

3.

すみません。ゆっくり　おねがいします。
SUMIMASEN. YUKKURI ONEGAISHIMASU.
   Excuse me.   Slowly, please.
ゆっくり YUKKURI means slowly.

4.

ちょっと　まって　ください。
CHOTTO MATTE KUDASAI.
   Please wait a minute.

5.

Thank you very much.

Depending upon the degree of politeness, parts of this expression may be omitted. Here are expressions of thanks listed from most formal to least formal.

どうも　ありがとう　ございます。
DOOMO ARIGATOO GOZAIMASU.
ありがとう　ございます。
ARIGATOO GOZAIMASU.
どうも　ありがとう。
DOOMO ARIGATOO.
ありがとう。
ARIGATOO.
どうも。
DOOMO.

6.

どういたしまして。
DOO ITASHIMASHITE.

You are welcome.

【＊オプショナルたんご: Optional Vocabulary】

1.

＊でんわばんごう
*DENWA BANGOO
telephone number

（きゅう・にい・なな・の・ろく・ごお・よん・ゼロ）
KYUU NII NANA NO ROKU GOO YON ZERO

When Japanese people read telephone numbers, they avoid similar sounds and short sounds. し SHI (four) and しち SHICHI (seven) sound alike. いち ICHI (one) and しち SHICHI (seven) sound alike. Thus, use よん YON for four, なな NANA for seven and きゅう KYUU for nine. The "dash" is pronounced as の NO. Single character numbers are lengthened to distinguish each number more easily (i.e., に NI to にい NII, ご GO to ごお GOO).

【 ● ぶんかノート : Cultural Notes】

1. Japanese depend heavily on set expressions and greetings.

   One of the most useful expressions in Japanese is すみません SUMIMASEN, because it carries so many meanings and can be used in a variety of situations. For example, it may be used to apologize for one's rude, inconsiderate, or thoughtless actions. It may also be used as a way to thank others for going through a lot of trouble to do something for you or give something to you. すみません SUMIMASEN may also be used to gain attention, much as English speakers use the expression, "Excuse me. (Are you there?) " or "Excuse me. (I hope you can help me.)"

2. Difference between もういちど MOO ICHIDO and もういちど おねがいします MOO ICHIDO ONEGAISHIMASU.

   もういちど MOO ICHIDO means "one more time." It is rude to say もういちど MOO ICHIDO when making requests to teachers and superiors. Instead, say もういちど おねがいします MOO ICHIDO ONEGAISHIMASU when you would like superiors to repeat something for you.

【 アクティビティー: Activities】

A. Class Work

   Play a game of Bingo with the numbers 1 through 10. Fill in each block with any number you like from 1 through 10. One student randomly reads numbers from 1 through 10. The other students listen and circle the numbers read until they have a bingo. Say できました DEKIMASHITA ("I made it") when you have Bingo.

で	き	ま	し	た
		☆		

で	き	ま	し	た
		☆		

B. Class Work

   Each student reads his/her own telephone number aloud and others write the numbers down. If you are not able to follow, ask your classmate to repeat his/her number. If the student speaks too quickly, ask the person to speak slowly. Thank the person for repeating his/her number and speaking. In return, the student should say, "You are welcome."

1 か

【たんご: Vocabulary】

1. Numbers

11　じゅういち 　　JUU-ICHI	
12　じゅうに 　　JUU-NI	20　にじゅう 　　NI-JUU
13　じゅうさん 　　JUU-SAN	30　さんじゅう 　　SAN-JUU
14　じゅうし, じゅうよん, (じゅうよー) 　　JUU-SHI,　JUU-YON,　　(JUU-YO~)	40　よんじゅう 　　YON-JUU
15　じゅうご 　　JUU-GO	50　ごじゅう 　　GO-JUU
16　じゅうろく 　　JUU-ROKU	60　ろくじゅう 　　ROKU-JUU
17　じゅうしち, じゅうなな 　　JUU-SHICHI, JUU-NANA	70　しちじゅう, ななじゅう 　　SHICHI-JUU, NANA-JUU
18　じゅうはち 　　JUU-HACHI	80　はちじゅう 　　HACHI-JUU
19　じゅうく, じゅうきゅう 　　JUU-KU, JUU-KYUU	90　きゅうじゅう 　　KYUU-JUU
	100 ひゃく 　　HYAKU

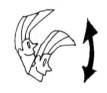

2. それ
SORE
that one
Refers to something
near the listener.

3. あれ
ARE
that one over there
Refers to something distant
from both speaker and listener.

4. はい, ええ
HAI, EE
Yes
ええ EE is less formal
than はい HAI.

5. いいえ
IIE
No

6. はい、そうです。
HAI, SOO DESU.
Yes, it is.
Expression of agreement. Used as a response.

7. いいえ、そうではありません。
IIE, SOO DEWA ARIMASEN.
or いいえ、そうじゃありません。
IIE, SOO JA ARIMASEN.
Expression of disagreement. Used as a response.

【*オプショナルたんご: Optional Vocabulary】
1.*Page numbers

page 1	いっページ	ip-peeji
2	にページ	ni-peeji
3	さんページ	san-peeji
4	よんページ	yon-peeji
5	ごページ	go-peeji
6	ろっページ	rop-peeji
7	ななページ	nana-peeji
8	はっページ	hap-peeji
9	きゅうページ	kyuu-peeji
10	じ(ゅ)っページ	jup-peeji, jip-peeji
page 11	じゅういっページ	juu-ip-peeji
. .		
page 20	にじ(ゅ)っページ	ni-jup-peeji, ni-jip-peeji
.		
what page?	なんページ	nan-peeji?

【ぶんぽう：Grammar】

A. これ／それ／あれ は ～です。 　　　　　This / That / That one over there is ~.

　　KORE / SORE / ARE WA ~ DESU.

これ KORE refers to something near the speaker. それ SORE refers to something near the listener. あれ ARE refers to something distant from both speaker and listener. これ KORE, それ SORE, あれ ARE cannot be used for people except for people in pictures and photos.

---

1. Teacher: 「これは　なんですか。」　　　　　What is this?
　　　　　KORE WA NAN DESU KA.

　Student: 「それは　<u>う</u>です。」　　　　　That is <u>U</u>.
　　　　　SORE WA <u>U</u> DESU.

2. Teacher: 「あれは　なんですか。」　　　　　What is that one over there?
　　　　　ARE WA NAN DESU KA.

　Student: 「あれは　<u>か</u>です。」　　　　　That is <u>KA</u>.
　　　　　ARE WA <u>KA</u> DESU.

B. Noun 1 は　Noun 2 ですか。　　　　　Is Noun 1 = Noun 2?

　Noun 1 WA　Noun 2 DESU KA.

　When the sentence ending particle か KA is added to a statement, a question is formed.

---

1. 「これは　<u>お</u>ですか。」　　　　　Is this <u>O</u>?
　　KORE WA <u>O</u> DESU KA.

　「はい、そうです。」　　　　　Yes, it is.
　　HAI, SOO DESU.

　「いいえ、そうではありません。」　　　No, it is not.
　　IIE, SOO DEWA ARIMASEN.

【 ● ぶんかノート : Cultural Notes】

Japanese Good Luck and Bad Luck Numbers

　In the Japanese culture, certain numbers are considered "bad luck" or "good luck," much like the number 13 is considered bad luck in Western culture. The "bad luck" numbers in Japanese are 4 (し SHI) and 9 (く KU). し SHI can also mean death, while く KU suggests suffering. Eight is considered good luck because of the mountain-like shape of the *kanji* character for eight (八). Mountains are regarded with reverence in Japan. Also, the character 八 resembles a fan shape, which is considered lucky because it suggests spreading out, growing and increasing, as in mounting good fortune.

【 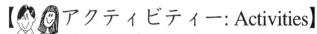 アクティビティー : Activities】

A. Pair Work

　Count from 1 to 100.

1 か

B. Class Work

Your teacher will write numbers from 1 to 100 at random on the board. Students will read them aloud.

C. Class Work

Let's play a Bingo game with the numbers 1 to 100. Fill in each block with any number you like from 10 to 100. One student randomly reads a number from 1 to 100. The other students circle the number being read until they have Bingo. Say できました DEKIMASHITA "I made it" when you have a Bingo.

で	き	ま	し	た
		☆		

で	き	ま	し	た
		☆		

D. Group Work - 3 Students

Form groups of 3. One student reads page numbers, while the other two race to see who can find the correct page more quickly. Keep track of points. Take turns so that each student will have a chance to be the page caller.

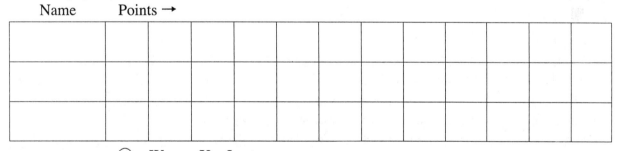

Name   Points →

○ = Won   X = Lost

E. ひらがな Pair Work

Spread a set of your *hiragana* flash cards on your desk, on your partner's desk and somewhere far from both of you. Ask each other what each card is. Use これKORE, それSORE, あれARE in both questions and answers.

1 か

【Expressions】

1. あついですねえ。

ATSUI DESU NEE.

It's hot!

2. さむいですねえ。

SAMUI DESU NEE.

It's cold!

3. すずしいですねえ。

SUZUSHII DESU NEE.

It is cool (temperature)!

4. そうですねえ。

SOO DESU NEE.

Yes, it is!

Indicates strong agreement.

5. (お)げんきですか。

(O)GENKI DESU KA.

How are you? (lit. Are you fine?)

This expression is used only when one meets a person after not seeing him/her for several days or more.

6. はい、げんきです。

HAI, GENKI DESU.

Yes, I am fine.

Notice that the polite prefix "お O" is removed here, since the speaker is talking about himself.

7. むしあついですねえ。

MUSHIATSUI DESU NEE.

It's hot and humid!

8. いい(お)てんきですねえ。

II (O)TENKI DESU NEE.

The weather is nice!

9. あめですねえ。

AME DESU NEE.

It's raining (a lot)!

1 か

1.＊いいえ、ぐあいが　わるいです。
*IIE, GUAI GA WARUI DESU.
No, I feel sick.

2.＊ねむいです。
*NEMUI DESU.
(I) am sleepy.

3.＊つかれています。
*TSUKARETE IMASU.
(I) am tired.

【ぶんぽう：Grammar】

A. Sentence ＋ねえ。
　　　NEE
The final particle ねえ NEE is used to express admiration, surprise, or exclamation.

1. あついですねえ。　　　　　　　　　　　　It is hot!
　　ATSUI DESU NEE.

2. さむいですねえ。　　　　　　　　　　　　It is cold!
　　SAMUI DESU NEE.

3. そうですねえ。　　　　　　　　　　　　　It is so!
　　SOO DESU NEE.

【 ● ぶんかノート : Cultural Notes 】

Why do Japanese people always discuss weather when they greet each other?

There are probably several explanations for this. First, Japanese do not like to get directly to the point when speaking with one another. Talking about the weather is a "safe" common ground from which to start a conversation. Another reason is the Japanese respect for nature. The native "religion" of Japan is *Shinto*, which among other things can be described as a form of nature worship. Japan has historically been very susceptible to the whims of nature, and the Japanese, especially in the past, felt a strong sense of awe and respect for natural phenomena. This "oneness" with nature is reflected even in everyday interactions such as greetings. Think of other ways in which nature plays a part in the Japanese lifestyle and culture.

【 アクティビティー : Activities 】

A. Pair Work

In the following scenarios, address the person involved, greet him/her properly, talk about the weather and ask how he/she is.

1. You enter the Japanese classroom in the morning. Your teacher is there. The room is very cold.

2. You meet your neighbor. It is morning and it is cool.

3. You meet your friend in the afternoon. It is a hot day.

4. You meet your Japanese friend Mari in the morning. It is cold.

5. You have not seen your teacher since the day before the weekend. Ask how he/she is.

JAPANESE CULTURE 1: WHERE IS JAPAN?

1. Where is Japan? Find Japan on the world map or on the globe.

2. What does Japan look like? Draw a simple map of Japan here.

3. What is the capital of Japan? Where is the capital of Japan? Mark the capital on the map you drew above.

4. How big is Japan compared to your state? Circle the correst answer.

   Japan is (bigger than, about the same size as, smaller than) the state I live in now.

5. Which U.S. state is about the same size as Japan? Circle the correct answer.

   (California, New Jersey, Florida)

6. What is the approximate population of Japan? What is the approximate population of the U.S.?
   Circle the correct answer.
   Japan   (100 million, 200 million, 300 million, 400 million, 500 million)
   U.S.   (100 million, 200 million, 300 million, 400 million, 500 million)

7. What natural disasters are common in Japan? Circle the correct answer.

   (typhoons, earthquakes, tsunamis, volcanic eruptions, floods)

1 か

おりがみ ORIGAMI means "folding paper". おり ORI is from the verb おります ORIMASU which means "to fold." がみ GAMI is from the word かみ KAMI which means "paper." *Origami* is a Japanese traditional craft which both adults and children enjoy. Enjoy folding *origami* such as animals, flowers, furniture, toys, etc.!

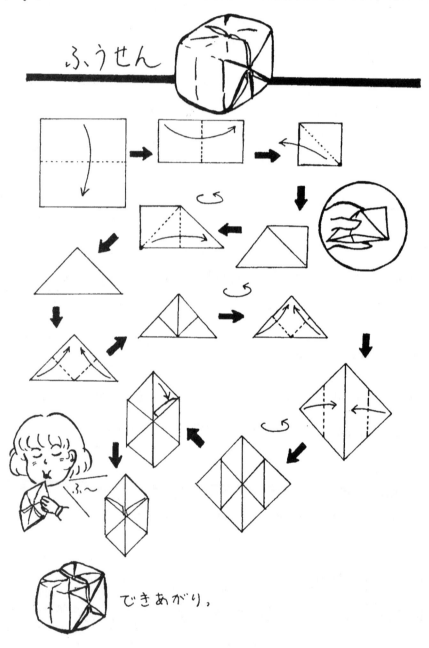

ふうせん

できあがり。

【アクティビティー: Activities】

1. Count in Japanese how many times you can bounce an *origami* balloon in the air.

2. Count in Japanese how many times you can bounce an *origami* balloon in the air with your partner.

By the end of this lesson, you will be able to communicate the information below in the given situations.

【1-2 タスク1】

Ask your teacher to give you another worksheet. The teacher scolds you and tells you where it is. You thank him/her.

【1-2 タスク2】

You lost (なくしました NAKUSHIMASHITA) your cap and bag. Go to the lost and found counter and tell the person in charge which one is yours.

【1-2 タスク3】

You are sitting at the back of the Japanese classroom. The teacher points to some small characters on the board and asks you if you can see them and what they are. The teacher then speaks softly and asks if you can hear what he/she says.

【1-2 タスク4】

You are getting help from a Japanese exchange student. You want to know the Japanese words for things around you. Point to things here and there and ask how to say them in Japanese. The Japanese student answers too quickly. Ask him/her to slow down and repeat the words. Then thank him/her for the help.

【Expressions】

1. わかりますか。

WAKARIMASU KA.

Do you understand?

2. はい、わかります。

HAI, WAKARIMASU.

Yes, I understand.

3. いいえ、わかりません。

IIE, WAKARIMASEN.

No, I do not understand.

4. しりません。

SHIRIMASEN.

I do not know.

"I know" is しっています

SHITTE IMASU.

5. みえません。

MIEMASEN.

I cannot see.

"I can see" is みえます

MIEMASU.

6. きこえません。

KIKOEMASEN.

I cannot hear.

"I can hear" is きこえます

KIKOEMASU.

7. いいです。

II DESU.

It is good.

8. だめです。

DAME DESU.

It is no good.

9. ええと.../あのう...

EETO. . . / ANOO. . .

Let me see . . ., Well . . .

When you need time to think of a response, use these expressions.

10. Tree は　にほんごで　なんと　いいますか。

Tree WA NIHONGO DE NAN TO IIMASU KA.

How do you say "tree" in Japanese?

にほんご NIHONGO means "Japanese language", で DE means "by means of," なん NAN means "what," と TO is a particle used for quotations, いいます IIMASU means "say" and か KA is a particle for questions.

【*Optional Expressions】

1.*わすれました。　　　　　2.*なくしました。
* WASUREMASHITA.　　　　* NAKUSHIMASHITA.
　　I forgot.　　　　　　　　　I lost (it).

3.

＊おてあらい／（お）トイレへ　いっても　いいですか。
* OTEARAI / (O)TOIRE E ITTE MO II DESU KA.
　May I go to the bathroom?

4.

＊ロッカーへ　いっても　いいですか。
*ROKKAA E ITTE MO II DESU KA.
May I go to the locker?

5.

＊（お）みずを　のんでも　いいですか。
* (O)MIZU O NONDE MO II DESU KA.
May I get a drink of water? (lit., "May I drink water?")

6.

＊えんぴつを　かして　ください。
* ENPITSU O KASHITE KUDASAI.
Please lend me a pencil.

7.

＊すみません。しつもんが　あります。
* SUMIMASEN. SHITSUMON GA ARIMASU.
Excuse me. I have a question.

2か

【ぶんぽう：Grammar】

> A. わかり<u>ます</u>。　　　　　　　　　I understand.
> WAKARIMASU.
> わかり<u>ません</u>。　　　　　　　　I do not understand.
> WAKARIMASEN.
>
> Japanese verbs consist of two parts, the verb stem and the portion which conjugates. The verb stem (the beginning part of a verb without the ます MASU) tells the meaning of the verb. [The conjugated portion (the verb ending, i.e., ます MASU) tells us the verb tense, whether the verb is affirmative or negative, etc.] The verb - ます MASU form is an imperfect affirmative form. Imperfect means present and future. It is translated "do, does, will do, going to do." The verb - ません MASEN form is an imperfect negative form. It is translated "do not, does not, will not do."

1. Teacher：みえ<u>ます</u>か。　　　　　　　Can you see it?

   MIEMASU KA.

   Student：はい、みえ<u>ます</u>。　　　　　Yes, I can see it.

   HAI, MIEMASU.

2. Student：すみません。せんせい、きこえ<u>ません</u>。　Excuse me. Teacher, I cannot

   SUMIMASEN. SENSEI, KIKOEMASEN.　　　hear it.

3. Teacher：これは　なんですか。　　　　What is this?

   KORE WA NAN DESU KA.

   Student：しり<u>ません</u>。　　　　　　I do not know.

   SHIRIMASEN.

4. Teacher：わかり<u>ます</u>か。　　　　　　Do you understand?

   WAKARIMASU KA.

   Student：いいえ、わかり<u>ません</u>。　　No, I do not understand.

   IIE, WAKARIMASEN.

【 ● ぶんかノート：Cultural Notes】

Manners in the Japanese Classroom.

   Classroom behavior is much more formal in Japan than in the U.S.

   1. Students never eat, drink or chew gum in class.
   2. Caps and hats are <u>always</u> removed.
   3. The teacher's permission is always asked before any action is taken by the students.
   4. Students do not freely stand up and move about in the middle of a class session.

【👧👦アクティビティー: Activities】

A. Pair Work

Do the following tests with your partner.

1. Eye test: Test your partner using the chart below.

2. Hearing test: Use a tape recorder or a CD player. Change the volume from low to high and test your partner. You may also adjust the volume of your own voice to test each other.

1	A	い
8	K	お
3	S	う
9	T	え
6	M	あ
4	N	く
7	E	こ
2	F	け
5	G	せ

B. Pair Work

Ask your partner if he/she knows the following words in Japanese. When your partner does not know the answer, he/she will say しりません SHIRIMASEN.

1. cat
2. You are welcome.
3. May I go to the bathroom?
4. teacher
5. telephone number
6. dog

2か

【Directions】

You are expected to understand and follow the directions your teacher will give you in class.

1. かいてください。
KAITE KUDASAI.
Please write.

2. よんでください。
YONDE KUDASAI.
Please read.

3. みてください。
MITE KUDASAI.
Please look.

4. きいてください。
KIITE KUDASAI.
Please listen.

5. すわってください。
SUWATTE KUDASAI.
Please sit.

6. たってください。
TATTE KUDASAI.
Please stand.

7. だしてください。
DASHITE KUDASAI.
Please turn in
(something).

8. みせてください。
MISETE KUDASAI.
Please show me
(something).

9. まどを　あけてください。
MADO O AKETE KUDASAI.
Please open the window.

10. ドアを　しめてください。
DOA O SHIMETE KUDASAI.
Please close the door.

11. しずかに　してください。
SHIZUKA NI SHITE KUDASAI.
Please be quiet.

12. よく　できました。
YOKU DEKIMASHITA.
Well done.

【* Optional Expressions】

1.*でんきを　つけてください。
　* DENKI O TSUKETE KUDASAI.
　　Please turn on the lights.

2.*でんきを　けしてください。
　* DENKI O KESHITE KUDASAI.
　　Please turn off the lights.

3.*おおきい　こえで　いってください。
　* OOKII KOE DE ITTE KUDASAI.
　　Please say it in a loud voice.

【● ぶんかノート: Cultural Notes】

More Manners in a Japanese Classroom.

Japanese students sit at full attention when in class.

They sit:

1. with both feet flat on the floor. (No feet resting on chairs, no crossed legs, etc.)
2. with their backs straight, resting only on seat backs. (No slouching, no resting heads on desk, no resting heads on one hand, etc.)
3. always facing the teacher. When called to answer a question or when speaking up, they will always stand before responding.

【アクティビティー: Activities】

A. Pair Work

　　Play the Simon Says game. Give commands to your partner using expressions you have learned.

B. Pair Work - Hiragana Speed Reading Contest

　　You show the *hiragana* cards one by one to your partner as your partner reads them aloud. Count how many he/she can read in 20 seconds. Take turns.

2か

【たんご: Vocabulary】

1.えんぴつ
ENPITSU
pencil

2.ボールペン
BOORUPEN
ballpoint pen

3.けしゴム
KESHIGOMU
(rubber) eraser

4.ほん
HON
book

5.かみ
KAMI
paper

6.きょうかしょ／テキスト
KYOOKASHO / TEKISUTO
textbook

7.じしょ
JISHO
dictionary

8.ノート
NOOTO
notebook

9.（お）かね
(O) KANE
money

10.しゃしん
SHASHIN
photo

11.バッグ
BAGGU
bag

12.ぼうし
BOOSHI
cap, hat

13.ごみ
GOMI
rubbish

【＊オプショナルたんご: Optional Vocabulary】

1.＊かばん
＊KABAN
bag, briefcase

2.＊とけい
＊TOKEI
watch, clock

3.＊かさ
＊KASA
umbrella

4.＊えんぴつけずり
＊ENPITSUKEZURI
pencil sharpener

5.＊ごみばこ
＊GOMIBAKO
wastebasket

【 ● ぶんかノート: Cultural Notes】

Japanese Word Order

The Japanese word order in a sentence is topic first, time word or adverb second, and verb last. Particles follow nouns. Correct particle usage is important in order to convey accurate information. Negations occur at the end of sentences. It is therefore hard for foreigners to know whether a sentence is affirmative or negative until the end of the sentence. When forming a question, the word order of the sentence is not changed as it is in English. Rather, the question marker is simply attached at the end of the sentence. Ex. みえます。MIEMASU. (I can see.) みえますか。MIEMASU KA. (Can you see?)

【 アクティビティー: Activities】

A. Pair Work

Point to things around you and ask what they are. Use これ KORE, それ SORE, あれ ARE for both questions and answers.

41

【たんご: Vocabulary】

1. この + Noun
   KONO + NOUN
   this ～

2. その + Noun
   SONO + Noun
   that ～

3. あの + Noun
   ANO + Noun
   that ～ over there

4. あなた
   ANATA
   you

Used to address persons of equal or lower status. Japanese people use names or titles to address persons of higher status. Whenever possible, avoid the use of あなた ANATA especialy when it is clear that the subject is "you."

5. わたしの
   WATASHI-NO
   mine

6. あなたの
   ANATA-NO
   yours

【ぶんぽう: Grammar】

A. The particle "の" indicates possession.

1. これは　わたしのです。　　　　This is mine.
   KORE WA WATASHI-NO DESU.

2. 「これは　あなたのですか。」　Is this yours?
   KORE WA ANATA-NO DESU KA.
   「はい、わたしのです。」　　　Yes, it is mine.
   HAI, WATASHI-NO DESU.

3. あれは　けいこさんのです。　That one over there is Keiko's.
   ARE WA KEIKO-SAN-NO DESU.

KONO / SONO / ANO＋ NOUN WA ~ DESU.

This is a variation of the Noun 1 = Noun 2 pattern. The pre-nominatives function as modifiers of the noun which they precede. "KONO," "SONO" and "ANO" cannot be used without nouns immediately following them.

1. その　えんぴつは　わたしのです。　　　That pencil is mine.

   SONO ENPITSU WA WATASHI-NO DESU.

2. あの　ぼうしは　ぼくのです。　　　　　That cap over there is mine.

   ANO BOOSHI WA BOKU-NO DESU.

3. この　おかねは　わたしのです。　　　　This money is mine.

   KONO OKANE WA WATASHI-NO DESU.

【 ● ぶんかノート: Cultural Notes】

1. Don't use あなた ANATA to your teacher.

   あなた ANATA is used to address persons of equal or lower status. It is rude to use あなた ANATA to your teacher. せんせい SENSEI should be used instead. Try to avoid using あなた ANATA in your conversations. Instead, use the listener's name to avoid being too direct.

2. Japanese students use したじき SHITAJIKI.

   Japanese students always go to school well equipped with school supplies. They carry pencils, pens, erasers, compasses, notebooks, pencil cases, etc. They also always carry their own supply of tissue. Another necessary item is the したじき SHITAJIKI, which is a smooth page-sized solid plastic sheet which is placed under paper so that one can write neatly. There may be several reasons for using a したじき SHITAJIKI. First, Japanese students rarely use loose "sheets of paper." They almost always use notebooks. したじき SHITAJIKI provides a solid backing when writing in a notebook. Second, Japanese traditionally always used both the back and front of a page of paper. By using the したじき SHITAJIKI, one can always have a clean piece (not one which is roughened by pressing heavily on the opposite side of the page). Japanese were conscious of recycling and environmental protection long before Americans because of their limited resources.

3. ちょうめん or ノート? Words change with time.

   Japanese language is constantly undergoing change, as it easily adopts words from other languages. This practice is also true historically, when Chinese words greatly enriched the Japan language. Now, English is a major source from which words are borrowed. For example, the word ちょうめん CHOOMEN, which is a practice writing tablet, is now called ノート NOOTO. The word "steak" was originally adopted as ビフテキ BIFUTEKI (beefsteak), but is now called ステーキ SUTEEKI. Gym shoes were called うんどうぐつ UNDOOGUTSU, but are now called スポーツシューズ SUPOOTSU SHUUZU or スニーカー SUNIIKAA.

【 アクティビティー: Activities】

A. Pair Work

You and your partner drop your belongings on the floor. Each of you claim your own possessions. Use この KONO, その SONO, あの ANO.

B. Class Work

Lost and Found. Each student loses one item. The lost items are at the lost & found corner. One student picks one item which does not belong to him/her and finds the person who lost it by asking questions such as:

「これ／この〜　は　あなたのですか。」

If it is yours, say 「はい、そうです。」 or 「はい、それは　わたしのです。」.

If it is not yours, say 「いいえ、そうではありません。」 or

「いいえ、わたしのではありません。」.

【たんご: Vocabulary】

1. ここ
KOKO
here

2. そこ
SOKO
there

3. あそこ
ASOKO
over there

4. ティッシュ
TISSHU
tissue

5. しゅくだい
SHUKUDAI
homework

6. しけん
SHIKEN
exam

7. しょうテスト
SHOOTESUTO
quiz

8. ワークシート
WAAKUSHIITO
worksheet

9. チョコレート
CHOKOREETO
chocolate

10. あめ or キャンディ
AME   KYANDII
candy

	11.	12. 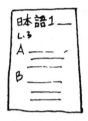
1	いちまい ICHIMAI	ひとつ HITOTSU
2	にまい NIMAI	ふたつ FUTATSU
3	さんまい SANMAI	みっつ MITTSU
4	よんまい YONMAI	よっつ YOTTSU
5	ごまい GOMAI	いつつ ITSUTSU
6	ろくまい ROKUMAI	むっつ MUTTSU
7	ななまい NANAMAI	ななつ NANATSU
8	はちまい HACHIMAI	やっつ YATTSU
9	きゅうまい KYUUMAI	ここのつ KOKONOTSU
10	じゅうまい JUUMAI	とお＊ TOO
?	なんまい NANMAI	いくつ IKUTSU
	Counter for flat objects.	Counter for round objects or other unclassified objects.
Ex.	paper, plates, CDs, tickets, shirts, tissue, etc.	keys, apples, candies, hamburgers, rings, etc.

＊ Exception: This long "OO" sound is spelled with an お instead of an う.

２か

13. 〜を　ください。
〜 O　KUDASAI.
Please give me 〜.

14. はい、どうぞ。
HAI, DOOZO.
Here, please. (Here you are.)

【ぶんぽう: Grammar】

A. Something を　(Counter)　ください。
O　　　　　　　KUDASAI.

This pattern is used when one requests something. を O is a particle which follows the direct object. The counter follows the object being requested. Particles do not follow counters.

1. せんせい、ティッシュを　ください。　　　　　Teacher, please give me some tissue.
SENSEI, TISSHU O KUDASAI.

2. すみません、ワークシートを　にまい　ください。　Excuse me, please give me
SUMIMASEN, WAAKUSHIITO O NIMAI KUDASAI.　　　　two worksheets.

3. あめを　ひとつ　ください。　　　　　Please give me one piece of candy.
AME O HITOTSU KUDASAI.

B. Something は　ここ／そこ／あそこ　です。
Something WA　　KOKO/SOKO/ASOKO DESU.

This is another variation of the Noun 1 = Noun 2 pattern. However, in this usage, Noun 2 is not the same object as Noun 1. Noun 2 indicates the location of Noun 1.

1. ティッシュは　あそこです。　　　　　The tissue is over there.
TISSHU WA ASOKO DESU.

2. しゅくだいは　ここです。　　　　　The homework is here.
SHUKUDAI WA KOKO DESU.

【 ● ぶんかノート: Cultural Notes】

1. When handing something to someone, it is polite to use both hands.
If the relationship between two persons is close, one hand may be used to hand over objects, but things are never thrown to others, as it is considered extremely impolite.

2か

2. Counting from 1 to 10 on one's hand, the Japanese way:

1   2   3   4   5

6   7   8   9   1 0

3. "Counters" are attached to numbers in Japanese. Depending on the item one counts, different counters are used.

This concept came from the Chinese language. However, Japanese counters are more complicated than Chinese counters. Some counters are based on the native Japanese counting system: ひとつ HITOTSU, ふたつ FUTATSU... Some are based on words brought from China: ICHI, NI, SAN. The counter changes depending on the kind of things being counted. Counters based on the native Japanese numbers are ひとつ HITOTSU, ふたつ FUTATSU which are used for counting things in general, and ひとり HITORI, ふたり FUTARI which are used for counting people. Examples based on the numbers borrowed from Chinese are いっぱい IPPAI, にはい NIHAI (cupfuls, bowlfuls, glassfuls, spoonfuls), いっぽん IPPON, にほん NIHON (long cylindrical objects), いちまい ICHIMAI, にまい NIMAI (thin flat objects), いっぴき IPPIKI, にひき NIHIKI (small animals), いっさつ ISSATSU, にさつ NISATSU (books), いっさい ISSAI, にさい NISAI (age), and いちだい ICHIDAI, にだい NIDAI (mechanically operated things). Note that there are also counters in English: cupfuls, pairs (of shoes or pants), heads (of cattle), and sheets (of paper).

2か

【アクティビティー: Activities】

A. Pair Work

You want the following things from your partner. Ask your partner for the things you want and your partner will hand them properly to you. You thank him/her and he/she responds, "You are welcome."

1. one sheet of paper

2. two sheets of tissue

3. three sheets of worksheets

4. one piece of candy

5. two pieces of chocolate

6. five cookies

7. (something of your choice)

B. Class Work

Your teacher has cookies. Ask your teacher to give you cookies. Be humble. The teacher will give you cookies only if you request them correctly. If you ask for more than one, count them in Japanese while you are receiving them. Don't forget to thank your teacher.

Say these expressions in Japanese.

1. How do you do? I am _____. Nice to meet you. [Bow.]

2. Mrs. (your teacher), good morning. [Bow.]

3. Mrs. (your teacher), good-bye. [Bow.]

4. Let's begin. Stand. Bow. Good afternoon. Sit down. [Do it!]

5. Jon, hurry.

6. Mike is tardy. Ben is absent.

7. Let's finish. Stand. Bow. Good-bye. [Do it!]

8. What is this? (Point to something near you.) / What is that? (Point to something near your

   teacher.) / What is that over there ? (Point to something distant from both you and your teacher.)

9. Excuse me. One more time please. [Bow slightly.]

10. Excuse me. Slowly please. [Bow slightly.]

11. Thank you very much (to your teacher). [Bow.]

12. You are welcome.

13. Teacher: Is this/ that/ that one over there ___? (Point to one *hiragana*)   You: (Answer.)

    [Use 3 *hiragana* cards.]

14. It's hot!

15. It's cold!

16. It's cool!

17. How are you?

18. Teacher: How are you?   You: (Answer).

19. Do you understand?

20. Yes, I understand.

21. No, I do not understand.

22. I do not know.

23. I cannot see.

24. I cannot hear.

25. How do you say "dog" in Japanese?

26. It is good.

27. It is no good.

28. Is this yours? [Point.] [Do not use あなた to your teacher!]

29. Is this money yours? [Point.] [Do not use あなた to your teacher!]

30. That one over there is mine. [Point.]

31. That pencil (near the teacher) is mine.

32. Please give me one sheet of paper.

33. Please give me one piece of candy.

34. Here, please. [Hand something to another person.]

35. The tissues are over there. [Point.]

36. The homework is here. [Point.]

37. [Read] 5, 9, 12, 43, 80   38. [Read] 7, 26, 54, 91, 100   39. [Read] 4, 38, 62, 75, 91

2 か   50

By the end of this lesson, you will be able to communicate the information below in the given situations.

【１-３ タスク１】

You meet a Japanese exchange student for the first time. Introduce yourselves and ask each other about your families. Discuss how many people are in your families, how they are related, what their jobs are, their grades, ages, names, etc. (When there are many siblings, talk about your parents and one sibling only.)

【１-３ タスク２】

You are hosting a student from another school. Introduce yourselves to one another and ask for names, schools, grades, and ages. Bring him/her to your Japanese class and introduce him/her to your teacher and classmates.

【おはなし：Story】

これは　わたしの　かぞくの　しゃしんです。
かぞくは　よにんです。
これは　ちちです。
ちちの　なまえは　ジャック JAKKU です。
ちちは　４５さいです。

KORE WA WATASHI NO KAZOKU NO SHASHIN DESU.

KAZOKU WA YONIN DESU.

KORE WA CHICHI DESU.

CHICHI NO NAMAE WA JAKKU DESU.

CHICHI WA YONJUUGO-SAI DESU.

【たんご：Vocabulary】

| 1. ちち
CHICHI
my father | 2. はは
HAHA
my mother | 3. あに
ANI
my older brother | 4. あね
ANE
my older sister | 5. おとうと
OTOOTO
my younger brother | 6. いもうと
IMOOTO
my younger sister |

 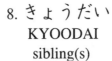

| 7. かぞく
KAZOKU
family | 8. きょうだい
KYOODAI
sibling(s) | 9. なまえ
NAMAE
name | 10. だれ
DARE
who? |

Counters

	11. People	12. Ages
1	ひとり　HITORI	いっさい　IS-SAI
2	ふたり　FUTARI	にさい　NI-SAI
3	さんにん　SAN-NIN	さんさい　SAN-SAI
4	よにん　YO-NIN *1	よんさい　YON-SAI
5	ごにん　GO-NIN	ごさい　GO-SAI
6	ろくにん　ROKU-NIN	ろくさい　ROKU-SAI
7	なな／しちにん　NANA/SHICHI-NIN	ななさい　NANA--SAI
8	はちにん　HACHI-NIN	はっさい　HAS-SAI
9	きゅうにん　KYUU-NIN	きゅうさい　KYUU-SAI *2
1 0	じゅうにん　JUU-NIN	じ(ゅ)っさい　JUS-SAI/JIS-SAI
1 1	じゅういちにん　JUUICHI-NIN	じゅういっさい　JUUIS-SAI
	＼	＼
2 0	＼	はたち　HATACHI
	＼	＼
?	なんにん　NAN-NIN?	なんさい　NAN-SAI? ／(お)いくつ　(O) IKUTSU?

*1 Do not use しにん SHININ for four people. しにん SHININ means "a dead person."

*2 Do not use くさい KUSAI for nine years old. くさい KUSAI means "is smelly."

3か

13. そうですか。

SOO DESU KA.

Is that so?

Used very often by a listener as a response to new information he/she receives, often used as one nods.

14. ほんとうですか。

HONTOO DESU KA.

Is that true?/ Really?

15. の

NO

A possessive and descriptive particle.
わたしのほん WATASHI NO HON
my book, にほんごのほん NIHONGO
NO HON Japanese language book

【＊オプショナルたんご: Optional Vocabulary】

		3. ＊どなた	＊DONATA	who?
				[polite form of だれ DARE]
		4. ＊ペット	＊PETTO	a pet
		5. ＊ぎりの〜	＊GIRI NO 〜	step 〜 (family)
1.＊いぬ	2.＊ねこ	6. ＊うえの〜	＊UE NO 〜	older (of two) 〜
＊INU	＊NEKO	7. ＊したの〜	＊SHITA NO 〜	younger (of two) 〜
dog	cat			

【ぶんぽう: Grammar 】

> A. NOUN 1 の　 NOUN 2
>
> 　 NOUN 1 NO　NOUN 2
>
> The particle の NO used here indicates possession or description. This の NO appears between two nouns. The first noun modifies the second.

1. これは　わたしの　かぞくの　しゃしんです。　　This is my family's photo.

　　KORE WA WATASHI NO KAZOKU NO SHASHIN DESU.

2. あにの　なまえは　マイクです。　　My older brother's name is Mike.

　　ANI NO NAMAE WA MAIKU DESU.

3.＊ぎりの　ははは　４０さいです。　　My stepmother is 40 years old.

　　＊GIRI NO HAHA WA YONJUS-SAI DESU.

【 ● ぶんかノート : Cultural Notes】

1. "In-group" vs. "Out-group"

The Japanese language reflects the structure, values and attitudes of the Japanese society. One of the primary forces which operates in Japanese society is "in-group" vs. "out-group." Japanese are constantly making distinctions between those people who are associated with themselves and those who are not. Members of the "in-group" may vary according to the circumstances. The "in-group" may be oneself, one's family, one's friends, one's school, one's company or even one's own country. The set of family terms which you are learning in this lesson is an example of how the language is used to make a distinction between one's own family and another's family.

2. Japanese *AIZUCHI*

"SOO DESU KA?" is but one example of *AIZUCHI*, or expressions which Japanese use frequently in conversations to indicate to the listener that they are listening to the speaker. Other words such as はい HAI or ええ EE are often also used as *AIZUCHI*. The use of *AIZUCHI* is similar to the English use of "uh huh", but is used much more frequently in Japanese. Using *AIZUCHI* is particularly important when talking over the phone.

【 アクティビティー : Activities】

A. Pair Work

Bring a photo or drawing of your family to class.

1. Describe what kind of photo or drawing it is.

2. Describe how many people there are in your family.

3. Describe each family member, including pets.

4. Give each family member's name and age.

3か

B. Class Work - Song

♪ ♪ ♪   Let's sing a counting song to the tune of "Ten Little Indians." ♪ ♪ ♪

1. ひとつ　ふたつ　みっつの　ハンバーガー
   HITOTSU FUTATSU MITTSU NO HANBAAGAA [1, 2, 3 hamburgers]
   よっつ　いつつ　むっつの　ハンバーガー
   YOTTSU ITSUTSU MUTTSU NO HANBAAGAA [4, 5, 6 hamburgers]
   ななつ　やっつ　ここのつの　ハンバーガー
   NANATSU YATTSU KOKONOTSU NO HANBAAGAA [7, 8, 9 hamburgers]
   とおの　ハンバーガー
   TOO NO HANBAAGAA [10 hamburgers]
   むしゃ　むしゃ　むしゃ　むしゃ　ハンバーガーは　おいしい
   MUSHA MUSHA MUSHA MUSHA HANBAAGAA WA OISHII
   　[munch, munch, munch, munch. Hamburgers taste good.]
   むしゃ　むしゃ　むしゃ　むしゃ　ハンバーガーは　おいしい
   MUSHA MUSHA MUSHA MUSHA HANBAAGAA WA OISHII
   むしゃ　むしゃ　むしゃ　むしゃ　ハンバーガーは　おいしい
   MUSHA MUSHA MUSHA MUSHA HANBAAGAA WA OISHII
   ハンバーガーは　おいしいね
   HANBAAGAA WA OISHII NE

2. ひとり　ふたり　さんにんの　こども
   HITORI FUTARI SANNIN NO KODOMO [1, 2, 3 children]
   よにん　ごにん　ろくにんの　こども
   YONIN GONIN ROKUNIN NO KODOMO [4, 5, 6 children]
   しちにん　はちにん　きゅうにんの　こども
   SHICHININ HACHININ KYUUNIN NO KODOMO [7, 8, 9 children]
   じゅうにんの　こども
   JUUNIN NO KODOMO [10 children]
   わいわい　がやがや　こどもは　たのしい
   WAIWAI GAYAGAYA KODOMO WA TANOSHII
   　[(Sound of children playing) Children have fun.]
   わいわい　がやがや　こどもは　たのしい
   WAIWAI GAYAGAYA KODOMO WA TANOSHII
   わいわい　がやがや　こどもは　たのしい
   WAIWAI GAYAGAYA KODOMO WA TANOSHII
   こどもは　たのしいね
   KODOMO WA TANOSHII NE

【かいわ: Dialogue】

エミ：ごかぞくは　なんにんですか。

ケン：よにんです。ちちと　ははと　あねと　ぼくです。

エミ：そうですか。

　　　おねえさんの　おなまえは　なんですか。

ケン：リサです。

エミ：おねえさんは　なんさいですか。

ケン：１８さいです。

EMI : GOKAZOKU WA NAN-NIN DESU KA.

KEN : YO-NIN DESU. CHICHI TO HAHA TO ANE TO BOKU DESU.

EMI : SOO DESU KA.

ONEESAN NO ONAMAE WA NAN DESU KA.

KEN : RISA DESU.

EMI : ONEESAN WA NAN-SAI DESU KA.

KEN : JUUHASSAI DESU.

【たんご: Vocabulary】

1. おとうさん
OTOOSAN
(someone's) father

2. おかあさん
OKAASAN
(someone's) mother

3. おじいさん
OJIISAN
grandfather, elderly man

4. おばあさん
OBAASAN
grandmother, elderly woman

5. おにいさん
ONIISAN
(someone's) older
brother

6. おねえさん
ONEESAN
(someone's) older
sister

7. おとうとさん
OTOOTOSAN
(someone's) younger
brother

8. いもうとさん
IMOOTOSAN
(someone's) younger
sister

３か

9. ジョンさんと　エミさん
JON-SAN <u>TO</u> EMI-SAN
Jon and Emi

10. ごかぞく
<u>GO</u>KAZOKU
(someone's) family

11. おなまえ
<u>O</u>NAMAE
(someone's) name

[ご and お are polite prefixes for nouns.]

12. そして　　　SOSHITE　　　And [Used only at the beginning of a sentence.]

【*オプショナルたんご: Optional Vocabulary】

1.*おじさん
*OJISAN
uncle

2.*おばさん
*OBASAN
aunt

3.*いとこ
*ITOKO
cousin

【ぶんぽう: Grammar】

A. NOUN 1 と NOUN 2　　　　　　　　　　Noun 1 and Noun 2
NOUN 1 TO NOUN 2
The particle と TO conjoins two or more nouns. It is translated as "and." It cannot ever be used to conjoin anything but nouns. It is not replaceable by commas, as is common in English when a string of nouns are listed together.

1. ベンさんと　エミさんは　おやすみです。 Ben and Emi are absent.

　　BEN-SAN <u>TO</u> EMI-SAN WA OYASUMI DESU.

2. かぞくは　ちちと　ははと　わたしです。 My family is my father, my mother and me.

　　KAZOKU WA CHICHI <u>TO</u> HAHA <u>TO</u> WATASHI DESU.

B. 〜は。🡕　　　　　　　　　　　　　　How about 〜?
〜WA？
When the predicate of a question is understood by both the listener and speaker, it is common to use this abbreviated form. This is used more frequently in speaking than in writing.

1. あなたは。🡕　　　　　　　　　　　　How about you?
　　ANATA <u>WA</u>.

2. おなまえは。🡕　　　　　　　　　　　What is your/his/her name?
　　ONAMAE <u>WA</u>.

3か

58

3. おねえさんは。↗ How about your older sister?
   ONEESAN <u>WA</u>.
4. しゅくだいは。↗ How about (your) homework?
   SHUKUDAI <u>WA</u>.
5. これは。↗ How about this?
   KORE <u>WA</u>.

C. Sentence 1。そして、 Sentence 2。 Sentence 1. And sentence 2.
   　　　　 SOSHITE
   そして SOSHITE which means "and" is only used at the beginning of sentences.

---

1. ちちは　４３さいです。<u>そして</u>、ははは　３８さいです。
   CHICHI WA YONJUUSAN-SAI DESU. <u>SOSHITE</u>, HAHA WA SANJUU-HAS-SAI DESU.
   My father is 43. And my mother is 38 years old.
2. あねの　なまえは　まゆみです。<u>そして</u>、１８さいです。
   ANE NO NAMAE WA MAYUMI DESU. <u>SOSHITE</u>, JUUHAS-SAI DESU.
   My older sister's name is Mayumi. And she is 18 years old.

【 ● ぶんかノート: Cultural Notes】

How do Japanese people address their family members?

When Japanese address family members, おとうさん OTOOSAN or パパ PAPA is used for father, おかあさん OKAASAN or ママ MAMA for mother, おにいさん ONIISAN for older brothers, おねえさん ONEESAN for older sisters and the given names for younger brothers and younger sisters. パパ PAPA and ママ MAMA are generally used by younger persons. Japanese do not use given names for family members older than themselves. Even spouses rarely use their given names when addressing one another. When children are smaller, they tend to use ちゃん CHAN instead of さん SAN to address others, i.e., おとうちゃん OTOOCHAN instead of おとうさん OTOOSAN, おねえちゃん ONEECHAN instead of おねえさん ONEESAN.

【 アクティビティー: Activities】

A. Pair Work

Ask about your partner's family and draw a family tree. Find out how many people are in the family, what their relationships are, and their names and ages.

「ごかぞくは　なんにんですか。」「〜にんです。」
GOKAZOKU WA NAN-NIN DESU KA.　〜NIN DESU.
「ごかぞくは　だれですか。」「ちちと　ははと　〜と　〜です。」
GOKAZOKU WA DARE DESU KA.　CHICHI TO HAHA TO 〜TO 〜DESU.
「おとうさんの　おなまえは　なんですか。」「ちちの　なまえは　〜です。」
OTOOSAN NO ONAMAE WA NAN DESU KA.　CHICHI NO NAMAE WA 〜DESU.
「おとうさんは　なんさいですか。」「ちちは　〜さいです。」
OTOOSAN WA NAN-SAI DESU KA.　CHICHI WA 〜SAI DESU.

【かいわ: Dialogue】

エミ：おなまえは？

ケン：ケンです。

エミ：ケンさんは　こうこうせいですか。

ケン：いいえ、ぼくは　こうこうせいでは　ありません。
　　　ちゅうがくせいです。

エミ：なんねんせいですか。

ケン：さんねんせいです。

エミ：そうですか。わたしも　ちゅうがくさんねんせいです。

EMI : ONAMAE WA?

KEN : KEN DESU.

EMI : KEN-SAN WA KOOKOOSEI DESU KA.

KEN : IIE, BOKU WA KOOKOOSEI DEWA ARIMASEN.
　　　CHUUGAKUSEI DESU.

EMI : NANNENSEI DESU KA?

KEN : SANNENSEI DESU.

EMI : SOO DESU KA. WATASHI MO CHUUGAKU SANNENSEI DESU.

【たんご: Vocabulary】

1. がっこう
GAKKOO
school

2. せいと
SEITO
elementary, intermediate,
or high school student

3. がくせい
GAKUSEI
college student

4. ちゅうがく CHUUGAKU intermediate school	6. ちゅうがくせい CHUUGAKUSEI intermediate student	8. ちゅうがく　いちねんせい CHUUGAKU　ICHINENSEI 7th grader
		9. ちゅうがく　にねんせい CHUUGAKU NINENSEI 8th grader
		10. ちゅうがく　さんねんせい CHUUGAKU SANNENSEI freshman, 9th grader
5. こうこう KOOKOO high school	7. こうこうせい KOOKOOSEI high school student	11. こうこう　いちねんせい KOOKOO　ICHINENSEI sophomore, 10th grader
		12. こうこう　にねんせい KOOKOO　NINENSEI junior, 11th grader
		13. こうこう　さんねんせい KOOKOO　SANNENSEI senior, 12th grader
		14. なんねんせい NANNENSEI? what grade?

15. 〜も　　　　〜MO　　　too, also

【*オプショナルたんご: Optional Vocabulary】

1.*だいがく　　　　*DAIGAKU　　　college, university

2.*だいがくせい　　*DAIGAKUSEI　　college student

3.*しょうがっこう　*SHOOGAKKOO　elementary school

4.*しょうがくせい　*SHOOGAKUSEI　elementary school student

5.*ようちえん　　　*YOOCHIEN　　kindergarten

6.*ほいくえん　　　*HOIKUEN　　preschool

3か

【ぶんぽう：Grammar】

A. Noun 1 は　　Noun 2 では　ありません／じゃ　ありません。　Noun 1 ≠ Noun 2
　　Noun 1 WA　Noun 2 DEWA ARIMASEN／JA ARIMASEN.

ではありません DEWA ARIMASEN is more polite and formal than じゃありません JA ARIMASEN. This pattern is the negative counterpart of NOUN 1 は WA NOUN 2 です DESU.

---

1. わたしは　こうこうせいでは　ありません。　　　　I am not a high school student.
   WATASHI WA KOOKOOSEI <u>DEWA ARIMASEN</u>.

2. ジョンさんは　おやすみでは　ありません。　　　　Jon is not absent.
   JON-SAN WA OYASUMI <u>DEWA ARIMASEN</u>.

3. ははは　５０さいでは　ありません。　　　　My mother is not 50 years old.
   HAHA WA GOJUSSAI <u>DEWA ARIMASEN</u>.

B. Noun 1 も　　Noun 2 です。　　　　　　　Noun 1 is <u>also</u> Noun 2. / Noun 1 is Noun 2 <u>too</u>.
　　Noun 1 MO　Noun 2 DESU.

　　Noun 1 も　　Noun 2 ではありません。　Noun 1 is not Noun 2, <u>either</u>.
　　Noun 1 MO　Noun 2 DEWA ARIMASEN.

も MO is used immediately after the noun to which the meaning of "also" applies. Mo is translated as "also" in positive sentences and "either" in negative sentences. も MO replaces particles を O, が GA, は WA.

　　Noun 1 も　　Noun 2 も　　Noun 3 です。　　　　<u>Both</u> Noun 1 <u>and</u> Noun 2 are Noun 3.
　　Noun 1 MO　Noun 2 MO　Noun 3 DESU.

　　Noun 1 も　　Noun 2 も　Noun 3ではありません。<u>Neither</u> Noun 1 <u>nor</u> Noun 2 are Noun 3.
　　Noun 1 MO　Noun 2 MO　Noun 3 DEWA ARIMASEN.

---

1. ゆみさんは　１４さいです。わたしも　１４さいです。
   YUMISAN <u>MO</u> JUUYON-SAI DESU. WATASHI MO JUUYON-SAI <u>DESU</u>.
   Yumi is 14. I am 14, too.

2. わたしは　ちゅうがくせいではありません。
   あにも　ちゅうがくせいではありません。
   WATASHI WA CHUUGAKUSEI DEWA ARIMASEN.
   ANI <u>MO</u> CHUUGAKUSEI <u>DEWA ARIMASEN</u>.
   I am not an intermediate school student. My older brother is not an intermediate student, either.

3. ちちも　ははも　４０さいです。
   CHICHI <u>MO</u> HAHA <u>MO</u> YONJUSSAI DESU.
   Both my father and mother are 40 years old.

4. わたしも　あにも　ちゅうがくせいではありません。
   WATASHI <u>MO</u> ANI <u>MO</u> CHUUGAKUSEI DEWA ARIMASEN.
   Neither I nor my older brother is an intermediate school student.

【 ● ぶんかノート: Cultural Notes】

1. The Structure of the Japanese School System

   The Japanese school system and the U.S. school system are not structured the same way. As in the U.S., an increasing amount of Japanese young children attend preschool. Almost all children attend kindergarten. Elementary school consists of six years. Intermediate school is three years, and high school is also three years. College is usually four years.

2. あなた ANATA ≠ You

   あなた ANATA is used to address persons of equal or lower status. Whenever possible, avoid the use of あなた ANATA, especially when it is clear that the subject is "you."

【 アクティビティー: Activities】

A. Class Work

   Ask your classmates for their full names and grades. Draw a seating chart with the names and the grades of each student in English. Later your teacher will ask you the grade level of each student. Answer in Japanese.

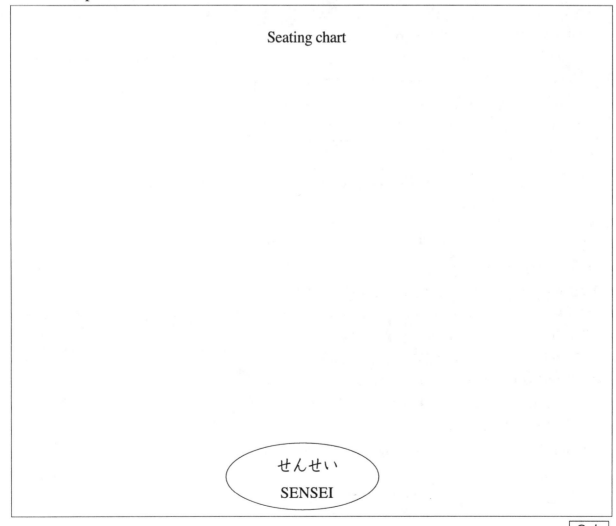

Seating chart

せんせい
SENSEI

3か

【かいわ: Dialogue】

ケン　　　：おなまえは？
なかむら：<u>なかむらあきこ</u>です。
ケン　　　：がっこうは　どこですか。
なかむら：<u>けいおう</u>こうこうです。
ケン　　　：なんねんせいですか。
なかむら：こうこういちねんせいです。

KEN　　　　：ONAMAE WA?
NAKAMURA：<u>NAKAMURA AKIKO</u> DESU.
KEN　　　　：GAKKOO WA DOKO DESU KA.
NAKAMURA：<u>KEIOO</u> KOOKOO DESU.
KEN　　　　：NAN-NENSEI DESU KA.
NAKAMURA：KOOKOO ICHI-NENSEI DESU.

こちらは　<u>なかむらあきこ</u>さんです。
<u>なかむら</u>さんは　にほんじんです。
にほんの　こうこういちねんせいです。

KOCHIRA WA <u>NAKAMURA AKIKO</u> SAN DESU.

<u>NAKAMURA</u> SAN WA NIHONJIN DESU.

NIHON NO KOOKOO ICHI-NENSEI DESU.

【たんご: Vocabulary】

1. どこ
DOKO
where?

2. こちら
KOCHIRA
this one
(Polite form of これ and may
be used to refer to a person.)

3. にほん
NIHON
Japan

4. にほんじん
NIHON-JIN
Japanese citizen

 ３か

5. アメリカ
AMERIKA
U.S.A.

6. アメリカじん
AMERIKA-JIN
U.S. citizen

7. なにじん
NANI-JIN?
What nationality?

8. ちゅうごく
CHUUGOKU
China

9. かんこく
KANKOKU
Korea

10. フランス
FURANSU
France

11. スペイン
SUPEIN
Spain

12. ドイツ
DOITSU
Germany

13. Months of the year

1	いちがつ	ICHI-GATSU	January
2	にがつ	NI-GATSU	February
3	さんがつ	SAN-GATSU	March
4	しがつ *1	SHI-GATSU	April
5	ごがつ	GO-GATSU	May
6	ろくがつ	ROKU-GATSU	June
7	しちがつ	SHICHI-GATSU	July
8	はちがつ	HACHI-GATSU	August
9	くがつ *2	KU-GATSU	September
10	じゅうがつ	JUU-GATSU	October
11	じゅういちがつ	JUUICHI-GATSU	November
12	じゅうにがつ	JUUNI-GATSU	December
?	なんがつ	NAN-GATSU?	what month?

14.

10月10日

～がつうまれ
～GATSU UMARE
born in (month)

*1 しがつ SHIGATSU,
never よんがつ
YONGATSU.

*2 くがつ KUGATSU,
never きゅうがつ
KYUUGATSU.

【*オプショナルたんご: Optional Vocabulary】
1.*ロシア　　　　　*ROSHIA　　　　　Russia
2.*イギリス　　　　*IGIRISU　　　　　England
3.*メキシコ　　　　*MEKISHIKO　　　Mexico
4.*フィリピン　　　*FIRIPIN　　　　　Philippines
5.*にっけいじん　　*NIKKEIJIN　　　　ethnically Japanese, but a citizen of another
　　　　　　　　　　　　　　　　　　　country, i.e., Japanese American

3か

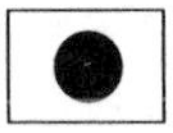

【 ● ぶんかノート: Cultural Notes】

にほんじん NIHONJIN and にっけいじん NIKKEIJIN

Do not confuse these two terms. にほんじん NIHONJIN is a person who is a Japanese citizen. A person who is ethnically Japanese, but a citizen of a country other than Japan (i.e., America, Brazil, etc.) is にっけいじん NIKKEIJIN. Japanese Americans are にっけいじん NIKKEIJIN.

【 アクティビティー: Activities】

A. Class Work

Ask your partner for his/her name, age, grade, and birth month. Then introduce him/her to the class.

B. Group Work

Ask each of your group members in what month they were born. Write each person's birth month on the chart below at the left. One student from each group will report. Tally the total numbers by month and group on the chart at the right. The teacher will ask you questions about the results you received.

Ex. 「なんがつうまれですか。」   Ex. 「〜がつうまれは　〜にんです。」
NANGATSU UMARE DESU KA.   〜GATSU UMARE WA 〜NIN DESU.

なまえ NAMAE	Birth month

month	G1	G2	G3	G4	month	G1	G2	G3	G4
1					7				
2					8				
3					9				
4					10				
5					11				
6					12				

【かいわ: Dialogue】

エミ：おとうさんの　おしごとは　なんですか？

ケン：いしゃです。

エミ：どこの　びょういんの　おいしゃさんですか。

ケン：<u>カイザー</u>びょういんです。

エミ：そうですか。おかあさんは？

ケン：ははは　いま　しゅふです。そして、まえ　せんせいでした。

EMI : OTOOSAN NO OSHIGOTO WA NAN DESU KA.

KEN : ISHA DESU.

EMI : DOKO NO BYOOIN NO OISHASAN DESU KA.

KEN : <u>KAIZAA</u>-BYOOIN DESU.

EMI : SOO DESU KA. OKAASAN WA?

KEN : HAHA WA IMA SHUFU DESU. SOSHITE, MAE SENSEI DESHITA.

【たんご: Vocabulary】

1.（お）しごと
(O) SHIGOTO
job

2. いしゃ
ISHA
medical doctor

When addressing a medical
doctor, one uses the doctor's
last name, followed by SENSEI,
i.e., ODA-SENSEI. ISHA is not
used.

3. おいしゃさん
OISHASAN
medical doctor

Polite form of ISHA. Often
used to refer to doctors
outside one's own family.

4. びょういん
BYOOIN
hospital

3か

5. べんごし BENGOSHI lawyer	6. かいしゃいん KAISHAIN company employee	7. しゅふ SHUFU housewife	8. エンジニア ENJINIA engineer

9. いま　　　　　　　IMA　　　　　　　　　　now
10. まえ　　　　　　　MAE　　　　　　　　　　before

【＊オプショナルたんご: Optional Vocabulary】
1.＊こうむいん　　　　＊KOOMUIN　　　　　government worker
2.＊かいけいし　　　　＊KAIKEISHI　　　　　accountant
3.＊ひしょ　　　　　　＊HISHO　　　　　　　secretary
4.＊パイロット　　　　＊PAIROTTO　　　　　pilot
5.＊スチュワーデス　＊SUCHUWAADESU　　flight attendant (female)
6.＊ふどうさんや　　　＊FUDOOSANYA　　　real estate salesperson
7.＊しゃちょう　　　　＊SHACHOO　　　　　company president
8.＊かんごふ　　　　　＊KANGOFU　　　　　nurse

【ぶんぽう: Grammar】

A. Noun1 は　Noun2 でした。　　　　　　　　　N1 was / were N2.
　　Noun1WA　Noun2 DESHITA.
　　Noun1 は　Noun2では／じゃ　ありませんでした。　N1 was not / were not N2.
　　Noun1WA　Noun2 DEWA/JA　ARIMASENDESHITA.
This pattern is a variation of the "N1 はWA N2 です DESU。" pattern. These new patterns are used when one expresses a statement in the past and the negative past form.

1. ちちは　まえ　かいしゃいんでした。　　　　My father was a company employee before.
　　CHICHI WA MAE KAISHAIN DESHITA.

2. ははは　まえ　せんせいでした。　　　　　　My mother was a teacher before.
　　HAHA WA MAE SENSEI DESHITA.

3. わたしは　まえ　この　がっこうの　せいとでは　ありませんでした。
   WATASHI WA MAE KONO GAKKOO NO SEITO <u>DEWA ARIMASENDESHITA</u>.

   I was not a student of this school before.

【 ● ぶんかノート: Cultural Notes】

Describing Occupations

Japanese tend to be very general about describing their occupations to others. Often, Japanese children know very little about the specifics of their father's jobs, except for the name of the company at which he works. Even spouses are sometimes not clear about the exact responsibilities of their spouses' jobs.

【 アクティビティー: Activities】

A. Class Work

Ask your partner about his/her family, what his/her parents do and what grade his/her siblings are in. Ask where his/her family members work or study.

Ex. 「おとうさんの　おしごとは　なんですか。」

   "What is your father's occupation?"

   「おしごとは　どこですか。」

   "Where does he work? (=Where is his work?)"

   「おにいさんは　なんねんせいですか。」

   "What grade is your older brother?"

   「おにいさんの　がっこうは　どこですか。」

   "What (=Where) is your older brother's school?"

Family	Job or Grade	Place of work or school

Introduce your partner and his/her family to the class.

Ex. 「～さんの　おとうさんは　(Working place)の　(Occupation)です。」

   「～さんの　おにいさんは　(School name)の　(Grade)です。」

３か

Find the answers by investigating books, by talking to friends, or by using the Internet.

1. Write down the members of your family (e.g., mom, dad, older brother, etc.).

2. What members of the family usually live under one roof in the U.S.?

3. What members of the family usually live under one roof in Japan?

4. What are the roles women and mothers usually play in U.S. families?

5. What are the roles women and mothers usually play in Japanese families?

6. What are the roles men and fathers usually play in U.S. families?

7. What are the roles men and fathers usually play in Japanese families?

8. In Japan, the eldest son usually gets certain benefits within the family, but also undertakes certain responsibilities. Name one benefit and one responsibility of eldest sons in Japan.

9. How long do children usually live with their parents in the U.S.?

10. How long do children usually live with their parents in Japan?

Ingredients: 2 cups uncooked rice
Umeboshi (pickled plum)
Salt
Strips of *nori* (seasoned dry seaweed)

1. You will need a rice cooker and uncooked rice. Place 2 cups of rice in the inner pot of the rice cooker. Two cups will make about 4 riceballs.

2. Briskly wash the rice in cold water. Rinse several times until water loses most of its cloudiness. Drain out water.

3. Pour cold water into rice pot until the line marked "2" on the side of the pot.

4. Cook rice.

5. After the button of the the rice cooker "pops," let stand for 5–10 minutes. When using a wet rice paddle, mix the rice. Cover and let stand a few minutes.

6. Sprinkle salt on your clean, moistened hands. Scoop about a 1/4 of the hot cooked rice on the palm of one of your hands. Place an *umeboshi* in the center of the rice. Be careful! The rice is hot!

3か

7. Using both hands, form your rice ball into a triangular shape. Use your hands as a mold and gently apply pressure as you shape the rice ball.

8. Apply a wide strip of *nori* around the rice ball.

でき あがり

9. Ready to eat — hot or cold!

Omusubi or *Onigiri*
Riceballs

Riceballs, a favorite food of Japanese, are called *omusubi* or *onigiri*. They are delicious, portable and fun to make!

Riceballs are most often triangular in shape, though in Japan they may also be oblong shaped. The rice is often seasoned, with salt or other flavorings. This not only adds flavor, but helps to preserve the rice. Inside the riceball, one usually places pickled plums, flavored strips of kelp, or dried bonito flakes.

One "wraps" the riceball with *nori* for extra flavoring and also to prevent the rice from sticking to other foods when packing the riceball or to prevent it from sticking to your hands as you eat it. Try this recipe and enjoy your *omusubi*!

My child made *omusubi*!

_____

Get your parent's signature.

By the end of this lesson, you will be able to communicate the information below in the given situations.

【1-4 タスク1】

You meet a student who has an international background. Ask him/her what languages his/her family speaks and what language the family speaks at home.

【1-4 タスク2】

In the morning you meet a friend who doesn't look well. Greet him/her and ask how your friend is and what he/she ate and drank last night.

【1-4タスク3】

You meet a Japanese exchange student. Ask him/her what the typical meals are for breakfast, lunch, and dinner in Japan. Describe typical meals in the U.S.

【1-4タスク4】

You were supposed to read newspapers and magazines and write a report for homework, but you didn't. You ask another student for help, but he/she didn't study at all either.

【かいわ: Dialogue 】

エミ：おとうさんと　おかあさんは　にほんごを
　　　　はなしますか。

ケン：ちちは　にほんごを　はなしません。
　　　　でも、ははは　にほんごを　よく　はなします。

エミ：あなたは　うちで　にほんごを　はなしますか。

ケン：いいえ。

EMI:　OTOOSAN TO OKAASAN WA NIHONGO O

　　　　HANASHIMASU KA.

KEN:　CHICHI WA NIHONGO O HANASHIMASEN.

　　　　DEMO, HAHA WA NIHONGO O YOKU HANASHIMASU.

EMI:　ANATA WA UCHI DE NIHONGO O HANASHIMASU KA.

KEN:　IIE.

【ぶんけい: Sentence Structures 】

Person は Place で Language を　はなします。	
WA DE O　HANASHIMASU.	
Sentence 1。でも、Sentence 2。	Sentence 1. However, Sentence 2.
DEMO	

【たんご: Vocabulary】

1. はなします [はなす]
HANASHIMASU [HANASU]
speak, talk

2. にほんご
NIHONGO
Japanese language

3. えいご
EIGO
English

4. うち
UCHI
house

5. ともだち
TOMODACHI
friend

6. ちゅうごくご	CHUUGOKU-GO	Chinese language
7. かんこくご	KANKOKU-GO	Korean language
8. スペインご	SUPEIN-GO	Spanish language
9. フランスご	FURANSU-GO	French language
10. ドイツご	DOITSU-GO	German language
11. なにご	NANI-GO	what language?
12. (Place +)で	(Place +) DE	at, in (a place)
13. よく	YOKU	well, often
14. すこし	SUKOSHI	a little
15. ちょっと	CHOTTO	a little [More colloquial usage than すこし SUKOSHI.]
16. でも	DEMO	But [Used at the beginning of the sentence.]

【*オプショナルたんご: Optional Vocabulary】

1.*ラテンご	*RATEN-GO	Latin language
2.*ロシアご	*ROSHIA-GO	Russian language

【ぶんぽう: Grammar】

A. Object + を (Object particle)
　　　　O

The particle を O immediately follows the direct object of a sentence.

1. ははは　にほんごを　はなします。　　　　My mother speaks Japanese.
   HAHA WA NIHONGO O HANASHIMASU.
2. わたしは　ちゅうごくごを　はなしません。　I do not speak Chinese.
   WATASHI WA CHUUGOKUGO O HANASHIMASEN.
3. 「すみません。かみを　ください。」　　　　"Excuse me. Please give me some
   SUMIMASEN. KAMI O KUDASAI.　　　　　　　paper."
   「はい、どうぞ。」　　　　　　　　　　　　"Yes, here you are."
   HAI, DOOZO.

B. Place + で + Action verb。　　at, in
　　　　DE

The particle で DE immediately follows the place word where the action of the sentence occurs.

75

4 か

1. わたしは　うち<u>で</u>　にほんごを　はなします。　　I speak Japanese at home.
   WATASHI WA UCHI <u>DE</u> NIHONGO O HANASHIMASU.
2. ぼくは　がっこう<u>で</u>　えいごを　はなします。　　I speak English at school.
   BOKU WA GAKKOO <u>DE</u> EIGO O HANASHIMASU.

C. Adverbs

よく	YOKU	well, often
すこし	SUKOSHI	a little
ちょっと	CHOTTO	a little (More colloquial usage than すこし SUKOSHI.)

Adverbs describe verbs. In Japanese sentences, adverbs generally come somewhere after the topic of the sentence and before the verb. No particles follow adverbs.

---

1. おばあさんは　にほんごを　<u>よく</u>　はなします。
   OBAASAN WA NIHONGO O <u>YOKU</u> HANASHIMASU.
   My grandmother speaks Japanese well.
2. あねは　<u>すこし</u>　スペインごを　はなします。
   ANE WA <u>SUKOSHI</u> SUPEINGO O HANASHIMASU.
   My older sister speaks a little Spanish.
3. <u>よく</u>　みえます。　　　　　　　　　　　　　I can see well.
   <u>YOKU</u> MIEMASU.

D. Sentence 1。でも、Sentence 2。　　　Sentence 1. However, sentence 2.
   DEMO
   でも DEMO which means "however" is only used at the beginning of sentences.

---

1. これは　わたしのです。<u>でも</u>、それは　あなたのです。
   KORE WA WATASHINO DESU. <u>DEMO</u>, SORE WA ANATANO DESU.
   This is mine. However, that is yours.
2. ははは　にほんごを　はなします。<u>でも</u>、ちちは　はなしません。
   HAHA WA NIHONGO O HANASHIMASU. <u>DEMO</u>, CHICHI WA HANASHIMASEN.
   My mother speaks Japanese. However, my father does not speak it.

E. Answering a verb-ending question.

   When a question ends with a verb, the answer should also be answered with a verb. そうです SOO DESU and そうではありません SOO DEWA ARIMASEN are incorrect responses.

Ex. Verb question: あなたは　にほんごを　<u>はなします</u><u>か</u>。　Do you speak Japanese?
   ANATA WA NIHONGO O <u>HANASHIMASU KA</u>.

   Positive answer: はい、<u>はなします</u>。　　　　　Yes, I do.
   HAI, <u>HANASHIMASU</u>.

Negative answer: いいえ、 <u>はなしません</u>。   No, I don't.
　　　　　　　 IIE, <u>HANASHIMASEN</u>.

【 ● ぶんかノート: Cultural Notes】

Verb MASU Form and the Dictionary Form

In this text you see another verb form in [   ] after the MASU form. The verb which appears in the brackets is called the dictionary form since this is the form used to look up verbs in the Japanese dictionary. The MASU form is a formal usage of verbs and is safe to use with any Japanese. However, if you listen to Japanese people's conversations on T.V. or Japanese tourists' conversations, you may notice that they are not always using the MASU form. Among close relatives or friends, plain forms are used instead of MASU forms. The dictionary form is the imperfect affirmative plain form. Using plain forms at the end of sentences does not change the meaning of the sentence. However, plain forms are not used with teachers and elderly Japanese strangers, as it would be considered rude. Correct usage of plain and polite MASU forms is important, as Japanese often judge you according to your correct usage of the language.

【 アクティビティー: Activities】

A. Pair Work

Ask your partner what language each family member speaks and what language he/she speaks at home.

Ex. Question: 「おとうさんは　うちで　なにごを　はなしますか。」
　　　　　　 OTOOSAN WA UCHI DE NANIGO O HANASHIMASU KA.

　 Answer:　「ちちは　（うちで）　えいごを　はなします。」
　　　　　 CHICHI WA (UCHI DE) EIGO O HANASHIMASU.

Family member	What language at home?

【かいわ: Dialogue 】

エミ：かぞくは　まいにち　ごはんを　たべますか。

ケン：いいえ、たいてい　パンを　たべます。

　　　　ときどき　ごはんを　たべます。

エミ：おちゃを　のみますか。

ケン：いいえ、おちゃは　のみません。

　　　　でも、ジュースと　ぎゅうにゅうを　よく　のみます。

EMI : KAZOKU WA MAINICHI GOHAN O TABEMASU KA.

KEN: IIE, TAITEI PAN O TABEMASU.

　　　　TOKIDOKI GOHAN O TABEMASU.

EMI : OCHA O NOMIMASU KA.

KEN: IIE, OCHA WA NOMIMASEN.

　　　　DEMO, JUUSU TO GYUUNYUU O YOKU NOMIMASU.

【ぶんけい: Sentence structures 】

Person は	まいにち everyday	×	food を	たべます。
WA	MAINICHI		O	TABEMASU
	たいてい usually		drink を	のみます。
	TAITEI		O	NOMIMASU
	ときどき sometimes			
	TOKIDOKI			
	いつも always			
	ITSUMO			
	よく often, well			
	YOKU			

【たんご: Vocabulary】

1. たべます ［たべる］
TABEMASU [TABERU]
to eat

2. のみます ［のむ］
NOMIMASU [NOMU]
to drink

3. ごはん
GOHAN
cooked rice

4. パン
PAN
bread

5. (お)みず
(O) MIZU
water

6. ジュース
JUUSU
juice

7. ぎゅうにゅう, ミルク
GYUUNYUU, MIRUKU
(cow's) milk

8. コーラ
KOORA
cola

9. おちゃ
OCHA
tea

10. コーヒー
KOOHII
coffee

11. まいにち
MAINICHI
everyday

12. ときどき 　　　　TOKIDOKI 　　　　sometimes
13. たいてい 　　　　TAITEI 　　　　usually
14. いつも 　　　　ITSUMO 　　　　always

4か

【ぶんぽう: Grammar】

A. Object + は + Negative predicate.
      WA

When a sentence ends in a negative predicate, the object particle を O may be replaced by the particle は WA.

1. わたしは にほんごを はなします。でも、ちゅうごくご<u>は</u> はなしません。
   WATASHI WA NIHONGO O HANASHIMASU. DEMO, CHUUGOKUGO <u>WA</u>
   HANASHIMASEN.
   I speak Japanese. But I do not speak Chinese.

2. わたしは まいにち コーヒーを のみます。でも、おちゃ<u>は</u> のみません。
   WATASHI WA MAINICHI KOOHII O NOMIMASU. DEMO, OCHA <u>WA</u> NOMIMASEN.
   I drink coffee everyday. But I do not drink tea.

【 ● ぶんかノート: Cultural Notes】

What do Japanese eat for breakfast, lunch and dinner?

Japanese traditionally have rice at all three meals. Recently, some of these dietary habits have changed, and some families have Western-style breakfasts and many have noodles and bread as alternates to rice for lunch and dinner. "Western-style breakfasts" in Japan, however, almost always include a vegetable salad, which sometimes replaces fruit. Cereals are becoming a more common sight, but are still not part of a typical Western breakfast meal in Japan.

【 アクティビティー: Activities】

A. Pair Work

Ask your partner if he/she eats or drinks the following items everyday. Your partner will respond using ときどき TOKIDOKI "sometimes" or たいてい TAITEI "usually" or いつも ITSUMO

4か

"always" as part of his/her answer.

Ex. Question: 「まいにち　ごはんを　たべますか。」
MAINICHI GOHAN O TABEMASU KA.

Answer: 「ときどき　ごはんを　たべます。」
TOKIDOKI GOHAN O TABEMASU.

	ときどき, たいてい, いつも
1. rice	
2. bread	
3. water	
4. juice	
5. milk	
6. cola	
7. tea	
8. coffee	

B. Pair Work

Find out what your partner's family members often eat and drink at home.

Ex. Question: 「おとうさんは　うちで　なにを　よく　たべますか。」
OTOOSAN WA UCHI DE NANI O YOKU TABEMASU KA.

Answer: 「ちちは　～を　よく　たべます。」
OTOOSAN WA ～O YOKU TABEMASU.

かぞく	Food	Drink

4か

【かいわ: Dialogue 】

エミ：きのう　ばんごはんに　なにを　たべましたか。

ケン：カレーライスを　たべました。

エミ：きょう　あさごはんに　なにを　たべましたか。

ケン：なにも　たべませんでした。

EMI : KINOO BANGOHAN NI NANI O TABEMASHITA KA.

KEN : KAREERAISU O TABEMASHITA.

EMI : KYOO ASAGOHAN NI NANI O TABEMASHITA KA.

KEN : NANI MO TABEMASENDESHITA.

【ぶんけい: Sentence Structures 】

| Person は | きょう today | × | あさごはん breakfast | に | food | を | たべました。|
| WA | KYOO | | ASAGOHAN | NI | | O | TABEMASHITA |

なにも　たべませんでした。
NANIMO TABEMASENDESHITA

【たんご: Vocabulary】

1. きのう
KINOO
yesterday

2. きょう
KYOO
today

3. あした
ASHITA
tomorrow

4. あさ
ASA
morning

5. (お)ひる
(O) HIRU
daytime

6. ばん
BAN
evening, night

7. よる
YORU
night

8. ゆうがた
YUUGATA
late afternoon, early evening

4か

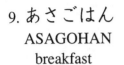

9. あさごはん
ASAGOHAN
breakfast

10. (お)ひる(ごはん)
(O)HIRU(GOHAN)
lunch

11. ばんごはん
BANGOHAN
dinner, supper

12. なにも + Neg.　　　NANI MO + Neg.　　　(not) anything, nothing

【*オプショナルたんご: Optional Vocabulary】

1.*べんとう	*BENTOO	box lunch
2.*むすび	*MUSUBI/ONIGIRI	rice ball
3.*ラーメン	*RAAMEN	Chinese noodles with soup
4.*うどん	*UDON	Japanese white noodles with soup
5.*ピザ	*PIZA	pizza
6.*ホットドッグ	*HOTTODOGGU	hot dog
7.*ハンバーガー	*HANBAAGAA	hamburger
8.*ステーキ	*SUTEEKI	steak
9.*さかな	*SAKANA	fish
10.*スパゲッティ	*SUPAGETI	spaghetti
11.*(お)すし	*(O)SUSHI	*sushi*
12.*てんぷら	*TENPURA	*tempura*

【ぶんぽう: Grammar】

A. Verb-ました 　Verb-MASHITA	did, have done [completed and affirmative form of verb]
Verb-ませんでした Verb-MASENDESHITA	did not, have not done [completed and negative form of verb]

1. 「あさごはんを　たべましたか。」　　　Did you eat breakfast?
　ASAGOHAN O TABEMASHITA KA.
「いいえ、たべませんでした。」　　　No, I did not eat.
　IIE, TABEMASENDESHITA.

4か

2. ちちは きょう コーヒーを のみ<u>ませんでした</u>。
   CHICHI WA KYOO KOOHII O NOMI<u>MASENDESHITA</u>.

My father did not drink coffee today.

B. <u>なにも</u> + Negative predicate。   (not) anything, nothing
    <u>NANI MO</u> + Negative predicate.

なにも NANI MO used with a negative predicate means "nothing" or "not anything."

---

1. 「あさ なにを たべましたか。」   What did you eat in the morning?
   ASA NANI O TABEMASHITA KA.

   「<u>なにも</u> たべませんでした。」   I did not eat anything.
   <u>NANI MO</u> TABEMASENDESHITA.

2. 「なにを のみますか。」   What will you drink?
   NANI O NOMIMASU KA.

   「<u>なにも</u> のみません。」   I won't drink anything.
   <u>NANI MO</u> NOMIMASEN.

C. General time words with no particle

One group of time words is called general time words. Words such as きょう KYOO "today," あさ ASA "morning," etc., which are not attached to a number, or do not suggest any degree of specificity, are in this category. General time words do not take any particles unless they are the topic of a sentence.

---

1. わたしは <u>きのう</u> なにも たべませんでした。   I did not eat anything yesterday.
   WATASHI WA <u>KINOO</u> NANIMO TABEMASENDESHITA.

2. きのうの <u>ばん</u> にほんごを はなしました。   I spoke Japanese last night.
   KINOO NO <u>BAN</u> NIHONGO O HANASHIMASHITA.

D. あさごはん／ひるごはん／ばんごはん＋<u>に</u>   for breakfast / lunch / dinner
    ASAGOHAN / HIRUGOHAN / BANGOHAN + NI

The particle に NI in this situation indicates "for what occasion."

---

1. 「おひるごはん<u>に</u> なにを たべますか。」
   OHIRUGOHAN <u>NI</u> NANI O TABEMASU KA.
   What are you going to eat for lunch?

   「ピザを たべます。」   I will eat pizza.

   PIZA O TABEMASU.

2. きのう ばんごはん<u>に</u> おすしを たべました。   I ate *sushi* for dinner yesterday.
   KINOO BANGOHAN <u>NI</u> OSUSHI O TABEMASHITA.

【 ● ぶんかノート : Cultural Notes 】

Lunch and Dinner in Japan

Lunch and dinner in Japan are extremely varied. They may be traditional, i.e., rice, *miso* soup, pickled vegetables and fish, or they may be a dish from any country in the world. Japanese meals have begun to take on a more Western appearance in recent years, with fewer vegetables and more beef and chicken. Likewise, "Western foods" as we know them (spaghetti, pizza, etc.) somehow still reflect a Japanese taste. Chinese foods, i.e., noodles, have become an important part of Japanese lunch and dinner menus, although they too have been altered significantly to suit the tastes of the Japanese.

【 アクティビティー : Activities 】

A. Pair Work

Ask your partner about his/her dinner menu for last night, this morning's breakfast menu and today's lunch menu.

Ex. Question: 「きのう　ばんごはんに　なにを　たべましたか。
KINOO BANGOHAN NI NANI O TABEMASHITA KA.
そして、なにを　のみましたか。」
SOSHITE, NANI O NOMIMASHITA KA.

Answer: 「〜と　〜を　たべました。そして、〜を　のみました。」
〜 TO 〜 O TABEMASHITA. SOSHITE, 〜 O NOMIMASHITA.

Yesterday's Dinner	Today's Breakfast	Today's Lunch

85

【かいわ: Dialogue 】

エミ：どこで　おひるごはんを　たべますか。
ケン：たいてい　カフェテリアで　たべます。
エミ：だれと　たべますか。
ケン：ともだちと　いっしょに　たべます。

EMI : DOKO DE OHIRUGOHAN O TABEMASU KA.

KEN : TAITEI KAFETERIA DE TABEMASU.

EMI : DARE TO TABEMASU KA.

KEN : TOMODACHI TO ISSHO NI TABEMASU.

【ぶんけい: Sentence structures 】

Person	は	today	X	place	で	Person	と(いっしょに)	thing	を	Action verb	。
	WA				DE		TO (ISSHO NI)		O		

【たんご: Vocabulary】

1. としょかん

2. カフェテリア

3. スナックバー

4. Person＋と
    (いっしょに)

TOSHOKAN
library

KAFETERIA
cafeteria

SUNAKKUBAA
snack bar

Person＋ TO (ISSHO NI)
(together) with (person)

5. しんぶん

SHINBUN

newspaper

6. ざっし

ZASSHI

magazine

7. ＣＤ

SHIIDII

CD

8. ＣＤプレーヤー

SHIIDII PUREEYAA

CD Player

9. よみます ［よむ］

YOMIMASU [YOMU]

to read

10. ききます ［きく］

KIKIMASU [KIKU]

to listen, hear

11. します ［する］

SHIMASU [SURU]

to do

12. べんきょう(を)します ［べんきょう(を)する］

BENKYOO (O) SHIMASU [BENKYOO (O) SURU]

to study

【＊オプショナルたんご: Optional Vocabulary】

1.＊テープ	TEEPU	tape
2.＊ウォークマン	WOOKUMAN	walkman
3.＊ランゲージラボ	RANGEEJI RABO	language lab

【ぶんぽう：Grammar】

A. Person ＋と　　（いっしょに）　　　　　　　　　　(together) with ~

　　Person ＋ TO　　(ISSHO NI)

The particle と TO follows a noun which names the person with whom an action is being done. Often いっしょに ISSHO NI "together with" appears after と TO.

1. 「だれと　おひるごはんを　たべますか。」　　　　With whom do you eat lunch?
   DARE TO OHIRUGOHAN O TABEMASU KA.

   「ともだちと　いっしょに　たべます。」　　　　　I eat with my friend.
   TOMODACHI TO ISSHO NI TABEMASU.

2. ベンさんと　いっしょに　しゅくだいを　しました。
   BEN-SAN TO ISSHO NI SHUKUDAI O SHIMASHITA.
   I did my homework with Ben.

B. Noun ＋（を）　します verbs.

　　Noun ＋ (O)　　SHIMASU verbs.

There are many verbs in this group such as べんきょう（を）します BENKYOO (O) SHIMASU "to study." べんきょう BENKYOO itself is a noun and します SHIMASU is the verb "to do." べんきょう（を）します BENKYOO (O) SHIMASU literally means "to do studies." Most Japanese sentences do not contain two を O. When there is something to study, を O follows the main direct object and is eliminated after べんきょう BENKYOO.

1. 「としょかんで　べんきょう（を）　しました。」　I studied at the library.
   TOSHOKAN DE BENKYOO (O) SHIMASHITA.

   「なにを　べんきょうしましたか。」　　　　　　What did you study?
   NANI O BENKYOOSHIMASHITA KA.

2. わたしは　にほんごを　べんきょうします。　　　I study Japanese.
   WATASHI WA NIHONGO O BENKYOOSHIMASU.

【 ● ぶんかノート：Cultural Notes】

Typical Japanese High School Student's School Day

Japanese students commute to school by bus, train, subway, bike, etc. Commuting by car is not common in cities. School regulations are quite strict. Students have to wear uniforms (せいふく SEIFUKU). Hair styles and hair length are sometimes decided by the school. The curriculum is set by the federal government and students do not have their own choice of subjects. All students in a given course are in the same grade. Mixed classes of students in different grade levels are not common in Japan. Even a one year age difference is significant in a Japanese school. Underclassmen call upperclassmen せんぱい SENPAI and upperclassmen call underclassmen こうはい KOOHAI. Students in one homeroom often all take the same courses. English is a required foreign lanugage and is taught beginning in the 7th grade. Recently, English is introduced at even earlier grades. Classes are usually as large as 40 or more students. Schools have many kinds of sports and cultural clubs. Many students belong to these clubs, which meet frequently. In Japan, school athletics do not have seasons; students play one sport all year long.

【アクティビティー: Activities】

A. Pair Work

Ask where and with whom your partner does the following things on a daily basis.

Ex. Eating breakfast.

Question 1: 「どこで　あさごはんを　たべますか。」

Question 2: 「だれと　（いっしょに）　あさごはんを　たべますか。」

	Where?	With whom?
1. Eating lunch		
2. Eating dinner		
3. Studying		
4. Doing homework		
5. Talking to friends		
6. Listening to music		
7. Reading books		
8. Reading newspapers/magazines		

*ひとりで　alone

4か

【かいわ: Dialogue 】

エミ : きのうの　ばん　うちで　なにを　しましたか。

ケン : テレビを　みました。

　　　そして、ともだちと　でんわで　よく　はなしました。

　　　でも、しゅくだいを　しませんでした。

エミ : だめですねえ。

EMI　: KINOO NO BAN UCHI DE NANI O SHIMASHITA KA.

KEN　: TEREBI O MIMASHITA.

　　　SOSHITE, TOMODACHI TO DENWA DE YOKU HANASHIMASHITA.

　　　DEMO, SHUKUDAI O SHIMASENDESHITA.

EMI　: DAME DESU NEE.

【ぶんけい: Sentence Structure 】

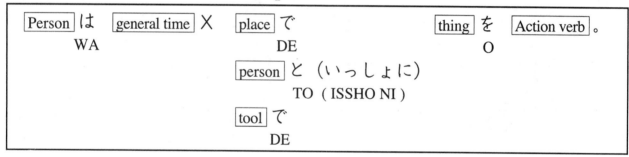

Person は	general time	X	place で		thing を	Action verb 。
WA			DE		O	
			person と （いっしょに）			
			TO (ISSHO NI)			
			tool で			
			DE			

【たんご: Vocabulary】

1. みます
　[みる]
MIMASU
[MIRU]
to watch, look, see

2. かきます
　[かく]
KAKIMASU
[KAKU]
to write, draw

3. タイプ(を)します
　[タイプ(を)する]
TAIPU (O) SHIMASU
[TAIPU (O) SURU]
to type

  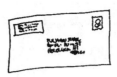 

4. テレビ	5. レポート	6. てがみ	7. ラジオ
TEREBI	REPOOTO	TEGAMI	RAJIO
TV	report, paper	letter	radio

8. でんわ	9. コンピューター	10. ＤＶＤ	11. means + で
DENWA	KONPYUUTAA	DIIBIIDII	DE
telephone	computer	DVD	by, with, on, in

【*オプショナルたんご: Optional Vocabulary】

1.*ニュース	*NYUUSU	news
2.*アニメ	*ANIME	cartoons
3.*テレビゲーム	*TEREBI GEEMU	video game
4.*まんが	*MANGA	comics
5.*ビデオ	*BIDEO	video

【ぶんぽう: Grammar】

| A. Means, Tool + で | by, with, on, in (means, tool, vehicle) |
| DE | |

で DE follows a noun that is used to do the action, i.e., tool, utensil, vehicle, language.

1. ともだちと　でんわで　よく　はなします。 I talk to my friend on the telephone a lot.
TOMODACHI TO DENWA <u>DE</u> YOKU HANASHIMASU.

2. コンピューターで　えいごの　レポートを　タイプしました。
KONPYUUTAA <u>DE</u> EIGO NO REPOOTO O TAIPUSHIMASHITA.

I typed my English paper by computer.

3. しけんを　えんぴつで　かきます。 I will write (take) the exam in pencil.
SHIKEN O ENPITSU <u>DE</u> KAKIMASU.

4か

【 ● ぶんかノート: Cultural Notes】

Typical Japanese High School Student Life after School

Many Japanese students go to じゅく JUKU "cram school" after school to prepare for college entrance exams. They study late and their whole family supports them in their efforts to perform well. In order that they can study, students (especially boys) are usually not expected to do chores around the home. Students who are not studying enjoy watching T.V., reading comics and playing video games at home. Students often also stay late in school when they are involved in club activities.

【 アクティビティー: Activities】

A. Pair Work

Ask your partner what he/she did last night at home.

Ex. 「きのうの　ばん　うちで　なにを　しましたか。」

B. Pair Work

Ask your partner whether he/she often does the following.

Ex. watch T.V.

「よく　テレビ TEREBI を　みますか。」

1. Watch videos		4. Type by computer	
2. Listen to the radio		5. Read the newspaper	
3. Talk on the telephone		6. Write letters	

C. Pair Work

Ask your partner how he/she does the following.

Ex. write papers

「なんで　レポート REPOOTO を　かきますか。」

1. Type papers (reports)	
2. Write letters	

Ask your partner these questions in Japanese.
Your partner answers in Japanese.

1. What is your name?

2. How old are you?

3. What school do you go to?

4. What grade are you in?

5. What month were you born?

6. What nationality are you?

7. How many people are there in your family?

8. Who is in your family?

9. What is your father's job?

10. What is your mother's job?

11. How old is your sibling(s)?

12. Do you speak Japanese at home?

13. What language do you speak at home?

4 か

14. Does your family eat rice everyday?

15. What do you usually drink ?

16. What did you eat for dinner yesterday?

17. Did you eat breakfast today?

18. Where do you usually eat lunch?

19. With whom do you eat lunch?

20. Do you read the newspaper everyday?

21. Do you listen to the walkman at the library?

22. Did you do yesterday's Japanese homework?

23. What do you do at the library?   [List at least two activities.]

24. Where do you talk with your friends?

25. Did you watch TV last night?

26. Do you talk to your friends on the phone everyday?

27. Do you type your English papers on the computer?

I. Conjugation

	Noun です。 [Copula]	Verb
Imperfect Affirmative	せんせいです。 (She) is a teacher.	たべます。 (She) will eat / is going to eat / eats.
Imperfect Negative	せんせいではありません。 or せんせいじゃありません。 (She) is not a teacher.	たべません。 (She) won't / does not eat.
Perfect Affirmative	せんせいでした。 (She) was a teacher.	たべました。 (She) ate.
Perfect Negative	せんせいではありませんでした。 or せんせいじゃありませんでした。 (She) was not a teacher.	たべませんでした。 (She) did not eat.

4 か

II. Particles   X = No particle

Topic は	General time Ⓧ	Occasion に "for"	Action verb
だれ？	まいにち	あさごはん	たべます
ちち	きのう	(お)ひる(ごはん)	のみます
はは	きょう	ばんごはん	はなします
あに	あした		よみます
あね	あさ	**Place で "at, in"**	ききます
おとうと	ひる	どこ？	します
いもうと	ばん	がっこう	べんきょう(を)します
ともだち		うち	みます
おじいさん	**Adverb Ⓧ**	としょかん	かきます
おばあさん	すこし	カフェテリア	タイプ(を)します
おとうさん	ちょっと	スナックバー	
おかあさん	よく		
おにいさん	ときどき	**Person と （いっしょに）**	
おねえさん	たいてい	"(together) with"	
おとうとさん	いつも	だれ？	
いもうとさん		ともだち　etc.	
		Means で "by, with"	
		なん？	
		でんわ	
		コンピューター	

Object を

なに？	あさごはん
にほんご	ひるごはん
えいご	ばんごはん
ごはん	しんぶん
パン	ざっし
(お)みず	ウォークマン
なにご？	テープ
ジュース	テレビ
ぎゅうにゅう	レポート
ミルク	てがみ
コーラ	ラジオ
おちゃ	ビデオ
コーヒー	

Noun 1 の Noun 2 [possessive and descriptive]

Noun 1 と Noun 2   "and"

も "also, too" replaces を, が, は.

4か   96

By the end of this lesson, you will be able to communicate the information below in the given situations.

【1-5 タスク1】

A Japanese student is going to stay at your home. The Japanese student wants to know about your family. He/She asks who your family members are and about each of their hobbies. He/She also asks whether your family understands any Japanese or not.

【1-5 タスク2】

You are a T.V. program host. Today's guest is a famous young singer. To make the interview interesting, ask all kinds of personal questions about what the singer did last night, what kind of things he/she likes or dislikes, what he/she is skillful and unskillful at, what his/her favorite color is, etc.

【かいわ：Dialogue 】

エミ EMI ：しゅみは　なんですか。

ケン KEN：そうですねえ… スポーツ SUPOOTSU と　おんがくです。

エミ EMI ：そうですか。

ケン KEN：エミ EMI さんの　しゅみは。

エミ EMI ：わたしの　しゅみは　えいがと　どくしょです。

【ぶんけい：Sentence structures 】

Person の　しゅみ は　～です。	Person's hobby is ~.
W-Question:	「しゅみは　なんですか。」
W-Answer:	「（わたしの　しゅみは）　～です。」
Yes/No Question:	「しゅみは　スポーツ SUPOOTSU ですか。」
Yes Answer:	「はい、そうです。or はい、スポーツSUPOOTSUです。」
No Answer:	「いいえ、そうでは／じゃありません。」
	or 「いいえ、スポーツ SUPOOTSUでは／じゃありません。」
	or 「いいえ、(your hobby)です。」

【たんご：Vocabulary】

1. しゅみ

hobby

2. スポーツ
SUPOOTSU
sports

3. おんがく

music

4. ダンス
DANSU
dance, dancing

5. うた
song, singing

6. えいが
movies

7. テレビゲーム
TEREBI GEEMU
video game

8. トランプ
TORANPU
(playing) cards

9. ピアノ
PIANO
piano

10. ギター
GITAA
guitar

11. どくしょ

reading

12. え

painting, drawing

13. ジョギング
JOGINGU
jogging

14. すいえい
swimming

15. そうですねえ...
Let me see . . .
Used when one is trying
to think of an answer.

【*オプショナルたんご: Optional Vocabulary】

1.*バイオリン	*BAIORIN	violin
2.*さいほう		sewing
3.*あみもの		knitting, crocheting
4.*おしゃべり		chatting, talking
5.*かいもの		shopping
6.*りょこう		traveling
7.*つり		fishing
8.*サーフィン	*SAAFIN	surfing
9.*スケートボード	*SUKEETOBOODO	skateboarding
10.*りょうり		cooking

5か

【 ● ぶんかノート: Cultural Notes】
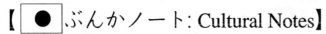

Japanese Hobbies

Japanese people's hobbies are not very different from Westerners' hobbies. Favorite sports of the Japanese are baseball, soccer and volleyball. Basketball is becoming increasingly popular as well. Football, however, has nowhere near the following it has in the U.S. Adults enjoy golf immensely, but the very high cost of playing golf restricts many from golfing as often as they would like. The most popular traditional "sport" of the Japanese, *sumoo*, also has a strong following, especially among adult Japanese.

【 アクティビティー: Activities】

A. Pair Work

Ask what hobbies your partner and his/her family members have. Write your partner's family members and their hobbies in the columns below.

Ex. 「あなたの　しゅみは　なんですか。」

「（わたしの　しゅみは）　〜です。」

かぞく	しゅみ

【かいわ: Dialogue 】

エミ EMI ：ケン KEN さんは　おすしが　すきですか。

ケン KEN ：いいえ、おすしは　すきでは　ありません。

エミ EMI ：そうですか。
　　　　　どんな　たべものが　すきですか。

ケン KEN ：そうですねえ...
　　　　　てんぷらが　すきです。

【ぶんけい: Sentence Structure 】

Person は	something が	すき	です。
どんな	something	だいすき	では／じゃありません。
		きらい	でした。
		だいきらい	では／じゃありませんでした。

【たんご: Vocabulary】

1. すき [なAdj.]
like

2. だいすき [なAdj.]
like very much, love

3. きらい [なAdj.]
dislike

4. だいきらい [なAdj.]
dislike a lot, hate

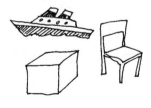

5. どんな〜
what kind of 〜 ?

6. もの
(tangible) things

7. たべもの
food

8. のみもの
a drink

9. (お)すし
sushi

10. さしみ
raw fish

11. てんぷら
tempura

【*オプショナルたんご: Optional Vocabulary】

1.*やさい		vegetable
2.*くだもの		fruit
3.*トマト	*TOMATO	tomato
4.*ほうれんそう		spinach
5.*にんじん		carrot
6.*りんご		apple
7.*オレンジ	*ORENJI	orange
8.*いちご		strawberry
9.*すいか		watermelon
10.*メロン	*MERON	melon
11.*アイスクリーム	*AISUKURIIMU	ice cream
12.*ケーキ	*KEEKI	cake
13.*ロック	*ROKKU	rock (music)
14.*ジャズ	*JAZU	jazz (music)
15.*クラシック	*KURASHIKKU	classical (music)

【ぶんぽう: Grammar】

A. な adjectives

A word which modifies a noun is called an adjective. There are two kinds of adjectives in Japanese: い adjectives and な adjectives. い adjectives are original Japanese adjectives such as あつい "is hot," さむい "is cold," etc. な adjectives are words of Chinese origin, such as すき "like," きらい "dislike," etc. い adjectives conjugate in one format and な adjectives conjugate exactly like nouns. How can you tell whether an adjective is an い adjective or a な adjective? All い adjectives end with -ai, -ii, -oi or -ui, while most of な adjectives do not have these endings, with a few exceptions. If you memorize those exceptions, you will not have any problems. きらい is one of these exceptions.

な adjective conjugation:

すき<u>です</u>。	(I) like (it).
すき<u>では／じゃありません</u>。	(I) do not like (it).
すき<u>でした</u>。	(I) liked (it).
すき<u>では／じゃありませんでした</u>。	(I) did not like (it).

い adjective conjugation will be introduced in the next lesson.

B. Noun 1 は Noun 2 が すき　　　　です。 N1 like N2.

だいすき　　　です。 N1 likes N2 very much./N1 loves N2.

きらい　　　　です。 N1 dislikes N2.

だいきらい です。 N1 dislikes N2 very much./ N1 hates N2.

N1 tells us who is being discussed, while N2 tells us what is under discussion. All four words used in the examples above as predicates are な Adjectives, even though some end in -ai.

1. わたしは　どくしょが　すきです。 I like reading (books).

2. おとうとは　テレビゲーム TEREBI GEEMU が　だいすきです。

My younger brother loves video games.

3. おばあさんは　テレビ TEREBI が　きらいです。 Grandmother does not like T.V.

4. ちちは　えいがが　だいきらいです。 My father hates movies.

C. どんな + Noun ? What kind/sort of ～?

1. 「どんな　たべものが　すきですか。」 What kind of food do you like?

「ちゅうごくの　たべものが　すきです。」 I like Chinese food.

2. 「どんな　スポーツ SUPOOTSU が　すきですか。」 What kind of sports do you like?

「フットボール FUTTOBOORU が　すきです。」 I like football.

【 ● ぶんかノート: Cultural Notes】

1. Seasonal Foods and Drinks in Japan

While some foods are enjoyed all year round, many foods are seasonal in Japan. For example, cold dishes, such as *somen* noodles or cold *soba* noodles are eaten only during the summer. Shaved ice and fruits such as watermelon, cherries and peaches are popular during the summer. Cold drinks, (fruit juices, iced tea and iced coffee) are consumed in far greater quantities during the summer. Even meals at home will vary according to the season, and are often also presented in different serving dishes according to the season.

2. *Sukiyaki* Song

There is a beautiful Japanese song titled 「うえを　むいて　あるこう」 sung by a famous male singer さかもときゅう. The song title means "Let's walk with our chins up." Since it was such a popular Japanese song, some U.S. musicians wrote words for this song in English and re-named it "Sukiyaki," which is also a favorite Japanese dish in the U.S. The song, however, makes no mention food.

5か

【🙂🙂アクティビティー: Activities】

A. Pair Work

Ask your partner if he/she likes foods from the following countries or not. Check the correct column.

Ex. 「にほんの　たべものが　すきですか。」

　　　"Yes" answer: 「はい、すきです。」

　　　"No" answer: 「いいえ、すきではありません／すきじゃありません。」

　　　　　　or 「いいえ、きらいです。」

	だいすき	すき	きらい	だいきらい
にほん				
ちゅうごく				
かんこく				
インド　INDO				
タイ　TAI				
アメリカ　AMERIKA				
メキシコ　MEKISHIKO				
イタリア　ITARIA				
フランス　FURANSU				

B. Pair Work

Ask what kind of foods and drinks your partner likes or dislikes. Write his/her answers in the blocks.

Ex. Question: 「どんな　たべものが　すきですか。」

　　　Answer: 「おすしと　てんぷらが　すきです。」

もの	すき	きらい
たべもの		
のみもの		

【かいわ: Dialogue 】

エミ EMI ：ケン KENは　なにが　とくいですか。

ケン KEN：ぼくは　やきゅうが　とくいです。エミ EMIさんは？

エミ EMI ：わたしは　バレーボール BAREEBOORU が　すきですが、
じょうずでは　ありません。

【ぶんけい: Sentence Structure 】

Person は	thing (intangible) が	じょうず	です。
	どんな こと	へた とくい にがて	ではありません。 or じゃありません。
			でした。
			ではありませんでした。 or じゃありませんでした。

Sentence 1＋が、Sentence 2。	Sentence 1, but Sentence 2.

【たんご: Vocabulary】

1. じょうず
[な Adj.]
skillful, be good at
Refers to someone else.
Never used to refer to
yourself.

2. へた
[な Adj.]
unskillful, be poor at

3. とくい
[な Adj.]
be strong in, can do well
May be used to refer to
oneself, though not
common.

4. にがて
[な Adj.]
be weak in
Used when one refers to
oneself. It also can be
used for persons, food,
etc., to which one has
a negative reaction.

5か

5. こと

thing (intangible)

6. フットボール
FUTTOBOORU
football

7. やきゅう

baseball

8. バスケット(ボール)
BASUKETTO (BOORU)
basketball

9. バレー(ボール)
BAREE (BOORU)
volleyball

10. サッカー
SAKKAA
soccer

11. テニス
TENISU
tennis

12. ゴルフ
GORUFU
golf

13. Sentence 1＋が、 Sentence 2。   Sentence 1, but Sentence 2. (Less formal than でも.)

　= Sentence 1。でも、 Sentence 2。   Sentence 1. But / However, Sentence 2.

【*オプショナルたんご: Optional Vocabulary】

1.*ボーリング　　　　　*BOORINGU　　　　　bowling

2.*スキー　　　　　　　*SUKII　　　　　　　skiing

3.*スケート　　　　　　*SUKEETO　　　　　　skating

4.*りくじょう　　　　　　　　　　　　　　　track

5.*きかいたいそう　　　　　　　　　　　　　gymnastics

【ぶんぽう: Grammar】

A. Sentence 1＋が、 Sentence 2。	Sentence 1, but Sentence 2. (Less formal than でも.)
= Sentence 1。でも、 Sentence 2。	Sentence 1. But / However, Sentence 2.

1. わたしは　サッカーSAKKAA が　すきですが、じょうずでは　ありません。
   I like soccer, but I am not skillful.
2. ちちは　ゴルフGORUFU が　じょうずですが、ははは　へたです。
   My father is good at golf, but my mother is poor at it.
3. おとうとは　テレビゲームTEREBI GEEMU が　だいすきですが、わたしは
   きらいです。
   My younger brother likes video games very much, but I do not like them.

【 ● ぶんかノート: Cultural Notes】

Does a Japanese person praise his/her own family?

A Japanese person does not praise his/her own family or himself/herself when talking to outsiders. Instead he/she may even portray himself/herself or family members as less than they actually are. This does not only apply to persons in the in-group, but belongings, works or acts of these persons. For example, when giving someone a gift one has chosen or made, one will always say that it is an insignificant gift, even if one has taken great care and effort to make or select it, or has spent a large sum of money for it.

【 アクティビティー: Activities】

A. Pair Work

Ask your partner what kind of activities each of his/her family member likes and if they are skillful at them or not. Write the family member in the first column, what they like in the second, and check either じょうず or へた in the last two columns.

Ex. Question 1: 「おとうさんは　どんな　ことが　すきですか。」

Answer 1: 「ちちは　ゴルフGORUFU が　すきです。」

Question 2: 「おとうさんは　ゴルフGORUFU が　じょうずですか。」

Answer 2: 「いいえ、じょうずでは　ありません。」

かぞく		すき	じょうず	へた

【かいわ: Dialogue 】

エミ EMI : にほんごが　とても　じょうずですねえ。
ケン KEN : いいえ、ぜんぜん　じょうずでは　ありません。
　　　　　とても　へたです。
エミ EMI : いいえ。じょうずですよ。

【ぶんけい: Sentence Structure 】

Person は	thing (intangible) が	とても すこし or ちょっと まあまあ	じょうずです。
		あまり	じょうずではありません。
		ぜんぜん	or じょうずじゃありません。

【たんご: Vocabulary】

1. とても ＋ Affirmative predicate.　　　　　very ～

2. まあまあ ＋ Affimative predicate.　　　　so, so ～

3. あまり ＋ Negative predicate.　　　　　not ～ very

4. ぜんぜん ＋ Negative predicate.　　　　not ～ at all

【＊オプショナルたんご: Optional Vocabulary】

1.＊とんでもないです。　　　　　　　　　Far from it!

【ぶんぽう: Grammar】

A. とても	＋ Affirmative predicate。	very ～
すこし／ちょっと	＋ Affirmative predicate。	a little ～
まあまあ	＋ Affimative predicate／です。	so, so (～)
あまり	＋ Negative predicate。	not very ～
ぜんぜん	＋ Negative predicate。	not ～ at all

1. おばあさんは　にほんごが　<u>とても</u>　じょうずですね。

Your grandmother is very good at speaking Japanese, isn't she?

2. ははは　にほんごが　<u>あまり</u>　じょうずでは　ありません。

My mother is not very good at speaking Japanese.

3. 「あなたは　すいえいが　じょうずですか。」　Are you good at swimming?

「<u>まあまあ</u>です。」　I'm so, so (at it).

4. ぼくは　バスケット BASUKETTO が　<u>ちょっと</u>　にがてです。

I am a little weak at basketball. [I cannot do it well and I do not like it so much.]

5. ぼくは　テニス TENISU が　だいすきですが、<u>ぜんぜん</u>　じょうずでは
ありません。

I love tennis but I am not good at all at it.

【　●　ぶんかノート: Cultural Notes】

1. *Karaoke*

   カラオケ KARAOKE is a word which originated in Japan.　カラ KARA means "empty" and
   オケ OKE is a short form of オーケストラ OOKESUTORA which means "orchestra." Literally, it
   means "empty orchestra." People enjoy singing with taped background music even if a live orchestra
   is present. *Karaoke* is now popular in other countries and people have adapted it to fit their own
   music.

2. とんでもないです。

   とんでもないです means "Far from it." When Japanese people praise your Japanese even though
   it is still inadequate, this is the appropriate response to give. In general, Japanese people are modest
   and refuse to accept compliments from other people.

【　アクティビティー: Activities】

A. Pair Work

Compliment your partner on at least three things. Your partner will respond by giving a modest
reply. Switch roles.

Ex.　「にほんごが　とても　じょうずですねえ。」

　　「いいえ、ぜんぜん　じょうずではありません。」

　　or 「いいえ、とんでもないです。」

5か

【かいわ: Dialogue 】

ケン KEN : エミ EMI さんは　なにいろが　すきですか。

エミ EMI : そうですねえ...
　　　　ピンク PINKU が　だいすきですが、しろも　すきです。
　　　　ケン KEN さんは？

ケン KEN : ぼくは　あおと　みどりが　すきです。

【ぶんけい: Sentence Structure 】

| Person | は | color / なにいろ | が | すき / きらい | です。/ ですか。 |

| Person | の | thing | は | color / なにいろ | です。/ ですか。 |

【たんご: Vocabulary】

1. いろ
color

?

2. なにいろ
What color?

3. あか
red

4. しろ
white

5. くろ
black

6. あお
blue

7. きいろ
yellow

8. ちゃいろ
brown
lit., "tea color"

9. みどり
green

10. むらさき
purple

11. ピンク
PINKU
pink

12. オレンジ(いろ)
ORENJI (IRO)
orange (color)

13. グレイ
GUREI
grey

14. きんいろ
gold (color)

15. ぎんいろ
silver (color)

５か

110

【＊オプショナルたんご: Optional Vocabulary】

These words are original Japanese color words, but recently Japanese people prefer to use the English borrowed equivalents instead, especially when describing modern, or Western items.

1.＊ももいろ   pink color (peach color)

2.＊だいだいいろ   orange color (tangerine orange color)

3.＊はいいろ   grey color (ash color)

4.＊ねずみいろ   grey color (mouse color)

【 ぶんかノート: Cultural Notes】

1. Japanese People's Image of Colors

Certain colors have significance in the Japanese culture. Red and white are used for happy occasions such as weddings, engagements, baby births, etc. Black is used for funerals. Purple is a noble color and is used by the imperial family. If you have a chance to meet the Imperial Family, avoid wearing purple as it is a color reserved for the Royal Family. Green has a clean, new and fresh image and therefore is used often to create a positive image. For example, グリーンしゃ GURIIN-SHA is the executive car of trains. The ticket window where one purchases green car tickets is called みどりのまどぐち.

2. あお has many meanings.

あお translates as "blue," but oftentimes also means green. The green color of traffic lights is considered あお in Japanese. New young leaves and fresh green grass are not described as みどり, but as あお. Also, young inexperienced people are sometimes referred to as being あおい (the adjective form of あお), because of their youth and lack of experience.

3. The Japanese Flag

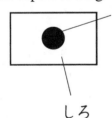

あか [This red circle represents the sun.]

しろ

The Japanese flag is called ひのまる which means "rising sun." The ancient Chinese referred to Japan as a "place where the sun rises" because of its relative geographical location. Since Japan is east of China, the sun appeared to rise from the direction of Japan. The name "Nihon" literally means "origin of the sun."

4. A Japanese Proverb 「じゅうにんといろ」

じゅうにん is a counter for ten people. といろ is an abbreviated form of とおいろ which means ten colors. 「じゅうにんといろ」 literally means "Ten men, ten colors." and may be interpreted as "Many men, many tastes."

【👥アクティビティー: Activities】

A. |Pair Work|

Ask for the colors of your partner's belongings.

Ex. 「あなたの　うちは　なにいろですか。」
　　「（わたしの　うちは）　しろです。」

Things	いろ
1. House	
2. Bag	
3. Cap or hat	
4. School colors	
5. Sports uniform (ユニフォーム UNIFOOMU)	
6. Eraser	
7. Car (くるま)	
8. * Dog or cat color	

＊ありません。I do not have (a pet).

B. |Class Work|

Let's find out what color is the most popular and the least popular in your class. Divide into groups and ask your classmates within your group to raise their hands as each of you take turns asking about each color. Tally the results on the chart. Then report the results to the entire class.

Ex. 「だれが　あかが　すきですか。」

いろ	すき	きらい	いろ	すき	きらい
1. あか			8. むらさき		
2. しろ			9. ピンク PINKU		
3. くろ			10. オレンジ ORENJI		
4. あお			11. グレイ GUREI		
5. きいろ			12. きんいろ		
6. ちゃいろ			13. ぎんいろ		
7. みどり					

JAPANESE CULTURE 3: EDUCATION AND SCHOOL

 Find the answers by investigating books, by talking to friends, or by using the Internet.

1. How much tuition do you pay a year?

2. What is the cost of one year of public high school education in the U.S.?

3. What is the cost of one year of public high school education in Japan?

4. What is the cost of one year of private high school education in the U.S.?

5. What is the cost of one year of private high school education in Japan?

6. Roughly what percentage of students in your city or state attend private schools?

7. Roughly what percentage of students in Japan attend private schools?

8. What days of the week do you go to school? What time does your school day begin and end?

9. What days of the week do Japanese students go to school? At what time does the school day begin and end in Japan?

10. Many Japanese students spend time outside of school at *juku*, or "cram schools. " Why do students go to *juku*?

11. Explain the Japanese phenomenon of "exam hell." Does a comparable experience exist in the U.S.?

5か

ぞうさん

まど　みちお　作詞
伊玖磨　作曲

By the end of this lesson, you will be able to communicate the information below in the given situations.
The person who asks the questions may look at this page, but the person who answers should not.

【1-6 タスク1】

You are planning to stay at the Japanese home of a student from Japan who is now at your school. You want to know his/her parents' characteristics — height, whether they are big or small, whether they are young or not, whether they are strict or not, etc. You also want to know his/her siblings' characteristics — whether they are smart or not, height, whether they are noisy or quiet, what things they like and dislike, etc. [Ask about only one parent and one sibling.]

【1-6 タスク2】

Your friend has a crush on someone you don't know. You want to know about your friend's new interest — age, appearance, nationality, height, size, personality, eye and hair color, hair length, hobbies, etc.

【かいわ: Dialogue 】

ケンKEN：おとうさんは　せが　たかいですか。

エミEMI：はい、ちちは　ちょっと　せが　たかいです。
でも、ははは　せが　ひくいです。

【ぶんけい: Sentence Structure 】　See next page.

【たんご: Vocabulary】　"Japanese *Sumo* Wrestler" *

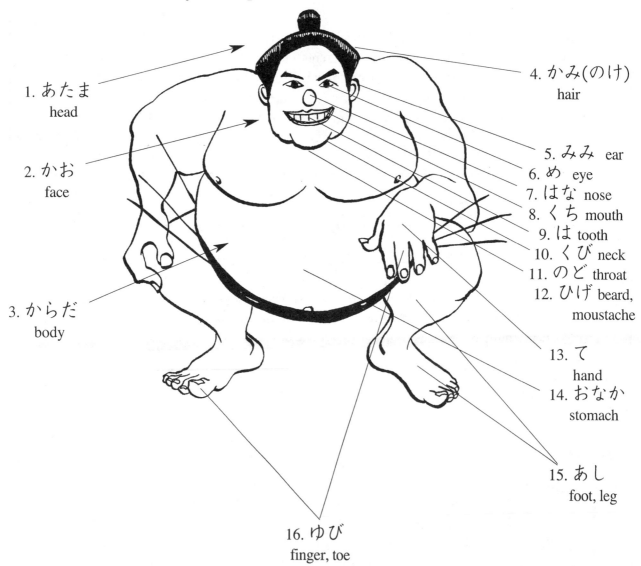

1. あたま head
2. かお face
3. からだ body
4. かみ(のけ) hair
5. みみ ear
6. め eye
7. はな nose
8. くち mouth
9. は tooth
10. くび neck
11. のど throat
12. ひげ beard, moustache
13. て hand
14. おなか stomach
15. あし foot, leg
16. ゆび finger, toe

* See Cultural Notes on page 127 and page 247.

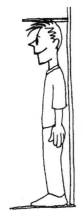    

17. せ（い）	18. こころ	19. こえ	20. たかい	21. ひくい
height	heart, spirit	voice	is tall	is short (height), low

【ぶんけい: Sentence Structure 】

Person は　せ（い）が	とても	たかい	です。
	すこし or ちょっと	ひくい	
	まあまあ		

【*オプショナルたんご: Optional Vocabulary】

1.*せなか	back	
2.*かた	shoulder	
3.*ひざ	knee	
4.*ひじ	elbow	
5.*まゆ（げ）	eyebrow	
6.*まつげ	eyelash	
7.*くちびる	lip	
8.*ほお	cheek	
9.*あご	chin	
10.*むね	chest	
11.*おしり	backside; butttocks	
12.*ほね	bone	
13.*きんにく	muscle	
14.*こし	waist	
15.*うで	arm	

6か

【ぶんぽう：Grammar】

A. Noun 1 (person) ＋ は　Noun 2 (part of body) ＋ が　～です。

Literally, this construction is translated "As for N1, N2 is . . . ", and is a sentence of description. This is commonly used to describe a person's physical characteristics. "As for so and so, his/her height is tall," etc.

The particle が is considered a subject marker. The topic particle は is often used to replace が. When this occurs, the noun preceding は becomes the topic of the sentence. N1 の N2 は ～ です。 has a slightly different meaning. Compare:

わたしは　せ（い）が　たかいです。　　As for me, I'm tall. [The topic is I.]
わたしの　せ（い）は　たかいです。　　My height is tall. [The topic is height.]

1. わたしは　すこし　せが　ひくいです。　　I am a little short.

2. あには　せが　とても　たかいです。　　My older brother is very tall.

【 ● ぶんかノート：Cultural Notes】

1. *Kanji* for Body Parts

Can you guess what these *kanji* mean? These *kanji* were derived from the shapes of body parts.

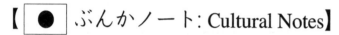

a. 口 (　　　) b. 目 (　　　) c. 耳 (　　　) d. 手 (　　　) e. 足 (　　　) f. 心 (　　　)

2. Singular/Plural Nouns

Unlike English where most nouns have a singular and plural form (i.e., boy/boys; woman/women), in Japanese, singular and plural forms are almost non-existent. One must use contextual cues to decide whether a noun is singular or plural. For example, は may mean one tooth or several.

【 アクティビティー：Activities】

A. Pair Work

As you name parts of the body, your partner points to the corresponding parts of his/her body. Take turns.

B. Pair Game → Group Game → Class Game

This game is played somewhat like "Simon Says." One student leader stands in front of the class as the others face him/her. The leader begins by pointing to his/her nose three times, saying はな each time. After the third はな, he/she chooses another body part, i.e., くち. At this point, the leader may either point correctly to his/her mouth or point incorrectly to another body part. Even if the leader points to a body part other than his/her mouth, the rest of the class must point to their mouths. If they follow the leader's incorrect action, they are "out" and must sit down. The last remaining standing student is the winner and becomes the next leader.

C. Pair Work

Ask whether your partner's family members are tall or short. Put a check mark in the correct box after writing the family member's name in the first column.

Ex. Aさん: 「ごかぞくは　なんにんですか。」
　　Bさん: 「よにんです。」
　　Aさん: 「だれですか。」
　　Bさん: 「ちちと　ははと　あねと　わたしです。」
　　Aさん: 「そうですか。おとうさんは　せが　たかいですか。」
　　Bさん: 「いいえ、ちちは　せが　すこし　ひくいです。」
　　Aさん: 「そうですか。」

かぞく		とてもたかい	すこしたかい	まあまあ	すこしひくい	とてもひくい

【かいわ: Dialogue 】

エミ EMI ：ケン KEN さんの　いもうとさんは　せが　たかいですか。

ケン KEN ：いいえ、たかくないです。

エミ EMI ：いもうとさんは　あたまが　いいですか。

ケン KEN ：いいえ、あまり　よくないです。

エミ EMI ：かみのけが　ながいですか。

ケン KEN ：はい、とても　ながいです。

【ぶんけい: Sentence Structure 】

Person は	part of body が	とても	いAdj. (－い) です。
		すこし or ちょっと	
		まあまあ	
		あまり	いAdj. (－く) ないです。 or
		ぜんぜん	いAdj. (－く) ありません。

Question:	「あなたは　めが　いいですか。」
Yes answer:	「はい、（めが）いいです。」 or 「はい、そうです。」
No answer:	「いいえ、（めが）よくないです。」 or
	「いいえ、そうではありません。」

【たんご: Vocabulary】

1. いい, よい [いAdj.]
   good
   Use よい in conjugations.

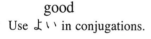

2. わるい [いAdj.]
   bad

3. おおきい [いAdj.]
   big

4. ちいさい [いAdj.]
   small

5. ながい [いAdj.]
   long

6. みじかい [いAdj.]
   short [not for height]

6か

【ぶんぽう：Grammar】

A. い Adjectives.

い adjectives and な adjectives describe nouns. い adjectives are original Japanese adjectives. Most end in -ai, -ii, -ui, or -oi. Some exceptional な adjectives end in -い. If you memorize these exceptions, you will not have any problems. So far, きらい "dislike" and とくい "be strong in" are the only exceptions you have learned. These look like い adjectives, but are actually な adjectives. They conjugate like nouns.

い adjective conjugation:

せ(い)が　たか<u>い</u>です。	(I) am tall.
せ(い)が　たか<u>くない</u>です。／たか<u>くありません</u>。	(I) am not tall.
せ(い)が　たか<u>かった</u>です。	(I) was tall.
せ(い)が　たか<u>くなかった</u>です。／たか<u>くありませんでした</u>。	(I) was not tall.

☆ いい "good" conjugates from the よい form.

い<u>い</u>です。／よ<u>い</u>です。	(It) is good.
よ<u>くない</u>です。／よ<u>くありません</u>。	(It) is not good.
よ<u>かった</u>です。	(It) was good.
よ<u>くなかった</u>です。／よ<u>くありませんでした</u>。	(It) was not good.

1. わたしは　せ(い)が　あまり　<u>たかくないです</u>。 I am not very tall.
2. やまださんは　とても　あたまが　<u>いいです</u>。 Mr. Yamada is very smart.
3. おばあさんは　めも　みみも　<u>よくないです</u>。
   My grandmother has bad eyesight as well as bad hearing.

B. Expressions using body part words

1. あたまが　いいです。　　is smart
2. あたまが　わるいです。　is unintelligent
3. かおが　いいです。　　　is good looking
4. かおが　わるいです。　　is homely
5. めが　いいです。　　　　has good eyesight
6. めが　わるいです。　　　has bad eyesight
7. みみが　いいです。　　　has good hearing
8. みみが　わるいです。　　has bad hearing
9. せ(い)が　たかいです。　is tall (height)
10. せ(い)が　ひくいです。　is short (height)

6 か

11. はなが　たかいです。　　　has a long (tall) nose
12. はなが　ひくいです。　　　has a short (flat) nose
13. こえが　おおきいです。　　has a loud voice
14. こえが　ちいさいです。　　has a soft voice
15. こころが　いいです。　　　is good natured
16. こころが　おおきいです。　is generous
17. こころが　ちいさいです。　is timid

【　●　ぶんかノート: Cultural Notes】

1. What does はなが　たかい mean?

   Japanese describe a nose as being tall or low, not long or flat as in English. Because having a nose with a high bridge (an aquiline or Roman nose) is not an important distinguishing characteristic for Westerners (almost everyone has "high" noses), an equivalent translation of はながたかい does not exist in common English vocabulary.

2. Is there a difference in meaning between the Japanese borrowed word スマート SUMAATO and the English word "smart"?

   When Japanese people say 「あなたは　スマートSUMAATO ですねえ。」, it does not mean "You are intelligent." It means "You are slim/stylish." It is similar to the English use of "smart" in the sentence "She is a smart dresser!" In addition, スマート SUMAATO in Japanese implies slenderness.

3. What is the standard of beauty for Japanese people?

   The standard of beauty has changed through history. Modern Japanese people's image of a beautiful woman is a person with large eyes, fair skin, a tall nose, a small mouth and long legs. The image of a handsome man is one who has thick, dark eyebrows, a tall nose, a well shaped mouth, dark skin, and long legs. In other words, "beauty in Japan" is now more similar to a Westerner's conception of "beauty."

【アクティビティー: Activities】

A. Pair Work

Ask your partner about his/her family members' characteristics. Write the names (titles) of each of your family members in the blocks in the top row and fill in the blocks below each with the correct description for each person <u>in Japanese</u>.

Ex. 「おとうさんは　せが　たかいですか。」
　　「はい、すこし　たかいです。」

かぞく				
1. Height				
2. Size (= body)				
3. Intelligence				
4. Looks (= face)				
5. Eyes				
6. Voice				
7. Hair				
8. Hands				
9. Legs (long/short)				
10. Heart				

【おはなし: Story 】

ちちの　めは　あおいですが、ははの　めは
ちゃいろいです。ぼくの　めも　ちゃいろいです。

【たんご: Vocabulary】

1. あかい [いAdj.]
   is red

2. しろい [いAdj.]
   is white

3. くろい [いAdj.]
   is black

4. あおい [いAdj.]
   is blue

5. きいろい [いAdj.]
   is yellow

6. ちゃいろい [いAdj.]
   is brown

【＊オプショナルたんご: Optional Vocabulary】

1.＊きんぱつ [Noun]	blonde (hair)
2.＊まっすぐ [なAdj.]	straight
3.＊カール KAARU しています [Verb]	is curly

【ぶんぽう: Grammar】

A. Colors

All colors have a noun form, but basic colors also have an い adjective form. When conjoining
more than two colors with と, the noun forms of the color must be used.

1. ぼくの　ぼうしは　<u>あかです</u>。	My cap is a red color.
2. ぼくの　ぼうしは　<u>あかいです</u>。	My cap is red.
3. ぼくの　ぼうしは　<u>あかと　しろです</u>。	My cap is red and white.

Negative form:

4. ぼくの　ぼうしは　<u>あかではありません</u>。	My cap is not a red color.
5. ぼくの　ぼうしは　<u>あかくないです</u>。	My cap is not red.
6. ぼくの　ぼうしは　<u>あかと　しろではありません</u>。	My cap is not red and white.

【 ● ぶんかノート: Cultural Notes】

"Grey Hair" is perceived as "White Hair" in Japan.

When one ages in America, one is concerned about one's hair turning "grey." However, the Japanese describe the same phenomenon as "having white hair" or "white hair appearing."

An interesting note: Take a look at photos of the older members of the Imperial Family of Japan. Notice that they allow their hair to grow "white" naturally. Because the Imperial Family must represent the beliefs of the Shinto religion, which espouses nature worship, they will not dye their hair because it is unnatural to do so.

【 アクティビティー: Activities】

A. Pair Work

Ask your partner about the eye color and hair color of each member of his/her family. Write the names of your partner's family members in the first column and the correct colors in the second and third columns.

Ex. Question: 「おとうさんは　めが　なにいろですか。」

　　　or 「おとうさんの　めは　なにいろですか。」

　Answer: 「（ちちは　めが）　ちゃいろいです。」

　　　or 「（ちちの　めは）　ちゃいろいです。」

かぞく		めのいろ	かみのいろ

B. Class Work - Game: 10 Questions

Gather pictures of ten famous people. One student volunteer chooses one of the 10 persons and only tells the teacher which person he/she has chosen. The rest of the class asks the student volunteer no more than 10 Yes/No questions as they try to guess which person was chosen. The student volunteer must give a Yes/No answer to every question asked.

【おはなし : Story 】

おじいさん

ぼくの おじいさんは 65さいです。とても
わかいです。ちょっと やせていますが、とても
げんきです。フットボールFUTTOBOORU が だいすきです。
そして、まいばん テレビTEREBI を みます。
そして、とても やさしいです。

【たんご : Vocabulary】

1. ふとっています [Verb]
is fat, heavy

2. やせています [Verb]
is thin

3. わかい [い Adj.]
is young

4. としを とっています [Verb]
is old (age)

5. きびしい [い Adj.]
is strict

6. やさしい [い Adj.]
is nice, kind

7. Question 1。 （それとも） Question 2。   Question 1, or Question 2.

	Affirmative	Negative
fat	ふとっています	ふとっていません
thin	やせています	やせていません
young	わかいです	わかくありません or わかくないです
old (age)	としを とっています	としを とっていません
strict	きびしいです	きびしくありません or きびしくないです
nice, kind	やさしいです	やさしくありません or やさしくないです

【ぶんぽう: Grammar】

A. Question 1。 （それとも）　 Question 2。　　 Question 1?, or Question 2?

それとも means "or" and is used at the beginning of a new sentence.

1. おとうさんは　ふとっていますか。それとも、やせていますか。

   Is your father fat? Or is he thin?

2. せんせいは　きびしいですか。それとも、やさしいですか。

   Is your teacher strict? Or is he/she nice?

3. ジュースを　のみますか。ミルクを　のみますか。

   Do you drink juice? Or do you drink milk?

4. おすしが　すきですか。きらいですか。

   Do you like *sushi?* Or do you dislike *sushi*?

【 ● ぶんかノート: Cultural Notes】

Why are すもうとり so heavy?

すもうとり are sumo wrestlers who are famous for their large size. A large すもうとり can weigh as much as 600 pounds. They wake up early in the morning to practice すもう. Young すもうとり, because of their low rank, must do all of the menial work, such as cleanup and cooking. This includes preparing ちゃんこなべ, which is a stew consisting of huge quantities of meat and vegetables. すもうとり may eat as many as eight to ten huge bowls of this a day. It is no wonder that they gain so much weight! When すもうとり retire, most lose weight and try to maintain a normal lifestyle at a reasonable weight.

【アクティビティー: Activities】

A. Pair Work

Ask the following questions. Use the cues to think of a specific person's name to substitute in the parenthesis. If your response is no, answer in the negative form. Take turns.

1. (Sumo wrestler) は　やせていますか。
2. (Famous person) は　ふとっていますか。
3. (Teacher) は　わかいですか。
4. (President) は　としを　とっていますか。

| 5. (Father or mother or teacher) は　きびしいですか。 |
| 6. (Friend, teacher) は　　やさしいですか。 |
| 7. (Student, father, teacher) は　　せ（い）が　たかいですか。 |
| 8. (Student, mother) は　　めが　あおいですか。 |
| 9. (Student) は　　おおきいですか。 |
| 10. (Student) は　　かみが　ながいですか。 |
| 11. (Partner) は　　あたまが　いいですか。 |

B. Pair Work

Ask your partner about his/her parents and grandparents. In the blanks, write a short response <u>in</u> <u>Japanese</u>.

Ex. 「おとうさんは　やせていますか。ふとっていますか。」
　　「ちちは　すこし　やせています。」

?	おとうさん	おかあさん	おじいさん	おばあさん
1. Heavy or thin				
2. Strict or nice				
3. Young or old				
4. Tall or short				
5. Hair color				
6. Eyesight				

【かいわ: Dialogue 】

エミ EMI : いもうとさんは　かわいいですね。
　　　　　　そして、とても　しずかですね。
ケン KEN : いいえ、きょう　しずかですが、
　　　　　　いつも　うるさいですよ。

【たんご: Vocabulary】

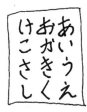

1. きれい [なAdj.]
is pretty,　　is clean,　　is neat, nice

2. きたない [いAdj.]
is dirty,　　is messy

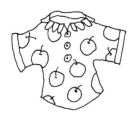

3. かわいい [いAdj.]
is cute

4. しずか [なAdj.]
is quiet

5. うるさい [いAdj.]
is noisy,
is annoying

6. じゃま [なAdj.]
is a hindrance, is a
nuisance, is in the way

7. いいです<u>ね</u>。

It is good, isn't it?

The sentence ending particle ね used when the
speaker wishes to seek agreement or confirmation
from the listener.

8. いいです<u>よ</u>。

It is good, you know.

The sentence ending particle よ
expresses emphasis or exclamation.

Vocabulary	Affirmative	Negative
pretty, clean, neat	きれいです	きれいではありません
dirty, messy	きたないです	きたなくありません or きたなくないです
cute	かわいいです	かわいくありません or かわいくないです
quiet	しずかです	しずかではありません
noisy	うるさいです	うるさくありません or うるさくないです
hindrance	じゃまです	じゃまではありません

【＊オプショナルたんご: Optional Vocabulary】

1.＊ハンサム   ＊HANSAMU   handsome

2.＊びじん   ＊BIJIN   a beauty, beautiful woman

【ぶんぽう: Grammar】

A. Sentence ＋ね。

　　Sentence ＋よ。

　　Sentence ＋ねえ。

The sentence ending particle ね is used when the speaker wants agreement from the listener. The sentence particle よ expresses emphasis. ねえ expresses exclamation and surprise. Do no confuse their usages!

Compare:　　あついですね。　　　It is hot, isn't it?

　　　　　　あついですよ。　　　It is hot, you know.

　　　　　　あついですねえ。　　It is so hot !

1. 「うるさいですよ。」　　　　　"You are noisy, you know. (Be quiet.)"

　 「すみません。」　　　　　　　"I am sorry."

2. 「かわいいですねえ。」　　　　"She is so cute!"

　 「そうですねえ！」　　　　　　"Yes, she is!"

3. 「あたまが　いいですね。」　　"You are smart, aren't you?"

　 「いいえ、よくないですよ。」　"No, I am not smart, you know."

B. Conjugation of な Adjectives.

There are two types of adjectives in Japanese. They are い adjectives and な adjectives. They are both adjectives and both describe nouns, but their conjugations are different. Adjectives which end in -ai, -ii, -oi or -ui are い adjectives and the adjectives which do not end with these endings are な adjectives. The two exceptional な adjectives so far are きらい "dislike" and とくい "strong at." The conjugations are as follows.

6か

130

	い adjectives	な adjectives
affirmative	おおきいです is big	しずかです is quiet
negative	おおきくありません or おおきくないです is not big	しずかではありません or しずかじゃありません is not quiet
other words	たかい　　　　しろい ひくい　　　　わかい いい,よい　　きびしい わるい　　　　やさしい おおきい　　　きたない ちいさい　　　かわいい ながい　　　　うるさい あかい　　　　etc.	すき　　　　じゃま きらい　　　　　etc. じょうず へた とくい にがて きれい しずか

---

*Summary

はい、そうです。	Yes, it is. [Used only in agreement to a です ending sentence.]
そうですか。	Is that so?
そうですねえ ...	Let me see ...
そうですねえ！	Yes, it is!
そうですね。	It is so, isn't it?
そうですよ。	It is so, you know.

【● ぶんかノート: Cultural Notes】

Why are Japanese people "reserved"?

Although this is a stereotype, Japanese are perceived as quiet or reserved as compared to Westerners. Japanese tend not to express their opinions freely. It may have to do partly with family upbringing and the educational system. At home, children are not always encouraged to form or express their own opinions, but must often subordinate themselves to their parents' thinking. At school, students are not provided time for much discussion because of traditional teaching styles and large class sizes. Often, class sizes exceed 40 students and there simply is not enough time for individual students to express their own opinions in discussion. Japanese value harmony over conflict, so will often refrain from expressing their opinions too freely.

6か

【アクティビティー: Activities】

A. Pair Work

Ask the following questions using the cues in the parenthesis as topics for your sentences. If the answer is "no," use the negative form. Take turns.

1. (Partner's hands, partner's mother, partner's <u>hiragana</u>) は　きれいですか。
2. (Partner's room へや, partner's <u>hiragana</u>) は　きたないですか。
3. (Classmate) は　かわいいですか。
4. (Library) は　しずかですか。
5. (Father, mother) は　うるさいですか。
6. (Partner's sibling) は　じゃまですか。

B. Pair Work

Ask your partner about his/her friend. Write <u>in Japanese</u> whether the person does or doesn't possess the qualities listed. Use the correct い adjective or な adjective affirmative or negative form in your responses.

Ex. A:「あなたの　ともだちは　だれですか。」
B:「～さんです。」
A:「～さんは　しずかですか。」
B:「いいえ、ぜんぜん　しずかではありません。」
A:「そうですか。」

1. Quiet	
2. Cute	
3. Nuisance	
4. Heavy, fat	
5. Intelligent	
6. Big	
7. Long haired	
8. Tall	

C. 10 Questions - Teacher to Students, Pair Work, Class Work

The teacher has one student in mind. Ask your teacher 10 Yes/No questions to find out which student the teacher has in mind. Second, play this game with a partner. Finally, have one student volunteer stand in front of the class as classmates ask the volunteer questions. Guess which classmate the student volunteer is thinking about. (Add. vocab.: おとこ male, おんな female.)

Ask your partner these questions in Japanese.
Your partner answers in Japanese.
You may substitute other family names in the following questions if they are inappropriate to your family situation. Be sure to let your teacher know ahead of time if you plan substitutions.

1. What is your hobby?

2. What is your father's job?

3. What is your mother's job?

4. Do you like *sushi*?

5. What kind of foods do you like?

6. What kind of drinks do you like?

7. What are you good at?

8. Are you good/skillful at baseball?

9. Do you like golf?

10. You are very good/skillful at speaking Japanese! [Respond to the compliment.]

11. What color(s) do you like?

12. What color(s) do you dislike?

13. Is your mother/father tall?

14. You are very smart! [Respond to the compliment.]

15. Is your father/mother's hair long?

6か

16. Are your eyes bad?

17. Do I have a pot belly (large belly)?

18. What color is your shirt (*shatsu*)?

19. Are your school's school colors white and blue?

20. Are your eyes blue?

21. What color is your mother's hair?

22. Am I fat?

23. Is your grandmother thin?

24. Is your Japanese teacher young?

25. Is your English teacher old?

26. Is your father strict?

27. Is your mother nice?

28. Is the library quiet?

29. You are noisy! [Respond to the comment.]

30. Are your hands clean?

31. That student over there is pretty, isn't she?   [Point to a pretty girl.]

32. Am I in your way?

33. Is your *hiragana* (writing) messy?

By the end of this lesson, you will be able to communicate the information below in the given situations.

【1-7 タスク1】

You invite your friend to a party. Your friend asks when it will be held, what time it begins, where it will be, who will come, and what time it will end. Your friend decides whether he/she will go based on these facts.

【1-7 タスク2】

You are going to do a home stay in Japan with the family of your Japanese friend. Ask about his/her family's time schedule, such as what time they get up, what time they eat breakfast, what time they go to work, what time they return home, what time they eat dinner, and what time they go to bed. Ask how you will be commuting to school.

【かいわ: Dialogue 】

ケン KEN：にほんごの　しけんは　いつですか。

エミ EMI：もくようびですよ。

ケン KEN：この　どようびに　えいがを　みませんか。

エミ EMI：はい、みましょう。

【たんご: Vocabulary】

1. にちようび	日曜日	Sunday	
2. げつようび	月曜日	Monday	
3. かようび	火曜日	Tuesday	
4. すいようび	水曜日	Wednesday	
5. もくようび	木曜日	Thursday	
6. きんようび	金曜日	Friday	
7. どようび	土曜日	Saturday	
8. なんようび	何曜日	What day of the week?	

9.

いつ

when?

No particle follows いつ.

10.

(お)やすみ

day off, vacation

11. Verb-ましょう。 　　　　　Let's do 〜. [Suggestion]

12. Verb-ませんか。 　　　　　Won't you do 〜?/Would you like to do 〜? [Invitation]

13. Specific time ＋ に　Verb。 　　do 〜 on, at (specific time)

【＊オプショナルたんご: Optional Vocabulary】

1.＊さいじつ 　　　　　　　　　(national, state) holiday(s)

2.＊しめきり 　　　　　　　　　deadline

3.＊いいえ、けっこうです。 　　No, thank you.

4.＊ざんねんですが... 　　　　　Unfortunately . . .

When you decline an invitation politely, you may use this (#4) as a preface. This by itself can be a complete sentence. Japanese prefer not to give a clear explanation, so this is particularly convenient to use when declining an invitation. No specific "excuse" needs to follow.

【ぶんぽう：Grammar】

A. Verb-ましょう。　　　　　　　　　　Let's do 〜. [Suggestion]

When -ましょう is attached to a verb stem (portion of the verb remaining after removing -ます), the verb means "let's do . . ." and is used when one makes a suggestion to others.

1. おひるごはんを　たべ<u>ましょう</u>。　　　Let's eat lunch!
2. えいがを　み<u>ましょう</u>。　　　　　　　Let's watch a movie!
3. おみずを　のみ<u>ましょう</u>。　　　　　　Let's drink water!

B. Verb-ませんか。　　　Won't you do 〜?/ Would you like to do 〜? [Invitation]

The negative -ませんか form plus か may have two interpretations. It may simply be a negative question. More often, however, it is used as an invitation to the listener to do something.

1. 「この　ざっしを　よみ<u>ませんか</u>。」　　"Won't you read this magazine?"
   「どうも　ありがとう。」　　　　　　　　"Thank you very much."
2. 「ジュース JUUSU を　のみ<u>ませんか</u>。」　"Won't you drink some juice?"
   「*いいえ、けっこうです。」　　　　　　　"No, thank you."

C. Specific time ＋ に　　　　　on, at

There are two types of time words in Japanese: general time and specific time.
General time words such as きょう "today," あさ "morning," いま "now," まいにち "everyday," etc. are not followed by the particle に.
Specific time words, such as いちじ "one o'clock," にちようび "Sunday," いちがつ "January" are followed by the particle に.

1. わたしは　どようび<u>に</u>　えいがを　みました。
   I watched a movie on Saturday.
2. にちようび<u>に</u>　としょかんで　えいごの　レポート REPOOTO を
   かきました。
   I wrote an English report at the library on Sunday.

7か

【 ● ぶんかノート: Cultural Notes】

Kanji (Chinese characters) for Days of the Week

Below are the original meanings of the words for the days of the week and the *kanji* for each of them. As noted earlier, some Chinese characters (*kanji*) depict a pictorial image of the words they represent. The illustrations below show how the *kanji* for the days of the week were derived.

→ 日 SUN   Sunday (also, day)

→ 月 MOON   Monday (also, month)

→ 火 FIRE   Tuesday

→ 水 WATER   Wednesday

→ 木 TREE   Thursday

→ 金 GOLD   Friday

→ 土 SOIL   Saturday

【🧑👩アクティビティー: Activities】

A. Pair Work

Look at the calendar of events below, and ask your partner what day of the week each event occurs. Fill in the blanks with the correct answers from the chart below. Your partner answers. Take turns.

Ex. Question: 「きょうは　なんようびですか。」

Answer: 「きょうは　〜ようびです。」

Sun	Mon	Tue	Wed	Thu	Fri	Sat
concert	[holiday] "day off"	Japanese exam	[today]	English paper	school dance	football

1. Today	_____ ようび
2. Tomorrow	_____ ようび
3. Yesterday	_____ ようび
4. Holiday ("day off")	_____ ようび
5. School dance	_____ ようび
6. Football	_____ ようび
7. Concert [konsaato]	_____ ようび
8. Japanese exam	_____ ようび
9. English paper	_____ ようび

7か

B. Pair Work

You want to do some activities together with your friend. Invite him/her to do each of the activities below. Decide which day of the week is convenient for both of you. Write your schedule on the chart below.

Ex. Question: 「～ようびに　いっしょに　おひるごはんを　たべませんか。」

　　Yes-answer: 「いいですよ。いっしょに　たべましょう。」

　　No-answer: 「いいえ、～ようびは　だめです。～ようびに　たべませんか。」

1. Eating lunch at the snack bar together.

2. Talking at the cafeteria together.

3. Doing Japanese homework together.

4. Listening to music together.

5. Watching a movie together.

Our schedule:

Sun	Mon	Tue	Wed	Thu	Fri	Sat

【かいわ: Dialogue 】

ケンKEN : いま　なんじですか。

エミEMI : １０じはんです。

ケンKEN : おそいですねえ。

じゃ、さようなら。

【たんご: Vocabulary】

A. Hours

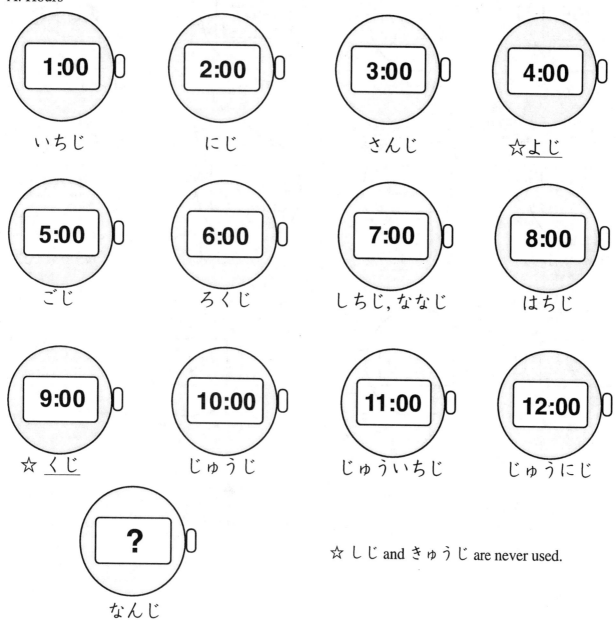

1:00 いちじ	2:00 にじ	3:00 さんじ	4:00 ☆<u>よじ</u>
5:00 ごじ	6:00 ろくじ	7:00 しちじ, ななじ	8:00 はちじ
9:00 ☆<u>くじ</u>	10:00 じゅうじ	11:00 じゅういちじ	12:00 じゅうにじ

? なんじ

☆ しじ and きゅうじ are never used.

B. Minutes

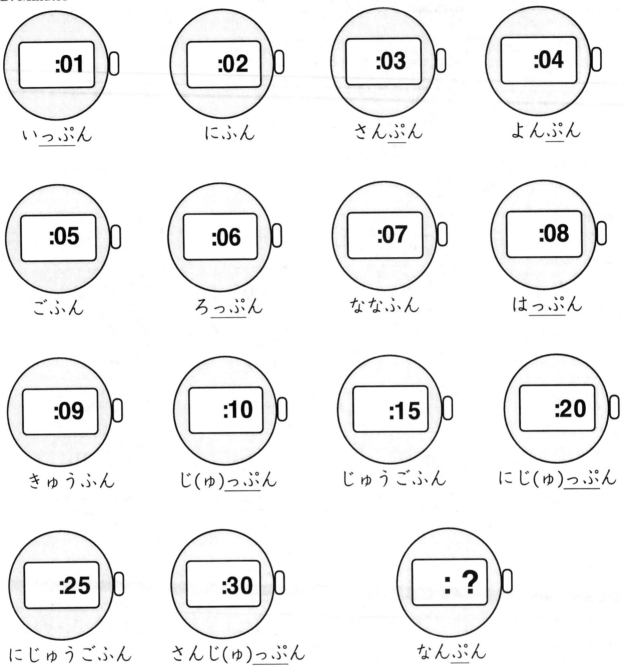

:01　いっぷん

:02　にふん

:03　さんぷん

:04　よんぷん

:05　ごふん

:06　ろっぷん

:07　ななふん

:08　はっぷん

:09　きゅうふん

:10　じ(ゅ)っぷん

:15　じゅうごふん

:20　にじ(ゅ)っぷん

:25　にじゅうごふん

:30　さんじ(ゅ)っぷん

: ?　なんぷん

C. Others

1. くじはん
half past 9:00

2. くじころ／ごろ
about 9:00

3. くじはんごろ
about half past 9:00

4. くじまえ
before 9:00

5. くじすぎ
after 9:00

6. くじ　ごふんまえ
five minutes before 9:00

☆ころ／ごろ "about," すぎ "past," まえ "before" appears between the specific time word and the particle に.

D.

1. はやい [いAdj.]
is early

2. おそい [いAdj.]
is late

3. こんばん
tonight

4. こんばんは。
Good evening.

5. ごぜん　　　　　　　　　a.m. [Ex. ごぜん１じ "1:00 a.m."]
6. ごご　　　　　　　　　　p.m. [Ex. ごご１じ "1:00 p.m."]

【*オプショナルたんご: Optional Vocabulary】

1. *ゆうべ　　　　　　　　last night
2. *とけい　　　　　　　　watch, clock
3. *じかんですよ。　　　　It is time (to do ...).

#3 may be used to indicate that it is time for an activity (i.e., class) to end.

7か

【 ● ぶんかノート: Cultural Notes】

Are Japanese always prompt?

Foreigners living in Japan quickly learn that it is important to be on time, particularly in the cities. Everything runs precisely on schedule — buses, trains, TV programming, etc. It is impolite to be late for appointments. In fact, Japanese always arrive early, before the agreed meeting time. Do not give excuses for being late. Simple apologies are more acceptable.

【 アクティビティー: Activities】

A. Class Work

The class wants to set up a standard curfew time for students. Some students suggest a time. Everyone has two flash cards: an おそい card and a はやい card. When a student suggests a curfew time, the other students raise their card and express their opinions. Try to make responsible decisions.

1. Curfew time on Monday, Tuesday, Wednesday, Thursday: _____

2. Curfew time on Friday and Saturday: _____

B. Pair Work

Ask your partner what time he/she eats breakfast, lunch and dinner everyday. Fill in the blanks.

Partner's meal time:

	Breakfast	Lunch	Dinner
Time			

C. Pair Work

You want to invite your friend to the following activities. Decide on an agreeable day and the time.

Activity	Day of the week	Time
1. Eating lunch together at the cafeteria		
2. Playing tennis together		
3. Watching a movie together		

* どようびの　いちじ　　one o'clock on Saturday

【かいわ: Dialogue 】

　　　ケンKEN：なんじに　うちへ　かえりますか。
　　　エミEMI：４じごろ　かえります。
　　　ケンKEN：じゃ、いっしょに　かえりましょう。

【ぶんけい: Sentence Structure 】

| Person | は | ～じ（ごろ） | に | Place | へ／に | Direction verb | 。 |

"to" 　いきます go
　きます come
　かえります return (to a place)

【たんご: Vocabulary 】

1. いきます［いく］
to go

2. きます［くる］
to come

3. かえります［かえる］
to return (place), to go/come home

4. おきます［おきる］
to wake up, get up

5. ねます［ねる］
to sleep, go to bed

6. かいしゃ
company

7. Place ＋ へ／に ＋ Direction verb。　　　　to (place)

8. Activity ＋ に ＋ Direction verb。　　　　to, for (activity)

9. Sentence 1。それから、 Sentence 2。　　　Sentence 1. And then Sentence 2.

【ぶんぽう : Grammar】

A. Direction verbs

Direction verbs are verbs which indicate direction or motion. There are three basic direction verbs - いきます "go," きます "come," かえります "return (place)."

B. Place ＋ へ／に ＋ Direction verb (いきます／きます／かえります)。 (go/ come/ return) to

Verbs used in this construction indicate direction or motion to the place of destination. The particles へ and に are used interchangeably and immediately follow the place of destination.

1. ぼくは　きょう　7じはんに　がっこう<u>へ</u>　きました。
   I came to school at 7:30 today.
2. ちちは　10じごろ　うち<u>に</u>　かえりました。
   My father came home about 10:00.
3. ともだちは　にちようびに　うち<u>へ</u>　きました。
   My friend came to my house on Sunday.

C. Activity ＋ に ＋ Direction verb。　　　　　　to, for

Shopping, movies, dancing, lunch, parties, classes, etc., are some examples of activities. Activities or events are followed by the particle に (not へ) when used with direction verbs.

1. どようびの　7じはんに　えいが<u>に</u>　いきました。
   I went to a movie at 7:30 on Saturday.
2. この　きんようびに　ともだちと　ダンス DANSU <u>に</u>　いきます。
   I will go dancing with my friend this Friday.
3. ちちは　まいにちようびに　ゴルフ GORUFU <u>に</u>　いきます。
   My father goes golfing every Sunday.

D. Sentence 1。それから、 Sentence 2。　　　Sentence 1. And then Sentence 2.

1. あさ　6じに　おきました。<u>それから</u>、あさごはんを　たべました。
   I got up at 6:00 in the morning. And then I ate breakfast.
2. あには　8じすぎに　うちへ　かえりました。<u>それから</u>、えいがに
   いきました。
   My older brother came home after 8 o'clock. And then he went to a movie.
3. わたしは　としょかんへ　いきました。<u>それから</u>、にほんごを
   べんきょうしました。
   I went to the library. And then I studied Japanese.

【 ● ぶんかノート: Cultural Notes】

1. Use of いきます and きます

   The Japanese usages of いきます and きます are slightly different from their usage in English. In Japanese, いきます is used to indicate motion away from the speaker's location, or a location associated with the speaker. きます is used to indicate motion toward the speaker, or toward a location associated with the speaker. When your friend invites you to a party at his house, he would say 「パーティー PAATII に　きませんか。」. What would your response be? Would it be 「はい、きます。」or 「はい、いきます。」? The correct answer is 「はい、いきます。」.

2. How do Japanese commute to school or work?

   Japanese people who live in urban areas do not usually commute by car. Public transportation such as buses, electric trains, and subways is common. In big cities such as Tokyo, Osaka, etc., the railway is most convenient because of its efficiency and dependability. One can almost set a clock by the arrival and departure of trains. Once you get on, you can study, sleep, listen to music, read a newspaper, etc. However, rush hour, which generally runs from 6:30 — 8:30 a.m. in Tokyo, can be a harrowing experience for those not used to massive crowds. Public transportation does not run all night long. If you are out late and miss the last bus or train, you may have to catch a taxi home.

【 アクティビティー: Activities】

A. Pair Work

   Ask your partner for the times he does the following activities on a normal school day. Write down the information you receive.

   Ex. Question: 「あさ　なんじに　おきますか。」

   　　Answer: 「～じに　おきます。」

Activity	Time
1. Get up in the morning	
2. Eat breakfast	
3. Come to school	
4. Go to the library	
5. Eat lunch	
6. Return home	
7. Eat dinner	
8. Go to bed	

7 か

B. Pair Work

Ask your partner what he/she did last Saturday and what time he/she did each activity. Write the information below. Start from early morning and end at bedtime.

_____ さん [partner's name] の　どようび

[Time]　　　　　　　　[Things he/she did.]

_____ に　おきました。

_____ に

_____ に

_____ に

_____ に　ねました。

【かいわ: Dialogue 】

At school.

ケン KEN ：なんで　がっこうへ　きますか。

エミ EMI ：バス BASU で　きます。

【ぶんけい: Sentence structures 】

Person は ～じ（ごろ）に	Place へ／に "to"	Direction verb 。
	transportation で "by"	
Subject / だれ が　～ます（か）。		

【たんご: Vocabulary】

1. くるま, じどうしゃ

car, vehicle

2. バス
BASU
bus

3. タクシー
TAKUSHII
taxi

4. じてんしゃ

bicycle

5. ちかてつ
subway

6. でんしゃ
electric train

7. ひこうき
airplane

8. ふね
boat, ship

9. あるいて　いきます
[あるいて　いく]
to go by walking

10. あるいて　きます
[あるいて　くる]
to come by walking

11. あるいて　かえります
[あるいて　かえる]
to return by walking

12. Transportation facility ＋ で   by (transportation facility)

13. Subject / だれ＋が　～ます（か）。   [Subject particle]

【＊オプショナルたんご: Optional Vocabulary】

1.＊しんかんせん

bullet train

【ぶんぽう: Grammar】

> A. Transportation facility ＋ で   by (transportation facility)
> The particle で immediately follows the noun which is the form of transportation, means, or tool by which an action occurs.

1. わたしは　バスBASUで　がっこうへ　きます。　　I come to school by bus.

2. ははは　くるまで　かいしゃに　いきます。　　My mother goes to her company by car.

3. おじいさんと　おばあさんは　きのう　ひこうきで　にほんへ　いきました。

My grandfather and grandmother went to Japan by airplane yesterday.

> B. Subject / だれ ＋ が
> が marks the subject of a sentence when the information expressed by the subject is introduced for the first time. When the subject is presented as the topic (that is, the information has already been introduced), however, the topic marker は replaces が.

1. だれが　がっこうへ　バスBASU で　きますか。　　Who comes to school by bus?

2. だれが　くるまで　きますか。　　　　　　　　Who comes by car?

【 ● ぶんかノート: Cultural Notes】

1. What is a しんかんせん?

The しんかんせん, literally translated at the "new trunk line," but more commonly known as the bullet train, stretches from northern Honshu to Kyushu in the south. It also connects eastern and western Japan. It is the fastest means of ground transportation, traveling at a maximum speed of about 175 mph.

2. Japanese cars drive on the left side of the street.

Unlike cars in the U.S., Japanese cars drive on the left lanes of the highway. Japanese cars have the steering wheel on the right side of the car.

3. Japanese Taxis

In Japan, there are many taxis on the street so they are easy to catch. Taxis with lighted red signs in their windows are available. Raise your hand and the taxi will stop for you. Because the door opens automatically, wait until it is opened by the driver. Do not stand close to the door, you may be hit! You do not have to give tips to taxi drivers in Japan. If you are unfamiliar with the Japanese language, it is recommended that you carry the business card of your place of destination, (or the correct address) and show it to the taxi driver when you enter the taxi. Many taxi drivers do not speak English well.

7か

【🧑‍🦱👩 アクティビティー: Activities】

A. Pair Work

Ask your partner how each member of his/her family goes to school or work and what time each leaves home.

Ex. Question 1: 「おとうさんは　しごとに　なんで　いきますか。」

Answer 1: 「ちちは　くるまで　いきます。」

Question 2: 「おとうさんは　なんじに　しごとに　いきますか。」

Answer 2: 「ちちは　〜じに　いきます。」

Family member	Transportation	Departure time

B. Pair Work

You want to go to the following places with your friend. Decide on your means of transportation, as shown in the example below.

Ex. A: 「えいがに　いきませんか。」

B: 「はい、いきましょう。」

A: 「なんで　いきますか。」

B: 「くるまで　いきましょう。」

Destination	Transportation	Destination	Transportation
1. Japan		4. Airport [くうこう]	
2. (Another state)		5. Library	
3. Alaska [Arasuka]		6. Movie	

C. Class Work

Ask all of your classmates how they come to school. Tally their responses below.

Ex. Who comes to school by bus?　「だれが　がっこうへ　バスBASUで　きますか。」

バス BASU	くるま	じてんしゃ	あるいて	ちかてつ

7か

【かいわ: Dialogue 】

ケン KEN ：この　どようびに　いっしょに　うみへ　いきませんか。
　　　　　　　そして、ピクニック PIKUNIKKU を　しましょう。

エミ EMI ：いいですねえ。

【たんご: Vocabulary】

1. うみ

beach, ocean, sea

2. やま

mountain

3. かわ

river

4. レストラン
RESUTORAN
restaurant

5. デパート
DEPAATO
department store

6. りょこう

trip, traveling

7. かいもの

shopping

8. しょくじ

meal, dining

9. パーティー
PAATII
party

10. ピクニック
PIKUNIKKU
picnic

11. キャンプ
KYANPU
camping

12. いそがしい
[い Adj.]
is busy

13. どこへも ＋ Neg. of direction verb。　　　do not go / return anywhere

1.*きっさてん		coffee shop
2.*ショッピングセンター	*SHOPPINGU SENTAA	shopping center
3.*コンサート	*KONSAATO	concert
4.*デート	*DEETO	dating
5.*ハイキング	*HAIKINGU	hiking
6.*ひま [な Adj.]		free (time), have nothing to do

【ぶんぽう: Grammar】

A. Noun ＋ （を） ＋ します Verbs

This object particle を is optional when used in this context. However if the sentence already has a direct object, this を should be omitted.

Noun form:

でんわ	a telephone
りょこう	a trip, travel, traveling
かいもの	shopping
しょくじ	a meal, dining

Verb form:

でんわ（を）します	to make a phone call
りょこう（を）します	to take a trip, to travel
かいもの（を）します	to shop
しょくじ（を）します	to have a meal, to dine

1. じゃ、あした でんわ（を）します。　　　Well then, I will call you tomorrow.
2. にほんへ りょこう（を）しましょう。　　Let's travel to Japan.
3. きのう かいもの（を）しました。　　　　I shopped yesterday.
4. レストラン RESUTORAN へ しょくじに いきましょう。

Let's go to a restaurant for a meal.

B. します has other translations besides "to do."

スポーツ SUPOOTSU を します	to play sports
テレビゲーム TEREBI GEEMU を します	to play video games
パーティー PAATII を します	to have a party
ピクニック PIKUNIKKU を します	to have a picnic
キャンプ KYANPU を します	to camp
デート DEETO を します	to have a date, to date, to go out on a date

1. ちちは ゴルフ GORUFU が だいすきです。そして、にちようびに
   いつも ゴルフ GORUFU を します。

My father loves golf. And he always plays golf on Sundays.

2. やまへ いきましょう。そして、キャンプ KYANPU を しましょう。

Let's go to the mountains. And let's camp.

C. どこへも ＋ Negative form of direction verb。　　　do not go/ return anywhere.
---

1. 「きんようびの　ばん　どこへ　いきましたか。」

　　　　　　　　　　　　　　　　　　　　　　"Where did you go on Friday night?"

　「どこへも　いきませんでした。」　　　"I did not go anywhere."

2. にちようびに　どこへも　いきませんでした。そして、なにも
しませんでした。

　　　I did not go anywhere on Sunday. And I did not do anything.

D. Specific time and general time words.

Specific time words take the particle に, but general time words do not take the particle に.

Specific time words are words such as いちじ "one o'clock," にちようび "Sunday," etc. General time words are words such as まいにち "everyday," きのう "yesterday," きょう "today," あした "tomorrow," あさ "morning," ひる "daytime," ばん "evening," etc. いつ "when?" does not take the particle に.
---

1. あした　ごじ(に)　おきます。　　　　　　I will get up at 5:00 tomorrow.

2. どようびの　しちじ(に)　いきましょう。　Let's go at 7:00 on Saturday.

3. 「いつ　パーティーPAATIIを　しますか。」　"When will you have a party?"

　or 「パーティー PAATII は　いつですか。」　"When is the party?"

【 ● ぶんかノート: Cultural Notes】

Japanese Weekends

　　Until several years ago, most Japanese only had one-day weekends. Adults worked six days a week and children went to school Monday through Saturday. Now, most schools take two-day weekends. More companies are beginning to give their employees two days off every weekend. Young people may stay home and watch television, read or play computer games. They often also go shopping or play sports. Fathers are able to spend more time with their families and couples are able to spend more time together.

【アクティビティー: Activities】

A. Pair Work

Invite your friend to do the following activities with you and decide where and when you want to do them.

Ex. A: 「いっしょに　かいものを　しませんか。」

B: 「はい。どこで　かいものを　しますか。」

A: 「(Shopping place)で　かいものを　しましょう。」

B: 「はい。いつ　かいものを　しますか。」

A: 「～ようびの　～じごろに　かいものを　しましょう。」

B: 「はい、いいですね。」

Activities	Where?	When?	
		～ようび	～じ
1. Shopping			
2. Dining			
3. Party			
4. Picnic			
5. Tennis			
6. Movies			

7か

Ask your partner these questions in Japanese.
Your partner answers in Japanese.

1. What day of the week is it today?

2. What time is it now?

3. What days of the week are days off?

4. When is the Japanese exam?

5. Let's eat lunch together at 12:00.

6. Would you like to go to a movie with me on Saturday? [Answer: Decline politely.]

7. What time does Japanese class (クラス KURASU) end?

8. What time did you get up this morning?

9. What time did you come to school today?

10. About what time will you go home today?

11. What time did you go to sleep last night?   Was it early?

12. What time do you usually go to bed?

13. What time does your father go to work?

14. How do you come to school?

15. What time do you usually eat lunch?

16. Do you walk to school?

17. How do you go to Japan?

18. Would you like to go to the beach on Saturday? And let's have a picnic.
    [Answer: Decline politely.]

19. Would you like to go to a restaurant tonight? And let's have a meal together.
    [Answer: Accept politely.]

20. What did you do on Saturday?

21. Where did you go on Sunday?

22. Where does your mother usually shop?

23. Are you busy now?

24. Where have you traveled before?

25. What do you do at the beach?

7 か

 Find the answers by investigating books, by talking to friends, or by using the Internet.

1. What religion do you practice?

2. What religions are dominant in the U.S.?

3. What religions are dominant in Japan?

4. What Japanese religion is associated with life and the living?

5. What Japanese religion is associated with death?

6. Can a Japanese person believe in more than one religion at once?

7. Is Christmas an important holiday in the U.S.?

8. Is Christmas an important holiday in Japan?

9. How is the New Year celebrated in your town?

10. How is the New Year celebrated in Japan? What ceremonies or rituals are undertaken during New Year's in Japan?

The game of *karuta* is a favorite activity of Japanese children and adults. The word *karuta* is derived from the word "card." *Karuta* is played in groups. There must be at least 3 persons: the reader and two contestants. Contestants may compete individually or in groups. The object of the game is to be the first to touch and grab the card which matches the proverb or poem called out by the reader. As the game proceeds, one accumulates as many cards as one can, and the winner is the one who has the most cards at the end of the game. During the New Year's season, adults play ひゃくにんいっしゅ *Hyaku-nin Isshu*, which is based on similar rules. In this game, however, contestants must be quick to match the second half of a classical poem with the first half of the poem which is read by the reader. National tournaments pitting skilled competitors are part of the New Year's celebrations in Japan.

7 か

Karuta, played by children, features famous Japanese proverbs. The card held by the reader has the entire proverb, while the playing card depicts the proverb with illustrations.

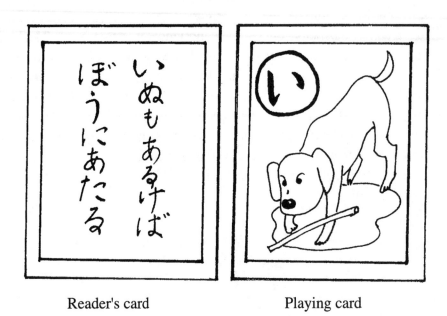

Reader's card   Playing card

In the example cards shown above, the reader would read the proverb "いぬも　あるけば ぼうに　あたる *Inu mo arukeba boo ni ataru..*" The contestants would listen for the first sound of the proverb, "い *i* ", then search quickly for the card marked "い *i* " from all of the cards which are randomly laid on the floor. The first person to lay his hands on the correct card takes it and keeps it. If one grabs the wrong card, one must return that card to the floor.

Literal meaning: When a dog walks, it, too, will stumble on a stick.
Interpretation: "Every dog has his day." or "A flying crow always catches something."
People may use proverbs in different contexts appropriate to their needs.

I. Sentence Patterns

Lesson 1

1-1わたし<u>は</u>　やまもと<u>です</u>。	I am Yamamoto.
1-4これは　<u>なんですか</u>。	What is this?
<u>1-6これ／それ／あれ</u>は　〜です。	This/That/That one over there is 〜.
1-6これは　お<u>です</u><u>か</u>。	Is this O?
1-7あついです<u>ねえ</u>。	It is hot!

Lesson 2

2-1わかり<u>ます</u>。	I understand.
2-1わかり<u>ません</u>。	I do not understand.
2-4これは　わたし<u>の</u>です。	This is mine.
<u>2-4この／その／あの</u>おかね　は　わたしのです。	This/That/That money over there is mine.
2-5ワークシート WAAKUSHIITO<u>を</u>　にまい　<u>ください</u>。	Please give me two worksheets.
2-5ティッシュ TISSHU は　<u>ここ／そこ／あそこ</u>です。	The tissue is here/there/over there.

Lesson 3

3-1あに<u>の</u>　なまえは　マイク MAIKU です。	My older brother's name is Mike.
3-2ベン BEN さん<u>と</u>　リサ RISA さんは　おやすみです。	Ben and Lisa are absent.
3-2あなた<u>は</u>？	How about you?
3-2ちちは　４３さいです。<u>そして</u>、ははは　３８さいです。	
	My father is 43. And my mother is 38 years old.
3-3わたしは　こうこうせい<u>では　ありません</u>。	I am not a high school student.
3-3わたし<u>も</u>　１４さいです。	I am 14 years old, too.
3-3ちち<u>も</u>　はは<u>も</u>　４０さいです。	Both my father and mother are 40 years old.
3-5ちちは　まえ　かいしゃいん<u>でした</u>。	My father was a company employee before.
3-5わたしは　まえ　この　がっこうの　せいと<u>では　ありませんでした</u>。	
	I was not a student of this school before.

4-1はは　にほんご<u>を</u>　はなします。　　　　My mother speaks Japanese.

4-1.わたしは　うち<u>で</u>　にほんごを　はなします。　I speak Japanese at home.

4-1おばあさんは　にほんごを　<u>よく</u>　はなします。　My grandmother speaks Japanese well.

4-1これは　わたしのです。<u>でも</u>、それは　あなたのです。This is mine. But that is yours.

4-2わたしは　にほんごを　はなします。でも、ちゅうごくご<u>は</u>　はなしません。

　　　　　　　　　　　　　　　　　　　I speak Japanese. But I do not speak Chinese.

4-3あなたは　あさごはんを　たべ<u>ました</u>か。　　Did you eat breakfast?

　いいえ、たべ<u>ませんでした</u>。　　　　　　　No, I did not eat (breakfast).

4-3<u>なにも</u>　たべませんでした。　　　　　　　I did not eat anything.

4-3わたしは　<u>きのう</u>　なにも　たべませんでした。I did not eat anything yesterday.

4-3きのう　ばんごはん<u>に</u>　おすしを　たべました。I ate sushi for dinner yesterday.

4-4ともだち<u>と</u>　<u>いっしょに</u>　たべます。　　I eat together with my friend.

4-4としょかんで　<u>べんきょう(を)　しました</u>。　I studied at the library.

4-4なにを　べんきょうしましたか。　　　　　　What did you study?

4-5しけんを　えんぴつ<u>で</u>　かきます。　　　　I will write the exam in pencil.

5-2すき<u>です</u>。　　　　　　　　　　　　　(I) like (it).

5-2すき<u>では／じゃありません</u>。　　　　　　(I) do not like (it).

5-2すき<u>でした</u>。　　　　　　　　　　　　(I) liked (it).

5-2すき<u>では／じゃありませんでした</u>。　　　(I) did not like (it).

5-2わたし<u>は</u>　どくしょ<u>が</u>　すきです。　　I like reading (books).

5-2あなたは　<u>どんな</u>　たべものが　すきですか。What kind of food do you like?

5-3ちちは　ゴルフGORUFUが　じょうずです<u>が</u>、ははは　へたです。

　　　　　　　　　My father is good at golf, but my mother is poor at it.

5-4おばあさんは　にほんごが　<u>とても</u>　じょうずです。

　　　　　　　　　My grandmother is very good at speaking Japanese.

5-4ぼくは　バスケットBASUKETTOが　<u>ちょっと</u>　にがてです。

　　　　　　　　　I am a little weak at basketball.

5-4ははは　にほんごが　<u>あまり</u>　じょうずでは　ありません。

　　　　　　　　　My mother is not very good at speaking Japanese.

5-4ぼくは　テニスTENISUが　<u>ぜんぜん</u>　じょうずでは　ありません。

　　　　　　　　　I am not good at tennis at all.

6-1わたしは　すこし　せが　ひくいです。　　　　I am a little short.

6-2たかいです。　　　　　　　　　　　　　　　　(I) am tall.

6-2たかくないです。／たかくありません。　　　(I) am not tall.

6-2たかかったです。　　　　　　　　　　　　　(I) was tall.

6-2たかくなかったです。／たかくありませんでした。　(I) was not tall.

6-2いいです。／よいです。　　　　　　　　　　(It) is good.

6-2よくないです。／よくありません。　　　　　(It) is not good.

6-2よかったです。　　　　　　　　　　　　　　(It) was good.

6-2よくなかったです。／よくありませんでした。　(It) was not good.

6-3ぼくの　ぼうしは　あかです。　　　　　　　My cap is a red color.

6-3ぼくの　ぼうしは　あかいです。　　　　　　My cap is red.

6-3ぼくの　ぼうしは　あかと　しろです。　　　My cap is red and white.

6-5「あなたは　あたまが　いいですね。」　　　"You are smart, aren't you?"

　　「いいえ、よくないですよ。」　　　　　　　"No, I am not smart, you know."

7-1おひるごはんを　たべましょう。　　　　　　Let's eat lunch!

7-1ジュースJUUSUを　のみませんか。　　　　　Won't you drink some juice?

7-1わたしは　どようびに　えいがを　みました。　I watched a movie on Saturday.

7-3ぼくは　きょう　７じはんに　がっこうへ　きました。

　　　　　　　　　　　　　　　　　　　　　　I came to school at 7:30 today.

7-3どようびの　７じはんに　えいがに　いきました。I went to a movie at 7:30 on Saturday.

7-3６じに　おきました。それから、あさごはんを　たべました。

　　　　　　　　　　　　　　　　　　　　　　I got up at 6:00. And then I ate breakfast.

7-4ははは　くるまで　かいしゃに　いきます。　My mother goes to her company by car.

7-5にほんへ　りょこう（を）しましょう。　　　Let's travel to Japan.

7-5ちちは　にちようびに　いつも　ゴルフGORUFUを　します。

　　　　　　　　　　　　　　　　　　　　　　My father always plays golf on Sundays.

7-5どこへも　いきませんでした。　　　　　　　I did not go anywhere.

II. Verbs, いAdjectives and なAdjectives

[The numbers appearing before each word indicate the lesson in which the word was introduced.]

A. Verbs

1-4 はじめます	begin, start	6-4 ふとっています	is fat, is heavy
1-4 おわります	finish	6-4 やせています	is thin
2-1 わかります	understand	6-4 としを　とっています	is old (age)
2-1 しりません	do not know	7-3 いきます	go
2-1 みえます	can see	7-3 きます	come
2-1 きこえます	can hear	7-3 かえります	return (place)
2-1 いいます	say	7-3 おきます	get up, wake up
4-1 はなします	speak, talk	7-3 ねます	go to bed, sleep
4-2 たべます	eat	7-4 あるいて　いきます	go by walking
4-2 のみます	drink	7-4 あるいて　きます	come by walking
4-4 よみます	read	7-4 あるいて　かえります	return by walking
4-4 ききます	listen, hear	7-5 スポーツ SUPOOTSU を　します	
4-4 します	do		play sports
4-4 べんきょう（を）します		7-5 パーティー PAATII を　します	
	study		have a party
4-5 みます	see, watch, look	7-5 りょこう（を）します	travel
4-5 かきます	write, draw	7-5 かいもの（を）します	shop
4-5 タイプ TAIPU （を）します		7-5 しょくじ（を）します	have a meal, dine
	type	7-5 でんわ（を）します	make a phone call

Verb Conjugation [Formal]

2-1　nonpast	のみ<u>ます</u>	drink, will drink, is going to drink
2-1　neg. nonpast	のみ<u>ません</u>	do not drink, will not drink, is not going to drink
4-3　past	のみ<u>ました</u>	drank, have drunk
4-3　neg., past	のみ<u>ませんでした</u>	did not drink, have not drunk
7-1　volitional	のみ<u>ましょう</u>	Let's drink. [Suggestion]
7-1　volitional	のみ<u>ましょうか</u>	Shall we drink? [Suggestion]
7-1　invitational	のみ<u>ませんか</u>	Would you like to drink? [Invitation]

8か　　　　　　　　　　164

B. い Adjectives

い Adjectives

1-7 あつい	hot		6-3 くろい	black	
1-7 さむい	cold		6-3 あおい	blue	
1-7 すずしい	cool		6-3 きいろい	yellow	
2-1 いい	good		6-3 ちゃいろい	brown	
6-1 たかい	tall, high		6-4 わかい	young	
6-1 ひくい	short (height), low		6-4 きびしい	strict	
6-2 よい	good		6-4 やさしい	kind, nice	
6-2 わるい	bad		6-5 きたない	dirty	
6-2 おおきい	big		6-5 かわいい	cute	
6-2 ちいさい	small		6-5 うるさい	noisy	
6-2 ながい	long		7-2 はやい	early	
6-2 みじかい	short (length)		7-2 おそい	late	
6-3 あかい	red		7-5 いそがしい	busy	
6-3 しろい	white				

い Adjective Conjugation [Formal]

6-2 nonpast	あついです	is hot
6-2 neg. nonpast	あつくないです or あつくありません	is not hot
6-2 past	あつかったです	was hot
6-2 neg. past	あつくなかったです or あつくありませんでした	was not hot

いい is never conjugated. よい is used in all conjugated forms.

6-2 nonpast	いいです	is good
6-2 neg. nonpast	よくないです or よくありません	is not good
6-2 past	よかったです	was good
6-2 neg. past	よくなかったです or よくありませんでした	was not good

C. な Adjectives

な Adjectives

1-7	げんき	healthy, fine	5-3	とくい	be strong in, does well in
2-1	だめ	no good	5-3	にがて	be weak in
5-2	すき	like	6-5	きれい	pretty, clean, neat
5-2	だいすき	like very much, love	6-5	しずか	quiet
5-2	きらい	dislike	6-5	じゃま	is a hindrance,
5-2	だいきらい	dislike a lot, hate			is a nuisance, is in the way
5-3	じょうず	skillful, be good at			
5-3	へた	unskillful, be poor at			

な Adjective Conjugation [Formal]

5-2 nonpast	すき<u>です</u>	like
5-2 neg. nonpast	すき<u>ではありません</u> or すき<u>じゃありません</u>	do not like
5-2 past	すき<u>でした</u>	liked
5-2 neg. past	すき<u>ではありませんでした</u> or すき<u>じゃありませんでした</u>	did not like

III. Nouns

A. Person		B. Thing	
1-1 わたし	I	1-2 これ	this one
1-1 ぼく	I (Used by male)	1-6 それ	that one
1-3 せんせい	teacher	1-6 あれ	that one over there
2-4 あなた	you	2-3 えんぴつ	pencil
3-1 ちち	my father	2-3 ボールペン BOORUPEN	ball point pen
3-1 はは	my mother	2-3 けしごむ	(rubber) eraser
3-1 あに	my older brother	2-3 ほん	book
3-1 あね	my older sister	2-3 かみ	paper
3-1 おとうと	my younger brother	2-3 きょうかしょ	textbook
3-1 いもうと	my younger sister	／テキスト TEKISUTO	
3-1 かぞく	my family	2-3 じしょ	dictionary
3-1 きょうだい	my siblings	2-3 ノート NOOTO	notebook
3-3 おとうさん	(someone's) father	2-3 おかね	money
3-3 おかあさん	(someone's) mother	2-3 しゃしん	photo
3-3 おじいさん	grandfather, elderly man	2-3 バッグ BAGGU	bag
3-3 おばあさん	grandmother, elderly lady	2-3 ぼうし	cap, hat
3-3 おにいさん	(someone's) older brother	2-3 ごみ	rubbish
3-3 おねえさん	(someone's) older sister	2-5 ティッシュ TISSHU	tissue
3-3 おとうとさん	(someone's) younger brother	2-5 しゅくだい	homework
3-3 いもうとさん	(someone's) younger sister	2-5 しけん	exam
3-3 せいと	student (not college)	2-5 しょうテスト TESUTO	quiz
3-3 がくせい	college student	2-5 ワークシート	worksheet
3-3 ちゅうがくせい	intermediate school student	WAAKUSHIITO	
3-3 こうこうせい	high school student	4-4 しんぶん	newspaper
3-4 こちら	this one (refers to a person)	4-4 ざっし	magazine
3-4 にほんじん	Japanese citizen	4-4 ウォークマン	walkman
3-4 アメリカ AMERIKA じん		WOOKUMAN	
	U.S. citizen	4-4 テープ TEEPU	tape
3-5 いしゃ	medical doctor	4-5 テレビ TEREBI	TV
3-5 おいしゃさん	medical doctor [polite]	4-5 レポート REPOOTO	report, paper
3-5 べんごし	lawyer	4-5 てがみ	letter
3-5 かいしゃいん	company employee	4-5 ラジオ RAJIO	radio
3-5 しゅふ	housewife	4-5 でんわ	telephone

8か

3-5 エンジニア	engineer	4-5 コンピューター	computer
ENJINIA		KONPYUUTAA	
4-1 ともだち	friend	4-5 ビデオ BIDEO	video

C. Food/Drink		D. Place	
2-5 チョコレート	chocolate	2-5 ここ	here
CHOKOREETO		2-5 そこ	there
2-5 あめ	candy	2-5 あそこ	over there
4-2 ごはん	cooked rice	3-3 がっこう	school
4-2 パン PAN	bread	3-3 ちゅうがく	intermediate school
4-2 （お）みず	water	3-3 こうこう	high school
4-2 ジュース JUUSU	juice	3-4 にほん	Japan
4-2 ぎゅうにゅう	(cow's) milk	3-4 アメリカ AMERIKA	U.S.A.
／ミルク MIRUKU		3-4 ちゅうごく	China
4-2 コーラ KOORA	cola	3-4 かんこく	Korea
4-2 おちゃ	tea	3-4 フランス FURANSU	France
4-2 コーヒー KOOHII	coffee	3-4 スペイン SUPEIN	Spain
4-3 あさごはん	breakfast	3-4 ドイツ DOITSU	Germany
4-3 ひるごはん	lunch	3-5 びょういん	hospital
4-3 ばんごはん	dinner, supper	4-1 うち	house, home
4-3 なにも + Neg.	(not) anything, nothing	4-4 としょかん	library
5-2 もの	(tangible) things	4-4 カフェテリア	cafeteria
5-2 たべもの	food	KAFETERIA	
5-2 のみもの	a drink	4-4 スナックバー	snack bar
5-2 すし	*sushi*	SUNAKKUBAA	
5-2 さしみ	raw fish	7-3 かいしゃ	company
5-2 てんぷら	*tempura*	7-5 うみ	beach, ocean, sea
		7-5 やま	mountain
		7-5 かわ	river
		7-5 レストラン RESUTORAN	restaurant
		7-5 デパート DEPAATO	department store
		7-5 どこへも + Neg.	(not) anywhere

E. Times		
3-5 いま	now	
3-5 まえ	before	
4-2 まいにち	everyday	
4-3 きのう	yesterday	
4-3 きょう	today	
4-3 あした	tomorrow	
4-3 あさ	morning	
4-3 （お）ひる	daytime	
4-3 ばん	evening	
4-3 よる	night	
4-3 ゆうがた	late afternoon, early evening	
7-1 にちようび	Sunday	
7-1 げつようび	Monday	
7-1 かようび	Tuesday	
7-1 すいようび	Wednesday	
7-1 もくようび	Thursday	
7-1 きんようび	Friday	
7-1 どようび	Saturday	
7-1 （お）やすみ	day off, vacation	
7-2 こんばん	tonight	
7-2 ごぜん	a.m.	
7-2 ごご	p.m.	

F. Activities/Events		
5-1 おんがく	music	
5-1 ダンス DANSU	dance, dancing	
5-1 うた	song, singing	
5-1 えいが	movie	
5-1 テレビゲーム TEREBIGEEMU	video game	
5-1 トランプ TORANPU	(playing) cards	
5-1 ピアノ PIANO	piano	
5-1 ギター GITAA	guitar	
5-1 どくしょ	reading	
5-1 え	painting, drawing	
5-3 こと	(intangible) thing	
7-5 りょこう	a trip, traveling	
7-5 かいもの	shopping	
7-5 しょくじ	meal, dining	
7-5 パーティー PAATII	party	
7-5 ピクニック PIKUNIKKU	picnic	
7-5 キャンプ KYANPU	camping	

G. Transportation	
7-4 くるま	car, vehicle
7-4 じどうしゃ	car, vehicle
7-4 バス BASU	bus
7-4 タクシー TAKUSHII	taxi
7-4 じてんしゃ	bicycle
7-4 ちかてつ	subway
7-4 でんしゃ	electric train
7-4 ひこうき	airplane
7-4 ふね	boat, ship

H. Sports		
5-1 スポーツ SUPOOTSU	sports	
5-1 ジョギング JOGINGU	jogging	
5-1 すいえい	swimming	
5-3 フットボール FUTTOBOORU	football	
5-3 やきゅう	baseball	
5-3 バスケット BASUKETTO	basketball	
5-3 バレーボール BAREEBOORU	volleyball	
5-3 サッカー SAKKAA	soccer	
5-3 テニス TENISU	tennis	
5-3 ゴルフ GORUFU	golf	

8 か

I. Colors			J. Parts of the body		
5-5 いろ	color		6-1 あたま	head	
5-5 あか	red		6-1 かお	face	
5-5 しろ	white		6-1 からだ	body	
5-5 くろ	black		6-1 かみ（のけ）	hair	
5-5 あお	blue		6-1 みみ	ear(s)	
5-5 きいろ	yellow		6-1 め	eye(s)	
5-5 ちゃいろ	brown		6-1 はな	nose	
5-5 みどり	green		6-1 くち	mouth	
5-5 むらさき	purple		6-1 は	tooth, teeth	
5-5 ピンク PINKU	pink		6-1 くび	neck	
5-5 オレンジ ORENJI	orange		6-1 のど	throat	
5-5 グレイ GUREI	grey		6-1 ひげ	beard, moustache	
5-5 きんいろ	gold (color)		6-1 おなか	stomach	
5-5 ぎんいろ	silver (color)		6-1 て	hand	
			6-1 あし	foot, leg	
			6-1 ゆび	finger, toe	
			6-1 せ（い）	height	
			6-1 こころ	heart, spirit	
			6-1 こえ	voice	

K. Languages		L. Others	
4-1 にほんご	Japanese	3-1 （お）なまえ	name
4-1 えいご	English	3-5 （お）しごと	job
4-1 ちゅうごくご	Chinese	5-1 しゅみ	hobby
4-1 かんこくご	Korean		
4-1 スペイン SUPEIN ご	Spanish		
4-1 フランス FURANSU ご	French		
4-1 ドイツ DOITSU ご	German		

Copula です Conjugation [Formal forms]

1-1 nonpast	せいと<u>です</u>	is a student
3-3 neg. nonpast	せいと<u>ではありません</u> or せいと<u>じゃありません</u>	is not a student
3-5 past	せいと<u>でした</u>	was a student
3-5 neg. past	せいと<u>ではありません</u><u>でした</u> or せいと<u>じゃありません</u><u>でした</u>	was not a student

IV. Adverbs, Question Words, Sentence Conjunctions, Suffixes and Prefixes

A. Adverbs		B. Question Words	
4-1 よく + Verb	well, often	1-4 なに／なん	what?
4-1 すこし	a little [formal]	2-5 なんまい	how many (sheets)?
4-1 ちょっと	a little [informal]	2-5 いくつ	how many (general things)?
4-2 ときどき	sometimes	3-1 だれ	who?
4-2 たいてい	usually	3-1 なんにん	how many (people)?
4-2 いつも	always	3-1 なんさい	how old?
5-4 とても + Adj./Adv.	very	3-1 (お)いくつ	how old?
5-4 まあまあ	so so	3-3 なんねんせい	what grade?
5-4 あまり + Neg.	(not) very	3-4 どこ	where?
5-4 ぜんぜん + Neg.	(not) at all	3-4 なにじん	what nationality?
		3-4 なんがつ	what month?
		4-1 なにご	what language?
		5-2 どんな	what kind of ?
		5-5 なにいろ	what color?
		7-1 なんようび	what day of the week?
		7-1 いつ	when?
		7-2 なんじ	what time?
		7-2 なんぷん	how many minutes?

8か

C. Sentence Conjunctions	D. Suffixes	E. Prefixes/Pre-Nominatives
3-2 そして　　　And	1-3 ～せんせい　　Mr./Mrs./Ms./Dr.	2-4 この～　this ～
4-1 でも　　　　But	1-3 ～さん　　　　Mr./Mrs./Ms.	2-4 その～　that ～
5-3 ～が、～　～, but ～	3-4 ～がつうまれ　born in (month)	2-4 あの～　that ～ over there
7-3 それとも　Q1 or Q2?	7-2 ～はん　　　　half past ～	3-2 ご～　　　[polite]
7-3 それから　And then	7-2 ～ころ, ごろ　about ～ (time)	3-2 お～　　　[polite]
	7-2 ～まえ　　　　before ～	
	7-2 ～すぎ　　　　after ～	

V. Particles

1-1 は	Topic particle
1-4 Sentence＋か。	Question particle
1-7 Sentence＋ねえ。	Sentence final particle used for admiration, surprise or exclamation
3-1 の	Possessive and descriptive particle
3-2 と	and [Noun and Noun only]
3-3 も	also, too [replaces を, が, は]
4-1 で	at, in (place) [with action verb]
4-4 と（いっしょに）	(together) with
4-5 means＋で	by, with, on, in
6-5 Sentence＋ね。	Sentence final particle for seeking agreement or confirmation
6-5 Sentence＋よ。	Sentence final particle of emphasis or exclamation
7-1 specific time＋に	at, on
7-3 place＋へ／に	to [with direction verb]
7-3 activity＋に	to, for (activity)
7-4 transportation＋で	by [with direction verb]
7-4 subject＋が	Subject particle

VI. Expressions

1-1 はじめまして。	How do you do?
1-1 どうぞ　よろしく。	Nice to meet you.
1-3 おはよう。	Good morning.
1-3 おはよう　ございます。	Good morning. [polite]
1-3 こんにちは。	Hello. Hi.
1-3 さようなら。	Good-bye.
1-3 はい。	Yes. [in response to roll call]
1-4 はじめましょう。	Let's begin.
1-4 きりつ。	Stand. [used at ceremonies]
1-4 れい。	Bow. [used at ceremonies]

8か

172

1-4 ちゃくせき。	Sit. [used at ceremonies]
1-4 （お）やすみです。	〜 is absent.
1-4 ちこくです。	〜 is tardy.
1-4 はやく。	Hurry.
1-4 おわりましょう。	Let's finish.
1-5 すみません。もう いちど おねがいします。	Excuse me. One more time, please.
1-5 すみません。ゆっくり おねがいします。	Excuse me. Slowly, please.
1-5 ちょっと まってください。	Please wait a minute.
1-5 どうも ありがとう ございます。	Thank you very much.
1-5 どういたしまして。	You are welcome.
1-6 はい。or ええ。	Yes.
1-6 いいえ。	No.
1-6 はい、そうです。	Yes, it is.
1-6 いいえ、そうではありません。or いいえ、そうじゃありません。	No, it is not.
1-7 あついですねえ。	It's hot!
1-7 さむいですねえ。	It's cold!
1-7 すずしいですねえ。	It is cool!
1-7 そうですねえ。	Yes, it is!
1-7 おげんきですか。	How are you?
1-7 はい、げんきです。	Yes, I am fine.
2-1 ええと ...	Let me see ...
2-1 あのう ...	Well ...
2-1 わかりますか。	Do you understand?
2-1 しりません。	I do not know.
2-1 みえません。	I cannot see.
2-1 きこえません。	I cannot hear.
2-1 Treeは にほんごで なんと いいますか。	How do you say "tree" in Japanese?
2-5 〜を ください。	Please give me 〜.
2-5 はい、どうぞ。	Here, please.
3-1 そうですか。	Is that so?
3-2 〜は。	How about 〜?
5-1 そうですねえ ...	Let me see ...
7-2 こんばんは。	Good evening.

VII. Counters

	1-5 1~10	1-5 11~20	1-5 10~100	2-5	2-5	3-1
1	いち	じゅういち	じゅう	いちまい	ひとつ	ひとり
2	に	じゅうに	にじゅう	にまい	ふたつ	ふたり
3	さん	じゅうさん	さんじゅう	さんまい	みっつ	さんにん
4	し、よん	じゅうし	よんじゅう	よんまい	よっつ	よにん
5	ご	じゅうご	ごじゅう	ごまい	いつつ	ごにん
6	ろく	じゅうろく	ろくじゅう	ろくまい	むっつ	ろくにん
7	しち、なな	じゅうしち, じゅうなな	ななじゅう	ななまい	ななつ	ななにん
8	はち	じゅうはち	はちじゅう	はちまい	やっつ	はちにん
9	く、きゅう	じゅうく	きゅうじゅう	きゅうまい	ここのつ	きゅうにん
10	じゅう	にじゅう	100　ひゃく	じゅうまい	とお	じゅうにん
?				なんまい？	いくつ？	なんにん？

	Age　3-1	Month　3-4	Grade　3-3	Hour　7-2	Minute　7-2
1	いっさい	いちがつ	いちねんせい	いちじ	いっぷん
2	にさい	にがつ	にねんせい	にじ	にふん
3	さんさい	さんがつ	さんねんせい	さんじ	さんぷん
4	よんさい	しがつ	よねんせい	よじ	よんぷん
5	ごさい	ごがつ		ごじ	ごふん
6	ろくさい	ろくがつ		ろくじ	ろっぷん
7	ななさい	しちがつ		しちじ、ななじ	ななふん
8	はっさい	はちがつ		はちじ	はっぷん
9	きゅうさい	くがつ		くじ	きゅうふん
10	じ(ゅ)っさい	じゅうがつ		じゅうじ	じ(ゅ)っぷん
11	じゅういっさい	じゅういちがつ		じゅういちじ	
12	20　はたち	じゅうにがつ		じゅうにじ	
?	なんさい？	なんがつ？	なんねんせい？	なんじ？	なんぷん？

Origin of *katakana*

Katakana is a phonetic alphabet. Each *katakana* character was made by simplifying or taking a portion of a *kanji* which represented the corresponding sound. For example, the *katakana* カ KA was taken from the kanji 加.

What is *katakana* used for?

Katakana is now used mainly to write words of foreign origin or names of foreigners. It is also sometimes used as a device to call attention to certain words (i.e., in advertising, announcements, etc.). It is also sometimes used to write onomatopoetic expressions.

How are *kanji*, *hiragana* and *katakana* used in the language?

Modern day Japanese sentences are composed of a combination of *kanji*, *hiragana* and *katakana* writing. Words which have strong semantic value, that is, nouns, verbs, adjectives and some adverbs, are written in *kanji*. Conjugated portions of verbs, adjectives or nouns (tenses, negations, etc.), particles, interjections, and most adverbs and other parts of sentences which do not convey the major message in the sentence are written in *hiragana*.

Ex. (WATASHI) WA TAITEI [GAKKOO] E (BASU) DE (KI)MASU.
私   は たいてい 学校 へ バス で 来ます。

Difficulty of *Katakana*

Katakana looks easy to foreigners, but *katakana* may be harder to learn than *hiragana* and *kanji*. *Katakana* words are created from the spelling or the pronounciation of foreign words. The way Japanese hear foreign words is often different from the way a native speaker hears them. There are some foreign sounds which do not exist in the Japanese language, i.e., "th," "f," "v," "r / l," "t," etc. Similar sounds from the native Japanese sound system had to be substituted for these sounds. For example, the English "v" sound often becomes a "b" sound in Japanese.

KATAKANA

	W	R	Y	M	H	N	T	S	K		
ン n	ワ	ラ	ヤ	マ	ハ	ナ	タ	サ	カ	ア	A
		リ		ミ	ヒ	ニ	チ chi	シ shi	キ	イ	I
		ル	ユ	ム	フ	ヌ	ツ tsu	ス	ク	ウ	U
		レ		メ	ヘ	ネ	テ	セ	ケ	エ	E
	ヲ particle	ロ	ヨ	モ	ホ	ノ	ト	ソ	コ	オ	O

P	B		D	Z	G	
パ	バ		ダ	ザ	ガ	A
ピ	ビ		ヂ ji	ジ ji	ギ	I
プ	ブ		ヅ zu	ズ zu	グ	U
ペ	ベ		デ	ゼ	ゲ	E
ポ	ボ		ド	ゾ	ゴ	O

カタカナ

R	M	H	N	C	S	K	
リ ャ	ミ ャ	ヒ ャ	ニ ャ	チ ャ	シ ャ	キ ャ	YA
リ ュ	ミ ュ	ヒ ュ	ニ ュ	チ ュ	シ ュ	キ ュ	YU
リ ョ	ミ ョ	ヒ ョ	ニ ョ	チ ョ	シ ョ	キ ョ	YO

P	B		J	G	
ピ ャ	ビ ャ		ジ ャ	ギ ャ	YA
ピ ュ	ビ ュ		ジ ュ	ギ ュ	YU
ピ ョ	ビ ョ		ジ ョ	ギ ョ	YO

カタカナ

ADDITIONAL KATAKANA COMBINATIONS FOR FOREIGN WORDS

va ヴァ	fa ファ			tsa ツァ				gwa グァ	kwa クァ		
vi ヴィ	fi フィ	di ディ	ti ティ							wi ウィ	
vu ヴュ		dyu デュ									
ve ヴェ	fe フェ			tse ツェ	che チェ	je ジェ	she シェ			we ウェ	ye イェ
vo ヴォ	fo フォ			tso ツォ					kwo クォ	wo ウォ	

Writing long vowel sounds in <u>katakana</u>:

Write a │ following the character you are lengthening if you are writing vertically, or ─ following the lengthened character if you are writing horizontally.

Example: チ　and　チーズ
チ
│
ズ

カタカナ

178

KATAKANA STROKE ORDER

	W	R	Y	M	H	N	T	S	K		
ン	ワ	ラ	ヤ	マ	ハ	ナ	タ	サ	カ	ア	A
N											
		リ		ミ	ヒ	ニ	チ	シ	キ	イ	I
		ル	ユ	ム	フ	ヌ	ツ	ス	ク	ウ	U
		レ		メ	ヘ	ネ	テ	セ	ケ	エ	E
	ヲ	ロ	ヨ	モ	ホ	ノ	ト	ソ	コ	オ	O
	O (Particle)										

179

カタカナ

あめふり

北原 白秋 作詞
中山 晋平 作曲

1. あ め あ め ふ れ ふ れ か あ さ ん が
　あ ら あ ら あ の こ は ず ぶ ぬ れ だ

じゃ の め で お む か い う れ し い な
や な ぎ の ね か た で な い て い る

ぴっ ち ぴっ ち ちゃっ ぷ ちゃっ ぷ らん らん らん
ぴっ ち ぴっ ち ちゃっ ぷ ちゃっ ぷ らん らん らん

あめ rain, ふれ fall [command form], かあさん mother, じゃのめ umbrella [waxed paper umbrella], おむかえ pick up, うれしい happy, な !, ぴっち & ちゃっぷ splash [onomatopoetic expression], らんらんらん skip [onomatopoetic expression], ずぶぬれだ soaking wet, やなぎ willow tree, ねかた foot of the tree trunk, ないている is crying

カタカナ

180

By the end of this lesson, you will be able to communicate the information below in the given situations.

【１-９ タスク１】

You want to know about your friend's English teacher from last semester (まえのがっき). You ask who his/her English teacher was, if that teacher was strict, if that teacher was good and if your friend liked that teacher. Your friend responds with his/her opinions.

【１-９ タスク２】

You ask your friend if he/she saw a movie last (まえの) Saturday, and your friend says he/she did. You ask if the movie was good, if it was long, what time he/she saw the movie and if he/she liked the movie. Your friend responds with appropriate replies.

【かいわ: Dialogue 】

ケンKEN : きのう　かいものに　いきましたか。

エミEMI : いいえ、いきませんでした。

えいがに　いきました。

ケンKEN : そうですか。

【＊ Review of Verb Conjugation [Formal Forms]】

nonpast	のみ<u>ます</u>	drink, will drink, is going to drink
neg. nonpast	のみ<u>ません</u>	do not drink, will not drink, is not going to drink
past	のみ<u>ました</u>	drank, have drunk
neg., past	のみ<u>ませんでした</u>	did not drink
volitional	のみ<u>ましょう</u>	Let's drink. [suggestion]
invitational	のみ<u>ませんか</u>	Would you like to drink? [invitation]

【 アクティビティー: Activities】

A. Pair Work

Interview your partner. The partner responds appropriately.

Ex. Did you eat sushi last night?

Question: 「きのうの　ばん　おすしを　<u>たべましたか</u>。」

Yes-Answer: 「はい、きのうの　ばん　おすしを　<u>たべました</u>。」

No-Answer: 「いいえ、きのうの　ばん　おすしを　<u>たべませんでした</u>。」

1. Did you see a movie on Saturday?	
2. Did you read a book last night?	
3. Did you eat breakfast today?	
4. Did you have a party on Saturday?	
5. Did you talk to your friend on the phone last night?	
6. Did you come to school by bus this morning?	
7. Did you study Japanese last night?	
8. Did you have a meal at a restaurant yesterday?	

B. Class Game

Prepare a set of cards as shown below for you and a partner. Each student takes one card. Do not show the card to anyone. Find the person who has the card which matches yours in the following way: One student invites another to do the activity written on the card. If that student has the same card, he/she accepts the invitation. If he/she does not have the same card, he/she declines the invitation politely. When you find your partner, give the cards to your teacher and sit down. The students who are first to sit are the winners.

Ex. テニス TENISU

Question: 「いっしょに　テニス TENISU を　しませんか。」
Yes-Answer: 「はい、しましょう。」
No-Answer: 「ざんねんですが、ちょっと　いそがしいです。」

テニス TENISU	カラオケ KARAOKE	テニス TENISU	カラオケ KARAOKE
えいが	バスケット BASUKETTO	えいが	バスケット BASUKETTO
ダンス DANSU	うみ	ダンス DANSU	うみ
トランプ TORANPU	にほん	トランプ TORANPU	にほん
レストラン RESUTORAN	スペイン SUPEIN	レストラン RESUTORAN	スペイン SUPEIN
パーティー PAATII	ピクニック PIKUNIKKU	パーティー PAATII	ピクニック PIKUNIKKU
コンサート KONSAATO	しょくじ	コンサート KONSAATO	しょくじ

9か

【かいわ: Dialogue 】

ケンKEN：えいがは　よかったですか。

エミEMI：いいえ、あまり　よくなかったです。

ケンKEN：そうですか。

【＊ Review of い Adjectives Conjugation [Formal forms]】

nonpast	あつ<u>いです</u>	is hot
neg. nonpast	あつ<u>くないです</u> or	is not hot
	あつ<u>くありません</u>	

*いい is conjugated from the よい form.

nonpast	<u>いいです</u>	is good
neg. nonpast	よ<u>くないです</u> or	is not good
	よ<u>くありません</u>	

【ぶんぽう: Grammar】

A. Past tense of い adjectives.

past	あつ<u>かったです</u>	was hot
neg. past	あつ<u>くなかったです</u> or	was not hot
	あつ<u>くありませんでした</u>	

*いい is conjugated from the よい form.

past	よ<u>かったです</u>	was good
neg. past	よ<u>くなかったです</u> or	was not good
	よ<u>くありませんでした</u>	

1. きのうは　とても　<u>さむかったです</u>ねえ。　　Yesterday was very cold!

2. きのうの　えいがは　<u>ながくなかった</u>です。　Yesterday's movie was not long.

3. きのうの　えいがは　とても　<u>よかった</u>ですよ。

　　　　　　　　　　　　　　　　　　　　Yesterday's movie was very good.

4. にほんごの　しけんは　あまり　<u>よくなかった</u>です。

　　　　　　　　　　　　　　　　　　　My Japanese exam was not very good.

【👩👩アクティビティー: Activities】

A. Pair Work

Ask your partner about a friend he/she had in elementary school. The partner responds appropriately. Take turns.

Ex. Was your friend smart?

Question:　「あなたの　しょうがっこうの　ともだちは　あたまが　よかったですか。」

Yes-Answer:「はい、あたまが　よかったです。」

No-Answer:「いいえ、あたまが　よくなかったです or よくありませんでした。」

1. Was smart?	
2. Was tall?	
3. Was nice?	
4. Was noisy?	
5. Was cute?	

B. Pair Work

Show a full-length picture of a person from a magazine. Show the picture to your partner for 5 seconds. Then ask your partner the questions below. Your partner responds relying on his/her memory of the picture.

Ex. Was this person tall?

Question:　「このひとは　せが　たかかったですか。」

Yes-Answer:「はい、たかかったです。」

No-Answer:「いいえ、たかくなかったです or たかくありませんでした。」

1. めが　おおきかったですか。	
2. かみのけが　ながかったですか。	
3. シャツが　あかかったですか。	
4. めが　あおかったですか。	
5. せが　たかかったですか。	
6. ふとっていましたか。	
7. はなが　たかかったですか。	
8. かおが　かわいかったですか。	
9. (Your own question)	

9か

【かいわ: Dialogue 】

ケンKEN：その　おとこのこが　すきでしたか。
エミEMI：いいえ、あまり　すきじゃありませんでした。
ケンKEN：そうですか。

【＊ Review of な Adjectives Conjugation [Formal Forms]】

nonpast	すきです	like
neg. nonpast	すきではありません or	do not like
	すきじゃありません	
past	すきでした	liked
neg. past	すきではありませんでした or	did not like
	すきじゃありませんでした	

【アクティビティー: Activities】

A. Pair Work

Reflect on your Japanese studies last semester. Ask your partner the following questions. Your partner answers. Switch and repeat.

1. あなたは　クラスで　にほんごを　よく　はなしましたか。	
2. あなたは　クラスで　うるさかったですか。	
3. にほんごの　しゅくだいを　いつも　しましたか。	
4. ときどき　ちこくを　しましたか。	
5. きょうかしょを　ときどき　わすれましたか。	
6. ランゲージラボに　いつも　いきましたか。	
7. ランゲージラボで　テープを　よく　ききましたか。	
8. まいにち　にほんごを　べんきょうしましたか。	
9. にほんごの　しけんは　よかったですか。	
10. にほんごの　べんきょうが　すきでしたか。	

B. Pair Work

What kind of child was your partner when s/he was an elementary student? Interview your partner using the following questions. When you finish, switch roles and repeat.

1. おおきかったですか。	
2. せが　たかかったですか。	
3. かみのけが　ながかったですか。	
4. やせていましたか。	
5. ほんが　すきでしたか。	
6. うるさかったですか。	
7. すいえいが　じょうずでしたか。	
8. げんきでしたか。	
9. あたまが　よかったですか。	
10. かわいかったですか。	

C. Pair Work

You want to know what kind of teacher your partner had last semester for English. Interview him/her using the following questions. Switch roles and repeat.

1. えいごのせんせいは　だれでしたか。	
2. ～せんせいは　きびしかったですか。	
3. ～せんせいは　じょうずでしたか。	
4. ～せんせいは　よかったですか。	
5. あなたは　～せんせいが　すきでしたか。	
6. あなたの　えいごの　せいせき(grade)は　よかったですか。	

9か

【かいわ: Dialogue 】

ケン KEN : そのえいがは　いいえいがでしたか。

エミ EMI : いいえ、あまり　いいえいがではありませんでした。

ケン KEN : そうですか。

【＊ Review of Copula です Conjugation [Formal Forms]】

nonpast	せいとです	is a student
neg. nonpast	せいとではありません or せいとじゃありません	is not a student
past	せいとでした	was a student
neg. past	せいとではありませんでした or せいとじゃありませんでした	was not a student

【アクティビティー: Activities】

A. Pair Work

You want to know about your partner's physical education teacher last semester. Ask the following questions. Then switch roles and repeat.

1. たいいく (P.E.) のせんせいは　だれでしたか。	
2. そのせんせいは　きびしい　せんせいでしたか。	
3. そのせんせいは　いいせんせいでしたか。	
4. あなたは　そのせんせいが　すきでしたか。	
5. たいいく(P.E.)の　クラス KURASU は　あさでしたか。	
6. あなたは　たいいくの　クラス KURASU が　すきでしたか。	

B. Pair Work

Interview your partner about a movie he/she saw recently. Switch roles and repeat.

1. なんのえいがを　みましたか。	
2. そのえいがは　よかったですか。	
3. そのえいがは　ながかったですか。	
4. (Main actress) は　きれいでしたか。	
5. (Main actor) は　じょうずでしたか。	

【アクティビティー: Activities】

A. Pair Work

The topic of this composition is "yesterday." The author wrote everything in the incorrect past tense form. Change the underlined portions to the correct past tense form.

きのうは　にちようびです。とても　さむいです。

わたしは　ごごいちじに　ともだちの　うちへ　いきます。

ともだちの　うちは　とても　おおきいです。そして、とても

しずかです。ともだちと　いっしょに　おんがくを　ききます。

おんがくは　とても　いいです。わたしは　その　おんがくが

すきですが、ともだちの　おかあさんは　その　おんがくが

すきではありません。その　おんがくは　とても　うるさいです。

わたしは　ごごろくじごろ　うちへ　かえります。そして、

かぞくと　ばんごはんを　たべます。ばんごはんは　よくありません。

あまり　たべません。わたしは　しゅくだいを　しません。　そして、

ごご１１じはんごろに　ねます。とても　おそいです。

きのうは　とても　ながいです。

B. Pair or Group Game

Copy the words below onto small cards. To start the game, stack the cards face down. Flip one card at a time and say the correct past form. If you produce the correct form, the card is yours. Continue until you make a mistake. Your partner now has a chance to give the correct answer. If he/she does, the card is hers/his, and your partner continues the game. If both players are unable to give the correct answer, the card is returned to the stack. The game continues until all cards in the stack are gone. The person with more cards wins. Play with the negative past form, too.

たべます	あついです	げんきです	せんせいです
いきます	いいです	すきです	いしゃです
きます	わるいです	きらいです	ちゅうがくせいです
ねます	きびしいです	へたです	ともだちです
はなします	うるさいです	とくいです	すしです
かきます	おそいです	きれいです	おやすみです
よみます	しろいです	じゃまです	しろです
べんきょうします	いそがしいです	しずかです	どようびです
かえります	きたないです	じょうずです	いいえいがです

Find the answers by investigating books, by talking to friends, or by using the Internet.

1. Draw a layout of your family's bathroom.

2. How is a traditional Japanese bathroom different from one in the U.S.?

3. Do your family members bathe/shower in a particular order?

4. According to Japanese tradition, does a family bathe in a particular order?

5. How do you usually spend your Saturday?

6. How does the average Japanese student spend his or her Saturday?

7. What do you usually do after school and at home during the week?

8. What does the average Japanese student do after school and at home during the week?

9. Do you do chores?   If so, what are your chores?

10. Do Japanese teens do chores? If so, what?

9 か

FUN CORNER 6: 早口ことば Tongue twisters

Can you say these Japanese tongue twisters?

Say each one three times as quickly as you can!

**② おやがめの うえに こがめ
こがめの うえに まごがめ**

おやがめ parent turtle
うえ top
こがめ child turtle
まごがめ grandchild turtle
[かめ turtle]

**① となりの きゃくは よく
かき くう きゃくだ。**

となり neighbor
きゃく guest
よく well
かき persimmon
くう eat
だ ＝ です [plain form]

**④ あかパジャマ きパジャマ
ちゃパジャマ**

あか red
き ＝ きいろ yellow
ちゃ ＝ ちゃいろ brown
パジャマ pajamas

③ なまむぎ なまごめ なまたまご

なま raw
むぎ wheat
ごめ ＝ こめ raw rice
たまご egg

9か

192

By the end of this lesson, you will be able to communicate the information below in the given situations.

【１-１０ タスク１】

You have a Japanese guest on campus today. Your guest wants to see the library, the cafeteria, the Japanese classroom, your locker, and the school office, and asks you where they all are. You take your guest to each place. Your guest gives his/her impressions of each place.

【１-１０ タスク２】

You will host a Japanese exchange student at your home. The Japanese student asks about your home, whether it is big or small, new or old, near school or not, how many rooms you have, how many cars you have, and whether you have a yard or not. The Japanese student also wants to know about the room he/she will stay in and asks whether the room is spacious or not and whether or not there is a bed, a desk, a chair and a T.V. You give a detailed description of your home and the room in which your guest will stay.

The counter for rooms: ひとつ、ふたつ、みっつ...、いくつ？

【かいわ: Dialogue 】

＜きょうしつで＞

ケンKEN：ジョンJONさんは　どこに　いますか。

エミEMI：ジョンJONさんは　そとに　いましたよ。

ケンKEN：また　ちこくですよ。

【ぶんけい: Sentence Structure 】

| Topic (Animate) は　Place に　います。 | (Animate object) is at a place. |
| Topic (Inanimate) は　Place に　あります。 | (Inanimate object) is at a place. |

★ You have learned two other particles which are used after place words. The type of verb one uses determines the particle used after the place word. Let's clarify their usage.

Place で　　　Action verb。　　(Ex. たべます eat, よみます read, はなします talk, etc.)

Place へ／に　Direction verb。　(Ex. いきます go, きます come, かえります return home)

Place に　　　Existence verb。　(Ex. います exist-animate, あります exist-inanimate)

【たんご: Vocabulary 】

1. います [いる]

there is, are (animate objects)

Verb of existence.

2. あります [ある]

there is, are (inanimate objects)

Verb of existence.

3. そと

outside

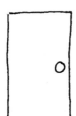

4. ドアDOA, と

door

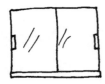

5. まど

window

6. つくえ

desk

7. いす

chair

8. えんぴつけずり	9. ごみばこ	10. いぬ	11. ねこ
pencil sharpener	trash can	dog	cat

12. Location に ＋ Existence verb。　　　in, at

13. また　　　again

【*オプショナルたんご: Optional Vocabulary】

1.*いらっしゃいます	there is, are (animate objects) [polite equivalent of います]
2.*こくばん	blackboard
3.*こくばんけし	blackboard eraser
4.*チョーク CHOOKU	chalk
5.*クーラー KUURAA	air conditioner
6.*でんき	electricity, lights
7.*スイッチ SUITCHI	(light) switch

【ぶんぽう: Grammar】

A. Topic (Animate) は＋ Location に ＋ います。

Topic (Inanimate) は＋ Location に ＋ あります。

います and あります are both existence verbs. います is used when the object being discussed is animate, while あります is used when it is inanimate. The particle に follows the place word where the object exists.
When the topic is a moving car, use the verb います.

1. 「えんぴつけずりは　どこに　ありますか。」　　Where is the pencil sharpener?
　「あそこに　ありますよ。」　　It is over there, you know.

2. 「ぼくの　きょうかしょは　ここに　あります。」　My textbook is here.

3. 「ジョンJONくんは　どこに　いますか。」　　Where is John?
　「ジョンJONさんは　そとに　います。」　　John is outdoors.

B. Topic (Animate) は ＋ Location に ＋ います。　　＝Topic (Animate) は ＋ Location です。

　Topic (Inanimate) は＋ Location に ＋ あります。＝Topic (Inanimate) は ＋ Location です。

You may replace に　います／あります by です. The meaning of the sentence does not change.

1. 「ごみばこは　どこですか。」　　　　Where is the trash can?
　「あそこです。」　　　　　　　　　　It is over there.
2. 「ジョンJONさんは　どこですか。」　Where is John?
　「ジョンJONさんは　そとです。」　　John is outdoors.

【 ● ぶんかノート: Cultural Notes】

1. Japanese Classroom

Most Japanese high school classrooms accommodate 40 students. Desks are situated in rows with narrow aisles facing the front of the classroom where the teacher stands. The front of the room may even be elevated so the teacher can easily see to the back of the classroom. When students arrive at school, they will change their shoes to "in school shoes." Their walking shoes are left in shoeboxes near the entrance. In Japan, students remain in one classroom while teachers shift from one class to another. Students are responsible for cleaning their own classrooms, hallways and bathrooms. Chores include sweeping, mopping and cleaning chalkboards.

2. Japanese Conversational Strategy

When Japanese people are asked where something is located, they often answer by first repeating the name of the thing before telling where it is.

Person 1: 「すみません。でんわは　どこに　ありますか。」
Person 2: 「でんわですか。でんわは　あそこに　あります。」

【アクティビティー: Activities】

A. Pair Work

Ask your partner where the following things are located. Write in the answers.

1. Pencil sharpener		4. Teacher's desk	
2. Trash can		5. (A student in class)	
3. (Box of) tissues		6. Teacher	

B. Pair Work

Select items from the list below, then draw them inside any or all of the drawings pictured in the first block. Do not show your picture to your partner. Ask your partner where his/her objects are located, then recreate your partner's picture in the second block. After you have both completed this exercise, compare your pictures and check that you have communicated accurately with one another.

Things to draw: **dog, cat, book, old man, homework, soccer ball, money, lunch** or any object you would like.

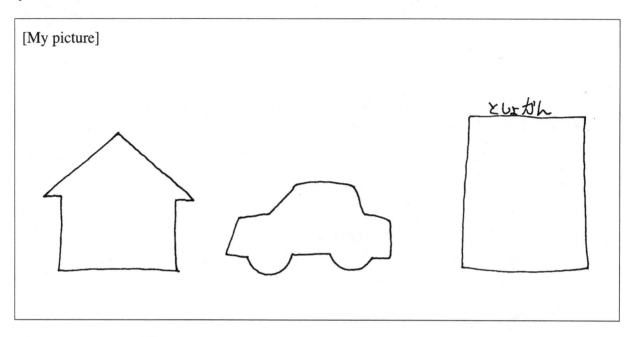

[My picture]

としょがん

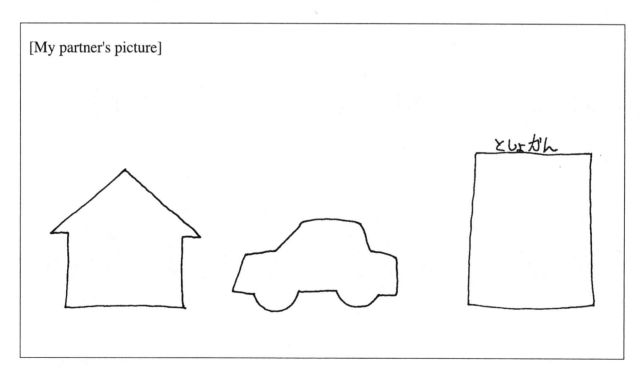

[My partner's picture]

としょがん

10か

【かいわ: Dialogue 】

エミEMI：あそこに　プールPUURU が　あります。
　　　　いきましょうか。
ケンKEN：はい、いきましょう。おおきいですねえ。
　　　　あそこに　かわいい　おんなのこが　いますよ。
エミEMI：あれは　ケリーKERIIさんです。

【ぶんけい: Sentence Structure 】

Place に Topic (Animate) が　います。	There is (animate object) at a place.
Place に Topic (Inanimate) が　あります。	There is (inanimate object) at a place.
Verb - ましょうか。	Shall we do 〜 ? [polite suggestion]

★ The difference between two similar sentence structures.

Topic (Animate) は Place に　います。	The (animate object) is at a place.
	[The place is the primary information.]
Place に Topic (Animate) が　います。	There is (animate object) at a place.
	[The emphasis lies on <u>what</u> exists.]

【たんご: Vocabulary】

1. おとこ
male

2. おんな
female

3. ひと
person

4. こども
child

5. おとこのひと
man

6. おんなのひと
woman, lady

7. おとこのこ
boy

8. おんなのこ
girl

9. (お)トイレ TOIRE、(お)てあらい   10. プール PUURU   11. 〜 かた

    toilet, bathroom, restroom   pool   person (Polite form of ひと.

                                                            Must be preceded by a word

                                                            such as この or あの.)

【*オプショナルたんご: Optional Vocabulary】

1.*どなた	who? [polite equiv. of だれ]
2.*たいいくかん	gym
3.*ちゅうしゃじょう	parking lot
4.*チャペル CHAPERU	chapel
5.*うんどうじょう	athletic field
6.*きょうぎじょう	track field
7.*コンピュータールーム KONPYUUTAA RUUMU	computer room
8.*ランゲージラボ RANGEEJI RABO	language lab
9.*テニスコート TENISU KOOTO	tennis court
10.*こうちょうせんせい	school principal

【ぶんぽう: Grammar】

A. Location に　Subject (Animate)　が　います。

   Location に　Subject (Inanimate)　が　あります。

The verbs います and あります indicate existence. います is used when the subject being discussed is animate. あります is used when the subject is inanimate. Often, these verbs are used with a place word which indicates where the subject exists. The particle に consistently follows the place word when it is the place of existence. When the subject follows the place word, the subject is followed by the particle が.

Compare:

   1. いぬは　あそこに　います。

      The dog is over there. [Place of existence is the primary information.]

   2. あそこに　いぬが　います。

      There is a dog over there. [The emphasis lies on what (the animate/inanimate object) exists.]

1. あそこに　プール PUURU が　あります。   There is a pool over there.

2. あそこに　かわいい　おんなの　こが　いますよ。 There is a cute girl over there.

B. Verb - ましょうか。　　　　　　　Shall we do 〜 ? [Polite suggestion]

This form of verb is used to politely suggest doing something together with others.
Compare:　1. いき<u>ましょうか</u>。　　　<u>Shall we go?</u> [Suggestion to others]
　　　　　　2. いき<u>ましょう</u>。　　　　<u>Let's go.</u> [Own suggested decision]
　　　　　　3. いき<u>ませんか</u>。　　　　<u>Would you like to go?</u> [Invitation]

1.「いま　おひるごはんを　たべ<u>ましょうか</u>。」　Shall we eat lunch now?
　「はい、たべましょう。」　　　　　　　　　　　Yes, let's eat.

2.「どようびに　うみへ　いき<u>ましょうか</u>。」　Shall we go to the beach on Saturday?
　「ええ、いきましょう。」　　　　　　　　　　　Yes, let's go.

【 ● ぶんかノート: Cultural Notes】

1. 男 and 女

In order to use a public restroom in Japan, it is important to know these two *kanji*. Which door will you choose to enter?

男	女

2. (お)トイレ TOIRE, (お)てあらい, (お)べんじょ

There are many Japanese words used to mean toilets, bathrooms and restrooms, much like English. The べん of (お)べんじょ means "human waste" and じょ means "place." So (お)べんじょ literally means a place for these functions. Modern Japanese people avoid the use of this word, as it sounds too direct and crude. If you go to the countryside in Japan, you may still find toilets referred to in this way. The て of (お)てあらい means "hands" and あらい is a stem form of あらいます which means "to wash." So (お)てあらい means "a place to wash hands." This is a more polite expression and it is quite commonly used by Japanese, especially women.

トイレ TOIRE is, of course, from the English word "toilet" and is used by young Japanese, especially young men. お attached to トイレ TOIRE adds politeness to the word. Females tend to use the word おトイレ(お TOIRE) more than males. Other euphemistic terms, such as WC (water closet, from British English) and けしょうしつ "powder room" are also used.

3. Japanese Toilets

Japanese-style toilets are becoming less common in Japan. To use them, one must squat (females) or stand (males) over a long rectangular porcelain receptacle which is installed into the floor. Most public restrooms now have Western-style sit down toilets. Modern homes are often now equipped with computerized toilets which can heat up, spray your bottom and flush automatically. Public restrooms often do not provide paper towels to use after washing your hands. Railroad station restrooms may not even supply toilet paper which must be purchased in vending machines.

Japanese toilet

10か

4. かれ and かのじょ

かれ means "he, him" and かのじょ means "she, her." Originally, these terms were not part of the Japanese language. These words were developed through Western influence and nowadays are quite commonly used when one refers to equals or inferiors, but never to superiors. Japanese young people have expanded the meaning of these words. わたしのかれ means "my boyfriend" and ぼくのかのじょ means "my girlfriend."

【アクティビティー: Activities】

A. Pair Work

You take your Japanese guest to the following places on your school campus. Explain where they are. Your guest gives his/her impressions of each place.

Ex. せいと ：「あそこに　プールPUURUが　あります。いきましょうか。」
にほんじん：「はい、いきましょう。」
せいと ：「プールPUURUは　ここです。」
にほんじん：「わあ、おおきいですねえ。」

Place	Location	Guest's Impression
1. Pool		
2. Gym		
3. Cafeteria		
4. Library		

B. Pair Work

You are visiting your friend's school and see the following people on campus. Ask who they are.

Ex. Visitor ：「すみません、あの　おんなのこは　だれですか。」
Host ：「あの　おんなのこですか。あのこは　～さんです。」
Visitor ：「そうですか。（かわいいですねえ。）」

People	Who?
1. Girl	
2. Boy	
3. Lady	
4. Distinguished man	

【かいわ: Dialogue 】

エミ EMI ：あそこに　はなが　たくさん　ありますねえ。
　　　　　　きれいですねえ。

ケン KEN ：いけに　さかなも　いますよ。

【ぶんけい: Sentence Structure 】

| Place | に | Subject | が | Counter Ⓧ | | います／あります |。

| Place | に | Counter | ((の)) | Subject | が | います／あります |。

【たんご: Vocabulary】

	1.	2.	3.	4.
1	いちだい	いちわ	いっぴき	いっぽん
2	にだい	にわ	にひき	にほん
3	さんだい	さんわ	さんびき	さんぽん
4	よんだい	よんわ	よんひき	よんほん
5	ごだい	ごわ	ごひき	ごほん
6	ろくだい	ろくわ	ろっぴき	ろっぽん
7	ななだい	ななわ	ななひき	ななほん
8	はちだい	はちわ	はっぴき	はっぽん
9	きゅうだい	きゅうわ	きゅうひき	きゅうほん
10	じゅうだい	じゅうわ	じ（ゅ）っぴき	じ（ゅ）っぽん
11	じゅういちだい	じゅういちわ	じゅういっぴき	じゅういっぽん
？	なんだい	なんわ	なんびき	なんぼん
	large mechanized goods	birds	small animals	long cylindrical objects

5. き
tree

6. はな
flower

7. いけ
pond

8. さかな
fish

9. とり
bird

10. たくさん
a lot, many

11. すこし
a few, a little

【ぶんぽう：Grammar】

A. Place に　Subject (Animate object) が　Counter　います。

Place に　Subject (Inanimate object) が　Counter　あります。

When a counter or quantity is included in this structure, it generally follows the subject. Particles do not follow counters or quantity words.

1. あそこに　おおきい　きが　<u>いっぽん</u>　あります。　There is a big tree over there.
2. そとに　ねこが　<u>2ひき</u>　います。　There are two cats outside.
3. うちに　くるまが　<u>にだい</u>　あります。　There are two cars at home.
4. ここに　はなが　<u>たくさん</u>　あります。　There are lots of flowers here.

B. ［Place］に　［Counter］（の）　［Subject］が　　います／あります。

When a counter describes the subject, it precedes the subject. In this case, the particle の sometimes follows the counter.

1. あそこに　おおきい　いっぽん<u>の</u>　きが　あります。　There is a big tree over there.
2. そとに　にひき<u>の</u>　ねこが　います。　There are two cats outside.
3. うちに　にだい<u>の</u>　くるまが　あります。　There are two cars at home.
4. ここに　たくさん<u>の</u>　はなが　あります。　There are lots of flowers here.

１０か

【 ● ぶんかノート: Cultural Notes】

Four Seasons in Japan

In Japan, people's lives are strongly influenced by the four distinct seasons. Spring is March, April and May. Summer is June, July and August. Autumn is September, October and November. Winter is December, January and February. The rainy season, called つゆ, is in June and July. Japanese people often remember memorable events in conjunction with the natural events of the season. For example, April, which marks the opening of the school year, is associated with cherry blossom season.

【 アクティビティー: Activities】

A. Pair Work

On each of the three pictures labeled "My Pictures," draw one or more of each of the items listed below the picture. Example: you may choose to draw 3 trees, 5 flowers and 2 fish. <u>Do not show your drawings to your partner.</u> After you and your partner have finished your drawings, ask your partner how many of each item are in his/her picture. Ask where they are located and draw them on the pictures labeled "My partner's pictures." Compare the corresponding pictures to see whether your communication was successful.

[My pictures]

| 1. tree, flower, fish | 2. fish, boat, people | 3. dog, boy, T.V. |

[My partner's pictures]

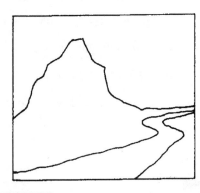 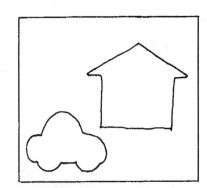

【かいわ: Dialogue 】

エミEMI ：がっこうの　じむしょは　どこに　ありますか。

ケンKEN ：あの　たてものに　あります。

　　　　　たてものは　ちょっと　ふるいです。

　　　　　<Enters building.>

エミEMI ：この　えは　うつくしいですねえ。

ケンKEN ：ええ、ゆうめいですよ。

【たんご: Vocabulary】

  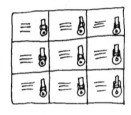

1. たてもの

building

2. じむしょ

office

3. きょうしつ

classroom

4. ロッカー ROKKAA

locker

5. あたらしい

[い Adj.]

is new

6. ふるい

[い Adj.]

is old (not for person's age)

7. うつくしい

[い Adj.]

is beautiful

8. ゆうめい

[な Adj.]

is famous

Negative form	5. あたらしくないです	is not new
	6. ふるくないです	is not old
	7. うつくしくないです	is not beautiful
	8. ゆうめいではありません	is not famous

【 ● ぶんかノート: Cultural Notes】

1. School Uniforms

   A majority of students in Japan wear school uniforms. Both private (しりつ) and public (こうりつ) schools may employ this custom. Traditionally, school uniforms have been conservative in style and color, often navy, black or gray. More recently, however, schools have had famous fashion designers create their uniforms, so they are more appealing to the students. Dress codes are still rather strict — no makeup, jewelry or permed hair. Hair style and length are also relatively restricted. Boys' uniforms often also include caps with the school insignia attached to the front of the cap. Students all own at least 2 sets of uniforms: a summer uniform and a heavier winter uniform. Students are required to switch from summer to winter uniforms in November and winter to summer uniforms in June.

2. A Japanese Proverb 「かえるのこはかえる」

   「かえるのこはかえる」 means "A frog's child is a frog." A child resembles his/her parents and will have a life like his/her parents. A child has the same kind of ability as his/her parents. Therefore, parents should not expect more of their child than they themselves could achieve. There is the similar Western expression: "The apple doesn't fall very far from the tree."

【🧑👩 アクティビティー: Activities】

A. Pair Work

Ask your partner where the following things are and what kind of places they are.

Ex. Question 1: 「<u>にほんごの　きょうしつ</u>は　どこに　ありますか。」

Question 2: 「どんな　<u>きょうしつ</u>ですか。」

Place	Where?	Impressions
1. Japanese classroom		
2. English classroom		
3. Locker		
4. School office		
5. Men's or women's restroom		
6. House		

B. Pair Work

Ask your partner where the following people are now and what kind of persons they are.

Ex. Question 1: 「<u>おかあさん</u>は　いま　どこに　いますか。」

Question 2: 「<u>おかあさん</u>は　どんな　ひとですか。」

Person	Where?	What kind of person?
1. Mother		
2. Father		
3. Friend		
4. (A famous or beautiful person)		

１０か

【かいわ: Dialogue 】

エミEMI：あなたの　うちは　ちかいですか。

ケンKEN：いいえ、ちょっと　とおいです。

エミEMI：うちは　ひろいですか。

ケンKEN：すこし　ひろいです。

でも、ぼくの　へやは　せまいです。

【たんご: Vocabulary 】

1. にわ
garden, yard

2. ガレージ GAREEJI
garage

3. へや
room

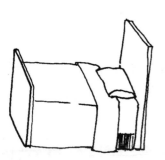

4. ベッド BEDDO
bed

5. ごきぶり
cockroach

6. ねずみ
mouse

7. ぶた
pig

8. ひろい [いAdj.]
is wide, spacious

9. せまい [いAdj.]
is narrow, small (room)

10. ちかい [いAdj.]

is near, close

11. とおい [いAdj.]

is far

【*オプショナルたんご: Optional Vocabulary】

1.*ポスター POSUTAA　poster

2.*ほんばこ　　　　　bookshelf

3.*かべ　　　　　　　wall

4.*ゆか　　　　　　　floor

5.*カーペット KAAPETTO　carpet

6.*てんじょう　　　　ceiling

7.*スピーカー SUPIIKAA　speaker (for sound)

【 ● ぶんかノート: Cultural Notes】

1. How do Japanese animals cry? Each culture perceives the sounds of animal cries differently. These are examples of Japanese perceptions of animal cries.

いぬ	ワンワン WANWAN
ねこ	ニャーニャー NYAANYAA
うし [cow]	モー MOO
うま [horse]	ヒヒーン HIHIIN
ぶた	ブーブー BUUBUU
ねずみ	チューチュー CHUUCHUU
（ちいさい）とり	ピーピー PIIPII
ライオン RAION	ワオー WAOO
さる[monkey]	キャッキャッ KYAKKYA
にわとり [chicken/rooster]	コケコッコー KOKEKOKKOO

2. A Japanese Proverb 「ねこに　こばん」

ねこ is a cat. こばん is a gold coin used during the Tokugawa period. 「ねこに　こばん」 means "to give a gold coin to a cat." It is used when someone receives something and cannot appreciate its value. This is similar to the Western expression: "to cast pearls before swine."

3. A Japanese Proverb 「さるも　きから　おちる」

さる is a monkey. も means "even." き is a tree. から means "from." おちる means "to fall." 「さるも　きから　おちる」 means "Even a monkey falls from a tree." This proverb means that even skillful people sometimes make mistakes.

【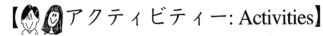アクティビティー: Activities】

A. Pair Work

First draw any of the listed items on the pictures marked "My picture." You may draw several items on each picture. <u>Don't show your drawings to your partner.</u> Ask your partner where the listed items are in his/her picture and draw them as he/she describes them on the pictures marked "My partner's pictures." Compare the two pictures to see whether your communication was successful or not.

[My picture]

1.

2.

3.

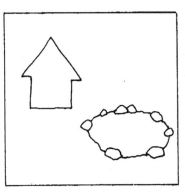

car	tree	mouse
cockroach	flower	cat
T.V.	dog	book
woman	fish	girl
trash can	boy	pencil

[My partner's picture]

1.

2.

3.

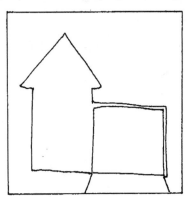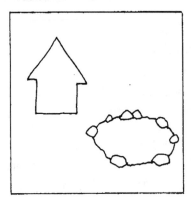

B. [Pair Work]

Interview your partner and ask about his/her house. Write down your partner's answers.

1. Big or small?	
2. Have a yard or not?	
3. New or old?	
4. What color?	
5. How many cars?	

C. [Pair Work]

Interview your partner. Ask about his/her room. Write down your partner's answers.

1. Have a bed?	
2. Have a desk and a chair?	
3. Have a TV?	
4. Have a computer?	
5. Have a telephone?	
6. Spacious or not?	
7. Messy or clean?	
8. What color?	

Ask your partner these questions in Japanese.
Your partner answers in Japanese.

1. Where is the men's / women's restroom?

2. Where is your Japanese teacher?

3. Where is the pencil sharpener?

4. What is over there? [Point to something distant.]

5. Who is that girl over there? [Answer: my friend]

6. Who is that (distinguished looking) man over there?   [Answer: my English teacher]

7. Shall we eat lunch together now?

8. Shall we go to a movie this Saturday?

9. Shall we do our Japanese homework together at the library?

10. How many students are there at your school?

11. How many male students are there in your Japanese class? And how many female students?

12. Are there many fish in the school pond?

13. Can you hear any birds? Where are the birds?

14. Where is the school office?

15. Is your school new?

16. Is your Japanese classroom clean?

17. Is your school well known (famous)?

18. Is your school football team [チーム] well known (famous)?

19. Is your house close?

20. Where is your house?

21. How many cars are there at your house?

22. Do you have a yard at your house?

23. Are there many flowers and trees in your garden?

24. Is your yard pretty (beautiful)?

25. Is your house big?

26. Is your room spacious?

27. What is there in your room? (Several things)

28. What color is your room?

29. Are there cockroaches and mice in your garage?

30. What time do you return home every day?

10か

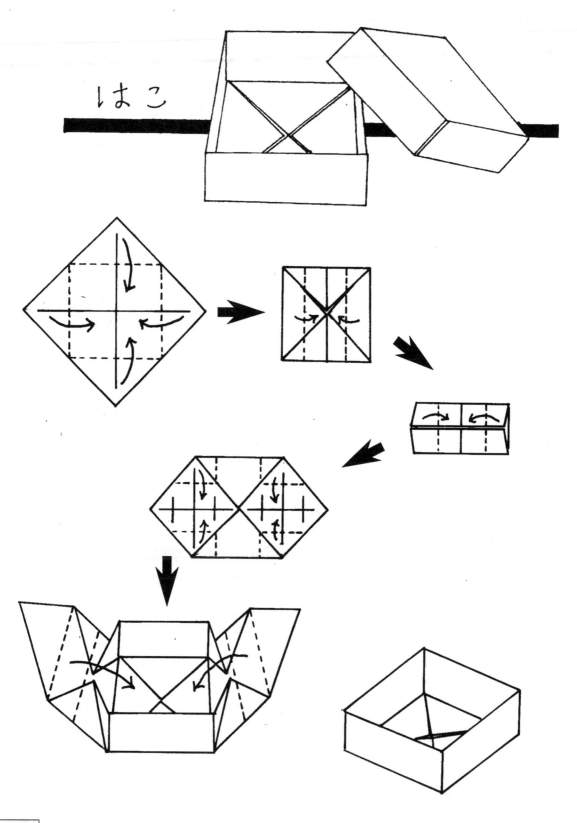

はこ

By the end of this lesson, you will be able to communicate the information below in the given situations.

【 I - 1 1 タスク 1 】

You are hosting a student from another school. The student is very curious and asks you various questions, especially about the class just after your Japanese class. The student asks questions such as: What is your next class, where is the classroom, how many students are there, who is the teacher, how is the teacher, from what time to what time is the class, is the class difficult or easy, is there lots of homework, and are your grades good? You answer these questions.

【 I - 1 1 タスク 2 】

Your friend asks you why you are so sad. You explain why. You are sad because you had a terrible grade on the social studies exam the day before yesterday. Your friend, however, is happy. You ask why he/she is happy. Your friend explains that his/her birthday is coming soon (すぐです) and invites you to his/her party. You ask when the party is. The party is from 4:00 to 7:00 next Saturday. Since he/she is a close friend, you ask what he/she wants for a present (プレゼント).

【かいわ: Dialogue 】

ケン：まりさんの　たんじょう日（び）は　いつですか。

エミ：３月３日〔さんがつみっか〕です。

【たんご: Vocabulary】

1. Days of the month.

ついたち 1日	じゅういちにち 11日	にじゅういちにち 21日
ふつか 2日	じゅうににち 12日	にじゅうににち 22日
みっか 3日	じゅうさんにち 13日	にじゅうさんにち 23日
よっか 4日	じゅうよっか 14日	にじゅうよっか 24日
いつか 5日	じゅうごにち 15日	にじゅうごにち 25日
むいか 6日	じゅうろくにち 16日	にじゅうろくにち 26日
なのか 7日	じゅうしちにち 17日	にじゅうしちにち 27日
ようか 8日	じゅうはちにち 18日	にじゅうはちにち 28日
ここのか 9日	じゅうくにち 19日	にじゅうくにち 29日
とおか 10日	はつか 20日	さんじゅうにち 30日
		さんじゅういちにち 31日
		なんにち？ なん日

2. (お)たんじょう日（び）

birthday

お is a polite prefix.

【かんじコーナー: *Kanji* Corner】

Kanji	Meaning	Readings	Examples		Stroke Order

1. 月　moon, month　がつ　１月〔いちがつ〕 January

2. 日　sun, day　にち　３０日〔さんじゅうにち〕 30th of the month
　　　　　　　　　　か　　２日〔ふつか〕 2nd day of the month
　　　　　　　　　　＊　　１日〔ついたち〕 1st day of the month

【＊オプショナルたんご: Optional Vocabulary】

1.＊(お)しょう月〔がつ〕　　　New Year's Day
2.＊クリスマス　　　　　　　Christmas
3.＊ひなまつり　　　　　　　Girl's Day (Doll Festival), March 3
4.＊こどもの日〔ひ〕　　　　Children's Day (Boy's Day), May 5

【＊オプショナルかんじ: Optional kanji】

1.＊年　　　year　　　ねん　　　２０１０年 the year of 2010

【 ● ぶんかノート: Cultural Notes】

1. Let's sing a Happy Birthday song in Japanese.

　　おたんじょう日〔び〕　おめでとう　　　♪♪♪　　　　♪♪♪
　　おたんじょう日〔び〕　おめでとう
　　おめでとう　(Name)さん
　　おたんじょう日〔び〕　おめでとう

　　[Sing to the tune of "Happy Birthday."]

2. Japanese Annual Events　　　◎ = National holiday

◎	１月　１日	(お)しょう月	New Year's Day
◎	１月 2nd Monday	せいじんの日	Coming-of-Age-Day [20 years old = adult]
	２月　３日	せつぶん	Bean-Throwing Ceremony
◎	２月１１日	けんこくきねん日	National Founding Day
	３月　３日	ひなまつり	Girl's Day
◎	３月２１日	しゅんぶんの日	Vernal Equinox Day
	４月　８日	はなまつり	Buddha's Birthday Festival
◎	４月２９日	しょうわの日	Showa Day (The Showa Emperor's Birthday)
◎	５月　３日	けんぽうきねん日	Constitution Memorial Day
◎	５月　５日	こどもの日	Children's Day
	７月　７日	たなばた	Star Festival
◎	７月 3rd Monday	うみの日	Marine Day
◎	９月 3rd Monday	けいろうの日	Respect-for-the-Aged Day
◎	９月２３日	しゅうぶんの日	Autumnal Equinox Day
◎	１０月 2nd Monday	たいいくの日	Health-Sports Day
◎	１１月　３日	ぶんかの日	Culture Day
	１１月１５日	しちごさん	Festival Day for 3, 5 and 7 Year Old Children
◎	１１月２３日	きんろうかんしゃの日	Labor Thanksgiving Day
◎	１２月２３日	てんのうたんじょう日	The *Heisei* Emperor's Birthday
	１２月３１日	おおみそ日	New Year's Eve

3. A Japanese Proverb 「みっかぼうず」

みっか means "three days" and ぼうず means "a monk."
「みっかぼうず」 is used to describe one who does not
persevere or one who is not a steady, reliable worker.

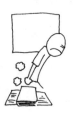

【アクティビティー: Activities】

A. Class Work

Everyone in class says their birthdates. Everyone writes the dates down in the spaces below. At the end, one student reads aloud everyone's birthdates to the class. Confirm your birthdates.

Ex. 「わたしの　たんじょう日〔び〕は　〜月〜日です。」

B. Pair Work

Ask your partner for the dates of the following days.

Ex. 「 きょう は　なん月〔がつ〕なん日〔にち〕ですか。」

　　「 クリスマス は　いつですか。」

1. Today

2. Your best friend's birthday

3. Tomorrow

4. Yesterday

5. Christmas

6. Halloween

7. Independence Day (どくりつきねん日〔び〕)

8. Valentine's Day

9. New Year's Day (おしょう月〔がつ〕)

10. Girl's Day (ひなまつり)

11. Boy's Day (こどもの日〔ひ〕)

12. This coming Saturday

１１か

【かいわ: Dialogue 】

エミ：きょう　なんの　じゅぎょうが　ありますか。
ケン：すうがくと　かがくと　えいごと　にほんごと　たいいくです。
エミ：おひるの　やすみじかんは　いつですか。
ケン：１１じはんから　１２じはんまでです。

【ぶんけい: Sentence Structure】

わたし は きょう えいごの じゅぎょう が １じ から ２じ まで あります。

I will have my English class from 1 o'clock to 2 o'clock today.

【たんご: Vocabulary】

1. しゃかい
social studies

2. かがく
science

3. すうがく
math

4. えいご
English

5. がいこくご
foreign language

6. びじゅつ
art

7. おんがく
music

8. たいいく
physical education

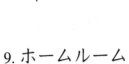

9. ホームルーム
homeroom

10. やすみじかん
a break

11. かもく
subject(s)

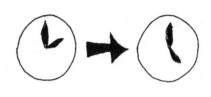

12. じゅぎょう, クラス
class, instruction

13. あります
have

14. 〜から〜まで
from 〜 to 〜

【*オプショナルたんご: Optional Vocabulary】

1.*〜を　とっています　　　　　is taking 〜

2.*れきし　　　　　　　　　　history

3.*アメリカし　　　　　　　　U.S. history

4.*アジアし　　　　　　　　　Asian history

5.*ヨーロッパし　　　　　　　European history

6.*けいざい　　　　　　　　　economics

7.*せいぶつ（がく）　　　　　biology

8.*ぶつり　　　　　　　　　　physics

9.*じしゅう　　　　　　　　　study hall

１１か

【ぶんぽう：Grammar】

A. Subject が あります "have"

The expanded meaning of あります is "have." は may replace が in negative sentences.

1. 「あした しけんが あります。」　　"I have an exam tomorrow."

2. 「きょう しゅくだいが ありますか。」　"Do we have homework today?"

   「いいえ、ありませんよ。」　　　　　　"No, we do not."

3. 「きょう たいいくの じゅぎょうは ありませんでした。」

   "We did not have P.E. class today."

B. Noun 1 から Noun 2 まで From N1 to N2.

N1 and N2 may represents times or places.

1. わたしは 10じから 11じまで えいごの じゅぎょうが あります。

   I have (my) English class from 10:00 to 11:00.

2. わたしの びじゅつの クラスは 1じはんから です。

   My art class is from 1:30.

【　●　ぶんかノート：Cultural Notes】

The Homeroom Teacher in Japanese Schools

The role of the homeroom teacher in a Japanese school is much more encompassing than in an American school. The relationship between students and their homeroom teacher is very close. There is a homeroom meeting every morning. Students have classes together with their homeroom classmates in the same classroom throughout most of the day. The subject teachers go from classroom to classroom and teach all classes in different rooms with th exception of P.E. and music. Homeroom students eat lunch together and clean their room and other places in the school together after school. The homeroom teacher takes care of the same homeroom students from entrance to graduation and becomes their personal, academic and college counselor. Elementary (and sometimes even higher level) school homeroom teachers visit parents of their students at home, too. The relationship of the homeroom student and his/her teacher lasts a lifetime. Students often invite their homeroom teachers to their weddings and keep in regular contact with them. Class reunions often are homeroom gatherings that include the teacher.

【👥アクティビティー: Activities】

A. Pair Work

Ask your partner about his/her schedule for today. Ask your partner what classes he/she has today and from what time to what time each class is and when his/her lunch break is. Write your partner's schedule in the chart below.

Ex. Question 1: 「きょう　なんの　じゅぎょうが　ありますか or ありましたか。」

Question 2: 「 Subject は　なんじから　なんじまで　ありますか
　　　　　　　or ありましたか。」

Question 3: 「おひるの　やすみじかんは　いつですか。」

[My partner's schedule for today]

Class	Time
	～
	～
	～
	～
	～
	～

B. Pair Work

Ask what subjects your partner likes and dislikes. Write your partner's favorite and least favorite subjects below.

Ex. Question: 「なんの　かもくが　すきですか。」

My partner's:

すき	
きらい	

【かいわ: Dialogue 】

エミ：つぎの　じゅぎょうは　なんですか。

ケン：かがくです。

エミ：せんせいは　だれですか。

ケン：スミスせんせいです。

エミ：どんな　せんせいですか。

ケン：ちょっと　きびしいですが、とても　いいです。

エミ：じゅぎょうは　どうですか。

ケン：おもしろいですが、ちょっと　むずかしいです。

【たんご: Vocabulary】

1. どうですか。
How is it?

2. つぎ
next

3. むずかしい [いAdj.]
is difficult

4. やさしい [いAdj.]
is easy

5. たのしい [いAdj.]
is fun, enjoyable

6. おもしろい [いAdj.]
is interesting

7. つまらない [いAdj.]
is boring, uninteresting

1.＊いじわる [なAdj.]		is mean
2.＊こわい [いAdj.]		is scary
3.＊へん [なAdj.]		is weird, strange
4.＊おかしい [いAdj.]		is funny (humorous), is weird
5.＊いかがですか。		How is it? [Polite equiv. of どうですか。]

【 ● ぶんかノート: Cultural Notes】

Foreign Language Education in Japanese Schools

English is a required course from 7th grade through 12th grade in Japan. More elementary schools are now also introducing English. English is one of the major subjects required for college entrance, so students take the study of English seriously. English language education in Japan is grammar oriented, and emphasizes mainly reading and writing. Many students can read difficult materials in English, but cannot speak or comprehend spoken English well. Students attend private English conversation schools （えいかいわがっこう）to brush up on their English speaking skills.

【 アクティビティー: Activities】

A. Pair Work

Ask your partner about his/her next class (つぎのクラス). If Japanese is your last class of the day, ask about your partner's previous class (まえのクラス). Write down your partner's answers.

1. What is your next class?	
2. Where is the classroom?	
3. Who is the teacher?	
4. How is the teacher?	
5. How is the class?	

B. Pair Work

Ask about the classes your partner will have/has had today. Write down your partner's responses.

Ex.　「きょう　なんの　クラスが　ありますか or ありましたか。」

　　　「(Subject)は　なんじから　なんじまで　ありますか or ありましたか。」

　　　「(Subject)の　きょうしつは　どこですか or どこでしたか。」

　　　「(Subject)の　せんせいは　だれですか or だれでしたか。」

　　　「(Teacher's name)せんせいは　どうですか or どうでしたか。」

　　　「(Subject)の　じゅぎょうは　どうですか or どうでしたか。」

Subject	Time	Classroom	(Who?) Teacher (How?)		Class (How?)

【かいわ: Dialogue 】

ケン：きょう ぼくは とても うれしいです。

エミ：なぜですか。

ケン：おとといの しゃかいの しけんの せいせきが
　　　よかったからです。

エミ：よかったですねえ。

【ぶんけい: Sentence Structure 】

い adjective -かったです	was 〜
い adjective -く なかったです or -く ありませんでした	was not 〜
Sentence 1 (Reason) から、 Sentence 2 (Result)。	Sentence 1, so Sentence 2.
Sentence 1 (Reason) からです。	It is because Sentence 1.

【たんご: Vocabulary】

1. なぜ／どうして
Why?

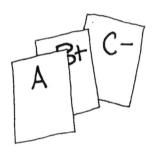

2. せいせき
grade

3. ひどい [い Adj.]
is terrible

Although both are used frequently,
どうして is used more often colloquially.

  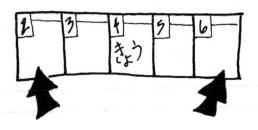

4. うれしい [いAdj.]
is glad, happy

5. かなしい [いAdj.]
is sad

6. おととい
the day before yesterday

7. あさって
the day after tomorrow

8. いいですねえ。
How nice!
Used when one receives good news of something which will soon occur.

9. よかったですねえ。
How nice!
Expression of happiness or support on a past event.

10. ざんねんですねえ。
How disappointing!, Too bad!
Expression of disappointment at something which won't happen.

11. ざんねんでしたねえ。
How disappointing!
Expression of disappointment at an unfortunate past occurrence.

12. Sentence 1 (Reason) ＋ から、Sentence 2 (Result)。

= Sentence 1 (Reason), so Sentence 2 (Result).

11か

228

【＊オプショナルたんご: Optional Vocabulary】

1.＊がっかりです。　　　　　　　I am disappointed.

2.＊こうへい [なAdj.]　　　　is fair

3.＊ふこうへい [なAdj.]　　　is unfair

【ぶんぽう: Grammar】

A. Sentence 1 (Reason)＋から、 Sentence 2 (Result)。

= Sentence 1 (Reason), so Sentence 2 (Result).

The conjunction から, which even in this construction originally meant "from," follows a reason or cause. から used in this context, however, is best translated as "so," or more literally "from the reason of." The second portion of this sentence structure, which expresses a result or consequence, may be omitted if it is understood. For example, as a response to a "why" question, only the reason is required in the response, so the second portion of the sentence is often dropped. When the first portion (reason) of the sentence ends with an いAdjective, the です before から is often omitted. However, if a noun or なadjective precedes です in the first part of the sentence, the です must not be dropped.

1. 「にほんごは　おもしろい（です）から、すきです。」

"Japanese is interesting, so I like it."

2. 「しけんは　あしたですから、こんばん　べんきょうします。」

"I have an exam tomorrow, so I'll study tonight."

3. 「なぜ　せいせきが　わるかったですか。」　　　"Why was your grade bad?"

「べんきょうしませんでしたから。」　　　　　"It is because I did not study."

Review: いAdjective Conjugation:

たかいです。	is tall
たかくないです。／たかくありません。	is not tall
たかかったです。	was tall
たかくなかったです。／たかくありませんでした。	was not tall

☆いい "good" conjugates in its よい form.

いいです。／よいです。	is good
よくないです。／よくありません。	is not good
よかったです。	was good
よくなかったです。／よくありませんでした。	was not good

1. きのうの　しけんは　むずかしかったです。　　　Yesterday's exam was difficult.

2. えいがは　とても　おもしろかったです。　　　The movie was very interesting.

3. その　せんせいは　ぜんぜん　きびし<u>くなかったです</u>。

That teacher was not strict at all.

【 ● ぶんかノート: Cultural Notes】

What is important to be accepted to a good college in Japan?

College admission in Japan is mainly decided by the results of an entrance exam which is usually held in Feburary. Many Japanese students go to じゅく (cram school) during after school hours in preparation for the entrance exam. Unlike major American colleges, Japanese colleges do not consider students' personal history, i.e., recommendations and extra-curricular activities. Only the results of the entrance exam are considered. When Japanese students fail in entrance exams and are not admitted to the college of their choice, they become ろうにん. (The original meaning of ろうにん is "a masterless samurai," but here it refers to an unsuccessful college entrant - a person who does not belong to a school.) ろうにん often attend よびこう (cram school for ろうにん) in their attempts to improve their chances of succeeding the next year. Some students remain ろうにん for as many as three or four years.

【アクティビティー: Activities】

A. Pair Work

Copy the following sentences on separate pieces of paper. Fold all the papers separately and put them on the desk or in a cap. Randomly pick one and say うれしいです or かなしいです depending on the message on your paper. Your partner asks なぜですか。 Explain the reason in Japanese. Take turns.

Ex.　Student A: 「わたしは　うれしいです。」

Student B: 「なぜ　うれしいですか。」

Student A: 「にほんごの　しけんが　Aでしたから、うれしいです。」

or 「にほんごの　しけんが　Aでしたからです。」

Ex. My Japanese exam grade was good.
1. My math exam was an F.
2. My friend does not like me now.
3. My dog died.　（died＝しにました）
4. I lost lots of money.　（lost＝なくしました）
5. Tomorrow is Saturday.
6. I have no homework today.

B. Class Work

Every student states whether he/she feels happy or sad. After each statement, members of the class will ask each other for a reason. Each student responds. Who can give the best reason for being happy or sad?

C. Class game

The class divides into four or five teams. Each team sends one of its members to the board to write answers to one of the questions below or some other similar question. The teacher will randomly ask a question. Assign each person on the team a number, starting with "one." Your number determines the order in which you will go to the board. The team which writes the correct answer on the board first earns 3 points. The team which finishes second with the correct answer earns 2 points, and the third team wins 1 point.

1. きょうは　なんよう日〔び〕ですか。

2. きょうは　なん日〔にち〕ですか。

3. きのうは　なんよう日〔び〕でしたか。

4. きのうは　なん日〔にち〕でしたか。

5. あしたは　なんよう日〔び〕ですか。

6. あしたは　なん日〔にち〕ですか。

7. おとといは　なんよう日〔び〕でしたか。

8. おとといは　なん日〔にち〕でしたか。

9. あさっては　なんよう日〔び〕ですか。

10. あさっては　なん日〔にち〕ですか。

11. クリスマスは　いつですか。

12. サンクスギビングは　いつですか。

13. こどもの日〔ひ〕 (Boy's Day) は　なん月なん日〔にち〕ですか。

14. ひなまつり (Girl's Day) は　なん月なん日〔にち〕ですか。

15. おしょう月 (New Year's Day) は　いつですか。

【かいわ: Dialogue 】

エミ：どうして　いつも　いそがしいですか。

ケン：しゅくだいが　とても　おおいからです。

　　　それに、こんしゅうの　きんようびに　しけんが　あります。

エミ：たいへんですねえ。

ケン：はやく　やすみが　ほしいです。

【ぶんけい: Sentence Structure】

| Person | は | Something | が | ほしい／ほしくない | です。 |

Person wants/does not want something.

| Person/Thing | は／が | | おおい／すくない | です。 There are many/few 〜.

【たんご: Vocabulary】

1. せんしゅう
last week

2. こんしゅう
this week

3. らいしゅう
next week

4. まいしゅう
every week

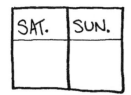

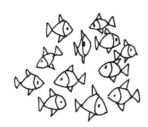

5. しゅうまつ
weekend

6. おおい [いAdj.]
are many, much

7. すくない [いAdj.]
are few, little

Although these are adjectives, they are not used before nouns in general.

Neg. form おおくないです　　　　Neg. form すくなくないです

8. (something)が　ほしい [いAdj.]
want (something)
Neg. form ほしくないです

9. たいへん [なAdj.]
is hard, difficult
Neg. form is たいへんではありません.
たいへん is used in situations which are
psychologically burdensome.

10. それに
Moreover, Besides

【＊オプショナルたんご: Optional Vocabulary】
1.＊ストレス　　　　　　　　　　　　　stress

【ぶんぽう: Grammar】

A. Noun が　　　ほしい(ん)です。　　　　　　　　　　　want ～
　　　　が/は　ほしくない(ん)です。/ほしくありません。　　do not want ～
　　　　が　　　ほしかった(ん)です。　　　　　　　　　　wanted ～
　　　　が/は　ほしくなかった(ん)です。/ほしくありませんでした。　did not want ～

ほしいです is used when one expresses a desire for <u>something</u>. The particle が generally follows the object
which the subject of the sentence wants. は often replaces が when ほしい is negated. ほしい is conjugated as
an い adjective. Do not use this pattern when you ask a superior what he/she wants. It is considered too direct and
rude. ん is often inserted when one wants to explain to the listener what one wants. This pattern is not to be
confused with the verb -TAI form, which is used when one wants <u>to do</u> something.

1.「なにを　のみますか。」　　　　　　"What will you have (to drink)?"

「いま　おみずが　<u>ほしいです</u>。」　　"I want water now."

2.「コーヒー<u>は</u>　<u>ほしくないです</u>。　ジュースを　ください。」

"I don't want coffee. Please give me some juice."

3.「はやく　やすみが　<u>ほしいです</u>。」　"I want a vacation soon."

B. Subject が＋　おおいです。　　　There are many / much ～.

　　Subject が＋　すくないです。　　There are few / little ～.

Both おおい and すくない are い adjectives. However they are not used before nouns in general.

1.すうがくは　しゅくだいが　とても　<u>おおいです</u>。

"There is a lot of math homework."

2. この　クラスに　おとこの　がくせいは　<u>すくない</u>ですね。
"There are few male students in this class, aren't there?"

【 ● ぶんかノート: Cultural Notes】

Sports in Japanese Schools

In Japan, students belong to one sports team and play that sport all year long. There are no seasonal sports in high school. The relationship among the team players is very special. In sports teams, an age difference of even a year among its players is significant. Younger students call the older students せんぱい and the older students call the younger students こうはい. こうはい are expected to arrive at games early and practice earlier than せんぱい. They must prepare the equipment for practice, greet せんぱい with respect and clean up after practice. This kind of vertical relationship also often exists in Japanese companies and other working environments.

【 アクティビティー: Activities】

A. Pair Work

Ask your partner about the courses he/she is taking. Ask what subjects he/she is taking, what kind of teachers he/she has, how the courses are, whether there is lots of homework, whether his/her grade is good, and what grade he/she wants.

Ex. 「なんの　かもくを　とっています (is taking) か。」
「せんせいは　どうですか。」
「じゅぎょうは　どうですか。」
「しゅくだいは　おおいですか。」
「せいせきは　どうですか。」
「どんな　せいせきが　ほしいですか。」

My partner's courses:

Subject	Teacher (How?)	Class (How?)	Homework (Lots?)	Grade (How?)	Grade (Wish?)

B. Pair Work

Using the "My Calendar" section below, fill in your schedule of exams and papers due within the specified 3 week period. Use the numbers to identify each exam or report. <u>Do not show your partner your calendar.</u> Ask your partner for his/her schedule of exams and papers and fill in "My Partner's Calendar" with the information you receive. When both of you finish, compare answers to see whether your communication was successful or not.

1. にほんごのしけん　2. えいごのレポート　3. しゃかいのレポート
4. かがくのしけん　　5. すうがくのしけん　6. たいいくのしけん

My calendar:

	Sunday	Monday	Tuesday	Wednesday	Thursday	Friday	Saturday
last week							
this week							
next week							

Ex. Question: 「にほんごの　しけんは　いつですか。」
　　Answer: 「〜しゅうの　〜ようびです。」

My partner's calendar:

	Sunday	Monday	Tuesday	Wednesday	Thursday	Friday	Saturday
last week							
this week							
next week							

１１か

Find the answers by investigating books, by talking to friends, or by using the Internet.

1. Name four Japanese national holidays.

2. Name two of your state holidays.

3. The Japanese "celebrate" a series of holidays that have become known as "Golden Week." What holidays fall during this week and when is "Golden Week" celebrated?

4. The traditional Japanese calendar revolves around the emperor. Eras are named after the emperor currently in power. What is the name of the present era? In what year did it start? What year is it now, according to the traditional Japanese calendar?

Bonus:

5. How is Valentine's Day celebrated in America?

6. In Japan, a holiday called "White Day" follows Valentine's Day by one month. What is the difference between Valentine's Day and White Day in Japan?

Microwave もち

Ingredients: 1 pkg. *mochiko*
2 cups water
1 cup sugar
1/4 tsp. vanilla
2 drops red or green food coloring
kinako (soy bean powder) / *katakuriko* (potato starch)

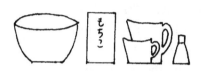

1. In a medium bowl, combine *mochiko*, water, sugar, vanilla and food coloring.

2. Mix until smooth.

3. Pour mixture into a greased 5 cup microwave tube pan.

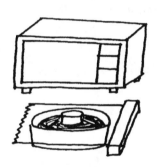

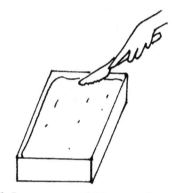

4. Cover with plastic wrap and cook on medium high for 10 minutes.

5. Pour *mochi* from tube pan into a rectangular baking pan and cool.

6. Loosen *mochi* by running a knife around the inner and outer edges of the pan.
* Use a plastic knife or a knife wrapped in saran.

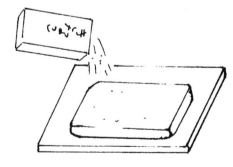

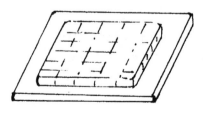

7. Remove to a board or platter dusted with *kinako* or *katakuriko* and cool.

8. Cut into serving pieces.

9. Coat with *kinako* or *katakuriko*.

１１か

What is Mochi?

Mochi, or rice cake, is made from a sticky variety of rice that is steamed, and kneaded by machine or pounded with a mallet in a mortar. It is usually formed into small round flattened mounds or cut into small rectangular blocks.

Mochi came to Japan from Southeast Asia at the same time rice cultivation was introduced. Originally, *mochi* was offered to the gods at shrines. Later, it was eaten on various festive occasions. *Mochi* first appeared at New Year's celebrations sometime during the eighth through tenth centuries. It was used primarily as a decoration called *kagamimochi*. One round *mochi* was placed on a slightly larger one, decorated festively with many symbolic foods and other items, and displayed in homes and businesses. Later, the tradition of eating *ozoni*, or *mochi* soup, on New Year's morning, began. Because *mochi* is considered good luck, it is also part of other festive occasions including weddings, children's festivals, housewarmings, special birthdays, and other happy celebrations. Though there are many theories, *mochi* is considered a good luck symbol, because of its round, never-ending shape (like a wedding band), its sticky consistency (which symbolizes a family or a couple who will always "stick together"), and the sound of the word, (the verb *mochimasu* means "to have or possess," suggesting wealth). Also, rice in any form is traditionally considered a symbol of prosperity in Japan. *Mochi* can be prepared in a variety of ways. It can be eaten plain, in soups, grilled, fried, flavored with various toppings or, most commonly, filled with sweetened black bean paste.

My child made *mochi*.

_____
Get your parent's signature.

By the end of this lesson, you will be able to communicate

the information below in the given situations.

【 I-１２ タスク１】

Your friend sees you are not well. Your friend asks you what happened. You have a bad headache. Your friend asks if you are all right or not. You tell him/her that you want to take some medicine so you want some water. Your friend gets a glass of water for you.

【 I-１２ タスク２】

You want to see an important college basketball game which will be held on Saturday during the spring vacation at the college gym (たいいくかん). You invite your friend and decide on a place and time to meet. The game will start at 6:00 p.m. You also invite your friend to a good movie after the game.

【 I-１２ タスク３】

Your friend had a soccer game yesterday and you want to know the results. Your friend explains that the other team was very strong and tells you that his/her team lost. You express your disappointment.

【かいわ: Dialogue 】

ケン：どう　しましたか。
エミ：ちょっと　あたまが　いたいです。
ケン：だいじょうぶですか。
エミ：ええ、だいじょうぶです。

【たんご: Vocabulary】

1. どう　しましたか。
What happened?

2. びょうき
illness, sickness
びょうきです means
"I am sick."

3. かぜ
a cold
When they catch colds,
Japanese wear gauze masks
to prevent spreading germs.
かぜです means "I have
a cold."

4. ねつ
fever
ねつが　あります。
means "I have a fever."
ねつが　たかいです。
means "I have a high
fever."

5. いたい
[い Adj.]
is painful, sore

6. だいじょうぶ
[な Adj.]
all right

7. しにます
[しぬ]
to die

8. かわいそうに。
How pitiful.
Sympathy to inferior.

【＊オプショナルたんご: Optional Vocabulary】

1.＊（お）きのどくに。　　　　I'm sorry. [Sympathy, formal expression]

2.＊かぜを　ひきました。　　　I caught a cold.

3.＊ねんざしました。　　　　　I sprained (something).

4.＊ほねを　おりました。　　　(I) fractured my bone.

【　●　ぶんかノート: Cultural Notes】

Japanese Medical Care

When Japanese catch colds, they generally go to pharmacies [くすりや] to get medicine. There are many pharmacies in town. Japanese do not go to the hospital as often as people in the U.S.; the family clinics are more frequently used. Most hospitals and clinics do not operate on an appointment system. Therefore, when Japanese go to a hospital or a clinic, they have to wait their turn. Physical examinations for students are all done at school. Students are visited by doctors and receive medical exams and immunization shots in school.

【 アクティビティー: Activities】

A. Pair Work

Your partner has a problem. Ask what happened. Your partner explains the problem. You express your concern.

Ex. Person A: 「～さん、どう　しましたか。」
　　Person B: 「かぜです。」
　　Person A: 「だいじょうぶですか。」
　　Person B: 「はい、だいじょうぶです。」
　　Person A: 「おだいじに。」

1. You have a cold.
2. You have a stomachache.
3. You have a sore throat.
4. You have a headache.
5. You have a slight fever.
6. Your eyes hurt.
7. Your dog died.
8. Your grandmother is very sick.

12か

【かいわ: Dialogue 】

ケン : きょう　はやく　うちへ　かえりたいです。

エミ : なぜですか。

ケン : すこし　ねつが　あります。

【ぶんけい: Sentence Structure 】

| Person | は | Object | が／を | Verb (Stem form) + | たい（ん）です | 。 want to do ～ |

Person は Object が／を Verb (Stem form) + たい（ん）です 。 want to do ～

Person は Object が／を Verb (Stem form) + たくない（ん）です 。

do not want to do ～

★ The verb stem is the portion of the verb preceding -ます.

★ ん appears when the speaker explains what he/she wants to do.

【たんご: Vocabulary】

1. やすみます
[やすむ]
to rest

2.（がっこうを）やすみます

to be absent (from school)

3. くすり(を　のみます)
[のむ]
(to take) medicine

Japanese ancient medicines were in
liquid or powder form. They literally
"drank" their medicine.
くすりや is a pharmacy.

4. ゆうべ
last night

5. けさ
this morning

6. こんばん
tonight

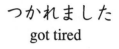

7. ねむい [い Adj.]
is sleepy
Neg. form ねむくないです

8. つかれています　　つかれました
is tired　　　　　got tired
Neg. form つかれていません

9. はやく [Adverb]
early

10. おそく [Adverb]
late

はやい is an adjective. It describes a noun. はやく is an adverb which most often describes a verb. Use はやい and はやく correctly. "I go home early" is 「はやく　かえります。」 and "It is early" is 「はやいです。」

【＊オプショナルたんご: Optional Vocabulary】
1.＊ほけんしつ　　　　　　　　　health room
2.＊アスピリン　　　　　　　　　aspirin

【ぶんぽう: Grammar】

A. Verb (Stem form) ＋たい(ん)です　　　　　　　want to do ～

Verb (Stem form) ＋たくありません／たくない(ん)です　　do not want to do ～

Verb (Stem form) ＋たかった(ん)です　　　　　wanted to do ～

Verb (Stem form) ＋たくありませんでした／たくなかった(ん)です

did not want to do ～

This structure is used when one wants to do a certain action. When one wants <u>something</u>, a different structure is used. たいです conjugates as an い adj. The object in this structure takes the particle が or を and sometimes は, if in a negative sentence. ん is often inserted when one explains to the listener what one wants to do. Warning! Do not use this pattern when you ask a superior what he/she wants to do. It is considered impolite and too direct.

12か

1. 「いま　テレビを　(or が)　みたいです。」
    "I want to watch TV now."

2. 「はやく　おひるごはんを　(or が)　たべたいです。」
    "I want to eat lunch early."

3. 「おちゃを　のみますか。」
    "Will you drink tea?"

    「すみません。おちゃは　のみたくありません。

    おみずが　(or を)　のみたいです。」

    "Sorry. I do not want to drink tea. I want to drink some water."

4. 「ゆうべ　フットボールを　みたかったんですが、いそがしかったんです。」
    "I wanted to watch football last night, but I was busy."

【 ● ぶんかノート: Cultural Notes】

1. Why don't Japanese use -たいですか and ほしいですか to superiors?
Japanese people tend to avoid directness in language and behavior. Japan is composed of small islands where many people live closely together and thus, they prefer to avoid conflict. Japanese are sensitive about living harmoniously and "keeping peace." Therefore, directness is sometimes not acceptable in Japanese society. For example, when asking a superior in Japanese "Do you want to drink coffee?," you would not say 「コーヒーをのみたいですか。」, but 「コーヒーは いかがですか。」. "What do you want to drink?" should not be 「なにを　のみたいですか。」, but 「おのみものは　なにが　いいでしょうか。」. The Japanese language abounds in expressions such as these which express messages in indirect ways. One is expected to be sensitive to others' needs by being observant and empathetic, not by asking others' directly of their needs.

2. A Japanese Proverb 「ばかに　つける　くすりは　ない」
ばか means "idiot." つける means "to apply." くすり means "medicine." ない means "does not exist." 「ばかに　つける　くすりは　ない」 means "There is no salve for stupidity" or "There is no cure for an idiot."

【👧👧アクティビティー: Activities】

A. Pair Work

You want to take the following actions. Your partner asks you why and you give reasons.

Ex. Person A: 「アスピリンを／が　のみたいです。」

Person B: 「なぜですか。」

Person A: 「あたまが　いたいからです。」

1. I want to take some aspirin （アスピリン）.
2. I want to rest a while.
3. I want to go to the hospital.
4. I want to return home early.
5. I do not want to eat anything.
6. I want to be absent tomorrow.
7. I want to sleep.
8. I do not want to take medicine.

B. Pair Work

Tell what you wanted to do. Your partner asks you why. You give a reason.

Ex. Person A: 「きのう　あなたと　はなしたかったです。」

Person B: 「なぜですか。」

Person A: 「パーティーが　ありますから。」

1. I wanted to talk to you yesterday.
2. I wanted to return home early yesterday.
3. I wanted to go to bed early last night.
4. I did not want to get up early this morning.
5. I did not want to eat anything this morning.
6. I wanted to come to school early.
7. I wanted to watch T.V. last night.

12か

【かいわ: Dialogue 】

ケン：きのうの　バスケットの　しあいは　どうでしたか。

エミ：わたしたちは　まけました。とても　つよい　チームでしたよ。

ケン：それは　ざんねんでしたねえ。

【ぶんけい: Sentence Structure 】

い Adjective X Noun
Ex. おおきい　ぼうし　　　　a big cap

【たんご: Vocabulary】

1. しあい

(sports) game

しあいをします "play a game"
しあいがあります "have a game"

2. わたしたち

we

たち is a suffix for animate plurals.

3. ぼくたち

we [used by males]

4. チーム

team

5. かちます [かつ]

to win

6. まけます [まける]

to lose

7. つよい [い Adj.]

is strong

8. よわい [い Adj.]

is weak

【ぶんぽう：Grammar】

> ### A. いAdjective ＋ Noun
> When an いadjective appears before a noun, no particle follows the いadjective.

1. <u>つよい　チーム</u>でした。　　　　(They) were a strong team.

2. とても　<u>おもしろい　えいが</u>です。　It is a very interesting movie.

3. わたしは　<u>あかい　はな</u>が　すきです。　I like red flowers.

【 ● ぶんかノート：Cultural Notes】

1. じゃんけんぽん Game

This is a popular game played when one needs to decide on a quick winner or "who goes first" and is much like "choosing straws."
One forms "paper," "stone" or "scissors" with one's fingers, in rhythm and unison with one's opponents. Winners are determined in the following way.
グー is stone, チョキ is scissors and パー is paper. Stone wins to scissors and loses to paper because scissors cannot cut stone, but paper can wrap stone. Scissors wins to paper and loses to stone because scissors can cut paper, but cannot cut stone. Paper wins to stone and loses to scissors because paper can wrap stone, but scissors can cut paper.

グー	チョキ	パー
stone	scissors	paper

「じゃんけんぽん」 to start a game.
「あいこでしょ」 to break a tie.

2. すもう

Sumo wrestling is the most popular of the Japanese traditional sports. It is the official national sport of Japan, and is several centuries old. *Sumo* wrestlers are called すもうとり and are famous for their huge bodies. *Sumo* wrestlers average between 250 — 350 pounds. Despite their massive appearance, they undergo rigorous training and must be agile, strong, quick and balanced if they are to be successful. They do, however, consume an extraordinary amount of food and drink. Names of すもうとり often end with やま (mountain), うみ (ocean), はな (flower), etc. Tournaments are held six times a year in different parts of Japan.

【 アクティビティー：Activities】

A. | Pair Work |

Do a *jan-ken-po* game with your partner five times and report who won most of the games.

Ex.「〜さんが　かちました。」

B. Group Work

   Make a *sumo* wrestler and have a tournament with wrestlers your group has made. Cut the
   すもうとり below and fold it in half. Name your すもうとり and color the まわし (sash).

How to play すもう:

1. Decide on a ぎょうじ (umpire).

2. Place the two すもうとり facing each other at the lines in the middle of the どひょう (*sumo*
   ring) which appears on the next page. [See below.]

3. For the purposes of this class, the ぎょうじ will signal the start of the match with a hand motion
   similar to a karate chop on the どひょう. The ぎょうじ repeats 「のこった　のこった」
   which means "Stay in" all during the match.

4. Tap the table top without touching the すもうとり.

5. The すもうとり who falls first or falls out of the どひょう is the loser.

6. The ぎょうじ (umpire) calls out the winner's name.

[すもう]

[すもうとり]

In real *sumo* tournaments, the two *sumo*
challengers wait for a designated time after
squatting at the starting line, stare at one
another and lunge at one another when they
are ready. If they do not do this on their own,
they are given a signal by the ぎょうじ to
start.

西
West

東
East

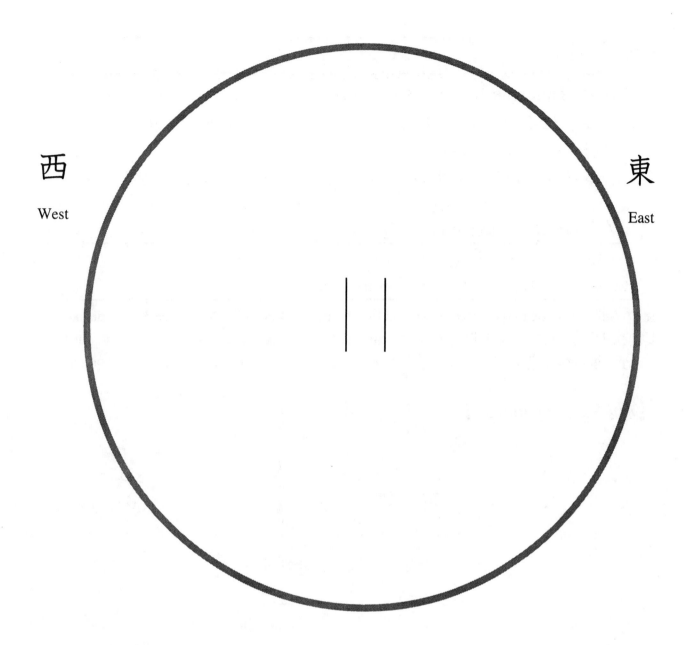

Tournament:
Have a tournament.

12か

【かいわ: Dialogue 】

ケン：はるやすみに　とても　だいじな　しあいが　あります。

エミ：がんばって　ください。

ケン：はい、がんばります。

【ぶんけい: Sentence Structure 】

| な Adjective | な | Noun |

Ex. きれい <u>な</u> ぼうし　　　　a pretty hat

★ な Adjectives you have learned so far are げんき fine, だめ no good, すき like, きらい dislike, じょうず skillful, へた unskillful, とくい strong at, にがて weak at, きれい pretty, しずか quiet, じゃま hindrance, ゆうめい famous, たいへん hard, だいじょうぶ all right, だいじ important.

【たんご: Vocabulary】

1. はる

spring

2. なつ

summer

3. あき

autumn, fall

4. ふゆ

winter

5. せんげつ

last month

6. こんげつ

this month

7. らいげつ

next month

8. まいつき

every month

9. だいじ [なAdj.]

is important

10. がんばって。

Good luck!

Do your best.

11. がんばります。

I will do my best.

【＊オプショナルたんご: Optional Vocabulary】
1.＊トーナメント tournament

【ぶんぽう: Grammar】

A. なAdjective + な + Noun

When なadjectives modify nouns, な appears between the なadjective and the noun.

1. あした だいじな しあいが あります。 I have an important game tomorrow.

2. 「すきな スポーツは なんですか。」 "What is your favorite sport?"

「ゴルフが すきです。」 "I like golfing."

3. きれいな ひとですねえ。 She is a pretty lady!

【 ● ぶんかノート: Cultural Notes】

はるやすみ, なつやすみ, ふゆやすみ in Japan

はるやすみ (spring vacation) is from about 20th of March to about the 10th of April and is the most relaxing vacation for Japanese students and parents. Because it is the vacation which marks the end of the one school year and the beginning of the next, there is no homework and no pressure from school. なつやすみ (summer vacation) is much shorter than summer vacation in the U.S. It is from about the 20th of July to the end of August. During the summer vacation, homework is assigned. ふゆやすみ (winter vacation) is from about the 20th of December to the 10th of January. Christmas is not a national holiday in Japan, but January 1st, 2nd, and 3rd is a time for family celebration, much like Christmas is in the West.

12か

【アクティビティー: Activities】

A. | Pair Work |

Interview your partner on his/her likes and dislikes. Write your partner's responses.

Ex. Question: 「すきな　たべものは　なんですか。」

　　　Answer:　「～です。」

1. すきな　たべもの　　　_____

2. きらいな　たべもの　　_____

3. すきな　くるま　　　　_____

4. すきな　ほん　　　　　_____

5. じょうずな　スポーツ　_____

6. へたな　スポーツ　　　_____

B. | Pair Work |

Ask your partner about the people below. Your partner will answer with descriptions based on the pictures below. You may use the cues below or make up your own descriptions.

Ex. Question: 「～さんは　どんな　ひとですか。」

　　　Answer:　「～さんは　_いAdj._　ひとです。」or

　　　　　　　「～さんは　_なAdj._（な）　ひとです。」

　　ベン　　　　　だいすけ　　ジェイン　　ゆか　　　Someone both of you know.

| うるさい, しずか, かわいい, きれい |

C. | Pair Work |

Randomly fill in the three month calendars on the following page with the activities and events below. Ask your partner when his/her activities and events occurred or will occur. Compare your two calendars to see if your communication was successful.

Ex. 「やきゅうの　しあいは　いつですか。」

1. today

2. vacation (spring)

3. piano concert

4. birthday party

5. important basketball game

6. good movie

7. Japanese exam

8. dog's death

9. basketball game

10. junior prom　（プラム）

My calendar:

Make Your Own Calendar

Last Month

日	月	火	水	木	金	土
			1	2	3	4
5	6	7	8	9	10	11
12	13	14	15	16	17	18
19	20	21	22	23	24	25
26	27	28	29	30		

This Month

日	月	火	水	木	金	土
					1	2
3	4	5	6	7	8	9
10	11	12	13	14	15	16
17	18	19	20	21	22	23
24	25	26	27	28	29	30
31						

Next Month

日	月	火	水	木	金	土
1	2	3	4	5	6	
7	8	9	10	11	12	13
14	15	16	17	18	19	20
21	22	23	24	25	26	27
28	29	30				

My partner's calendar:

Last Month

日	月	火	水	木	金	土
			1	2	3	4
5	6	7	8	9	10	11
12	13	14	15	16	17	18
19	20	21	22	23	24	25
26	27	28	29	30		

This Month

日	月	火	水	木	金	土
					1	2
3	4	5	6	7	8	9
10	11	12	13	14	15	16
17	18	19	20	21	22	23
24	25	26	27	28	29	30
31						

Next Month

日	月	火	水	木	金	土
1	2	3	4	5	6	
7	8	9	10	11	12	13
14	15	16	17	18	19	20
21	22	23	24	25	26	27
28	29	30				

12か

【かいわ: Dialogue 】

ケン：あした　ここのだいがくと　スタンフォードだいがくの
　　　バレーボールの　しあいが　あります。
　　　いっしょに　いきませんか。

エミ：どこで　ありますか。

ケン：だいがくで　あります。

エミ：じゃ、５じに　わたしの　うちで　あいましょうか。

ケン：ええ。そして、しあいの　あとで　えいがに　いきましょう。

【ぶんけい: Sentence Structure】

| Activity | は | Place | で | あります。 | There is an activity at ～. |

【たんご: Vocabulary】

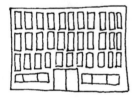

1. だいがく

college, university

2. だいがくせい

college student

3. ～のまえに

before ～

4. ～のあとで

after ～

5. (Place で) あいます
　　　[あう]

to meet (at a place)

6. れんしゅう(を)します
　　　　　　　[する]

to practice

7. はしります
　　[はしる]

to run

【ぶんぽう: Grammar】

> A. Place ＋で　Activity/Event ＋が　あります。
>
> When an activity or event occurs at a place, the particle で (not に) is used after the place word.

1. 「きょう　しあいは　どこで　ありますか。」　　"Where is the game today?"

　「マッキンレーこうこうで　あります。」　　"It will be at McKinley High School."

2. きんようびの　ダンスは　カフェテリアで　あります。

　　　　　　　　　　　　　　　　Friday's dance will be at the cafeteria.

【 ● ぶんかノート: Cultural Notes】

High School and College Sports in Japan

　Japanese high school sports are very popular. Japanese high school baseball and soccer are especially popular. Kooshien Baseball Stadium in Kobe is famous for high school national tournaments held there. There are two national tournaments a year. One is in March and one is in August. Many Japanese people watch these games on TV and cheer for their home teams. Japanese college sports games are not as popular as high school sports. They are also not as popular as U.S. college sports games. Except for major tournaments, people are not charged admission to attend high school or college games.

【 アクティビティー: Activities】

A. Pair Work

You want to do the following activities with your friend. Discuss with your partner the place and the time the event will start and decide on where and when to meet.

Ex. Question 1: 「えいがは　どこで　ありますか。」
　　Question 2: 「えいがは　いつですか。」
　　Question 3: 「どこで　あいましょうか。」
　　Question 4: 「なんじに　あいましょうか。」

	Place	Time	Place to meet	Time to meet
1. movie				
2. concert （コンサート）				
3. college basketball game				
4. dancing （ダンス）				
5. running				
6. tennis practice				

Grammar Review

I. Verb Conjugation

nonpast	いきます
neg. nonpast	いきません
past	いきました
neg., past	いきませんでした
let's ~	いきましょう
Shall we ~?	いきましょうか
Would you like to ~?	いきませんか

II. Noun + Copula

Noun +です
Noun +ではありません or じゃありません
Noun +でした
Noun +ではありませんでした or じゃありませんでした

Noun +(の)+ Noun

III. Adjectives

	い Adjective		な Adjective
	おおきい	いい	しずか
nonpast	おおきいです	いいです	しずかです
neg. nonpast	おおきくないです	よくないです	しずかではありません
	おおきくありません	よくありません	しずかじゃありません
past	おおきかったです	よかったです	しずかでした
neg. past	おおきくなかったです	よくなかったです	しずかではありませんでした
	おおきくありませんでした	よくありませんでした	しずかじゃありませんでした
prenominal	おおきい　ひと	いい　ひと	しずか(な)　ひと
words	あつい　くろい　いそがしい　つまらない さむい　あおい　あたらしい　ひどい すずしい　きいろい　ふるい　うれしい たかい　ちゃいろい　うつくしい　かなしい ひくい　わかい　ひろい　おおい わるい　きびしい　せまい　すくない おおきい　やさしい　ちかい　ほしい want ちいさい　きたない　とおい　いたい ながい　かわいい　むずかしい　ねむい みじかい　うるさい　やさしい　つよい あかい　はやい　たのしい　よわい しろい　おそい　おもしろい　Verb stem+たい want to do		げんき　きれい だめ　しずか すき　じゃま きらい　ゆうめい じょうず　たいへん へた　だいじょうぶ とくい　だいじ にがて

Ask your partner these questions in Japanese.
Your partner answers in Japanese.

1. What is the date today?

2. What subjects do you have today?

3. What is your next class?

4. Who is your math teacher? How is that teacher?

5. What kind of teacher is your English teacher?

6. How is your social studies teacher?

7. Where is your science classroom? Is it nearby?

8. Is your Japanese grade good?

9. I am sad because my exam yesterday was terrible.

10. I am happy because my exam the day before yesterday was very good.

11. Why are you so busy? [Give two reasons.]

12. Is there a lot of homework this week?

13. When is spring vacation?

14. What do you want to do during spring vacation?

15. What (thing) do you want now?

16. Are you sick now?

17. My dog died last week. [Respond to the comment.]

18. I have a slight stomachache. [Respond to the comment.]

19. I have a slight fever. [Respond to the comment.]

20. I have a cold. [Respond to the comment.]

21. Do you want to rest now?

22. I just took some medicine now. [Respond to the comment.]

23. Did you go to bed late last night? What time did you go to bed?

24. Did you get up early this morning? What time did you get up?

25. Is our school baseball team strong?

26. [Do じゃんけんぽん.] Who won?

27. What do you want to do this weekend?

28. What did you do during the winter vacation?

29. I have an important exam tomorrow. [Respond to the comment.]

30. Where will they have the (university name) and (university name) baseball game?

31. Let's go to a dance tonight. Where shall we meet?

32. Do you practice Japanese everyday?

33. Are you tired now?

By the end of this lesson, you will be able to communicate the information below in the given situations.

【 I-1 3 タスク 1 】

You are a customer at a watch shop. You see some watches you like in the showcase. Ask the clerk to show you those watches. The clerk asks you which two you want to see. There are two different colors. You ask for the prices. The clerk gives you the prices and comments on each watch. You decide to buy one of them.

【 I-1 3 タスク 2 】

You are a Japanese food promoter at a supermarket. You are selling *sushi* and Japanese tea. You tell the customer to try them and you try to sell the products. The customer asks for prices, comments on the food and decides to buy one of each.

【 I-1 3 タスク 3 】

Your Japanese friend is wearing a nice pair of shoes. You compliment him/her on the shoes, but your humble Japanese friend denies it. You ask where he/she bought them. Your friend describes the shop and says they were not very expensive.

【ぶんぽう：Grammar】

A. Verb TE Form

The verb TE form is an important verb form, as it is used in many ways. When the TE form is followed by ください, it is a request form which means "Please do such and such." When the TE form is followed by もいいですか, it means "May I do such and such?" and is used to ask permission. The TE form is also used to string together sequences of verbs. The TE form has many more functions. The tense of the TE form is determined by the final tense of the sentence.

Example: たべて is the TE form of たべます.

1. たべて　ください。　　　Please eat. (request)

2. たべても　いいですか。　May I eat? (permission)

3. たべて、ねました。　　　I ate and slept. (sequence)

How is the TE form derived from MASU form? Japanese verbs are divided into three groups according to the way they conjugate: Group 1 verbs, Group 2 verbs and Irregular verbs.

1. Group 1 Verbs

Group 1 verbs are identified by the verb stem ending. The verb stem is that portion of the verb which remains after dropping the -ます. If there are more than 2 *hiragana* characters remaining in the verb stem after dropping the ます, and the final sound of the verb stem is an い ending sound, the verb can usually be categorized as a Group 1 verb. To obtain the TE form, one first must group the verbs into those whose stems end in 1) み, に or び; 2) い, ち or り; 3) き; 4) ぎ and 5) し. Verb stems which end in み, に and び drop the び(ます), み(ます) and に(ます) and replace them with んで. Verb stems which end in い, ち or り change to って, き ending verb stems change to いて, ぎ ending verb stems change to いで and し ending verb stems change to して. The exception in Group 1 is いきます, which becomes いって. See the chart on page 261 for examples.

[☐ -i ます]

	MASU form	Meaning	TE form
[み]	のみます	to drink	のんで
	よみます	to read	よんで
	やすみます	to rest, be absent	やすんで
[に]	しにます	to die	しんで
[び]	あそびます*	to play*	あそんで*
[い]	あいます	to meet	あって
[ち]	かちます	to win	かって
[り]	わかります	to understand	わかって
	しります	to get to know	しって
	かえります	to return (place)	かえって
	あります	to be (inanimate)	あって
	がんばります	to do one's best	がんばって
	はしります	to run	はしって
[き]	ききます	to listen, hear	きいて
	かきます	to write	かいて
	いきます	to go	いって★
	あるきます	to walk	あるいて
[ぎ]	およぎます*	to swim*	およいで*
[し]	はなします	to talk	はなして

★ Exception

* Not introduced yet.

2. Group 2 Verbs

Group 2 verbs can be identified by a verb stem (verb without ます) which ends in an
"えsounding" *hiragana*, or a verb stem which contains only one *hiragana*. See examples below. A
few exceptions do exist. They must simply be learned as exceptions on a case by case basis.
Group 2 verb TE forms are created simply by adding て after removing the -ます.

	MASU form	Meaning	TE form
[☐ -e ます]	みえます	can be seen	みえて
	きこえます	can be heard	きこえて
	たべます	to eat	たべて
	ねます	to sleep	ねて
	まけます	to lose	まけて
[☐ ます]	みます	to see, watch	みて
	います	to be (animate)	いて
[Exceptions]	おきます	to get up	おきて

3. Irregular Verbs

Only きます, します and a noun + します verbs belong to this group. Memorize the TE form as irregular forms.

MASU form		Meaning	TE form	
	きます	to come		きて
	します	to do		して
べんきょう（を）	します	to study	べんきょう（を）	して
タイプ（を）	します	to type	タイプ（を）	して
りょこう（を）	します	to travel	りょこう（を）	して
かいもの（を）	します	to shop	かいもの（を）	して
しょくじ（を）	します	to have a meal	しょくじ（を）	して
れんしゅう（を）	します	to practice	れんしゅう（を）	して

【 アクティビティー: Activities】

A. Let's sing the TE form song!

TE Form Song *   (For Group 1 & Irregular verbs)

Oh, み, に, び
Oh, み, に, び
み, に, び to んで!

Oh, い, ち, り
Oh, い, ち, り
い, ち, り to って!

き to いて
ぎ to いで
し to して
And きて, して

Oh, み, に, び
Oh, み, に, び
Now we know our TE forms!

* Sing to the tune of <u>Oh, Christmas Tree</u>.

B. Pair or Group Game

Copy the verbs from this page onto small cards. To start the game, stack cards face down. Flip one card at a time and say the correct TE form. If you produce the correct form, the card is yours. Continue until you make a mistake. Your partner now has a chance to give the correct answer. If he/she does, your partner takes the card and continues the game. If both players are unable to give correct answers, the card is returned to the stack. The game continues until all the cards in the stack are gone. The person with more cards wins.

のみます	しにます	みます
おきます	ねます	かちます
やすみます	はなします	かきます
います	きます	かえります
あいます	よみます	たべます
いきます	わかります	します
おわります	まけます	ききます
あります	かいもの（を）します	はしります
がんばります	べんきょう（を）します	りょこう（を）します

のんで [のみます]	しんで [しにます]	みて [みます]
おきて [おきます]	ねて [ねます]	かって [かちます]
やすんで [やすみます]	はなして [はなします]	かいて [かきます]
いて [います]	きて [きます]	かえって [かえります]
あって [あいます]	よんで [よみます]	たべて [たべます]
いって [いきます]	わかって [わかります]	して [します]
おわって [おわります]	まけて [まけます]	きいて [ききます]
あって [あります]	かいもの（を）して [かいもの（を）します]	はしって [はしります]
がんばって [がんばります]	べんきょう（を）して [べんきょう（を）します]	りょこう（を）して [りょこう（を）します]

【かいわ: Dialogue 】

＜おみせで＞

ケン 　　　　: すみません。これを　みせてください。

みせのひと : これですか。はい、どうぞ。

【たんご: Vocabulary】

1. すわってください。
Please sit.
すわります [すわる]

2. たってください。
Please stand.
たちます [たつ]

3. だしてください。
Please turn in
(something).
だします [だす]

4. みせてください。
Please show me
(something).
みせます [みせる]

5. まどを　あけてください。
Please open the window.
あけます [あける]

6. ドアを　しめてください。
Please close the door.
しめます [しめる]

7. しずかに　してください。
Please be quiet.
しずかに　します [する]

8. もう　いちど　いってください。
Please say it one more time.
いいます [いう]

9. ちょっと　まってください。
Please wait a minute.
まちます [まつ]

10. (お)みせ

store

11. すみません。

Excuse me! (to get attention)

【かんじコーナー: *Kanji* Corner】

Kanji	Meaning	Readings	Examples	Stroke Order
1. 一	one	いち	一月〔いちがつ〕January	
		ひと	一つ〔ひとつ〕one (general counter)	
		*	一日〔ついたち〕1st day of the month	

一 → 一 → ▬ → 一   ¹⟍

2. 二	two	に	二月〔にがつ〕February	
		ふた	二つ〔ふたつ〕two (general counter)	
		ふつ	二日〔ふつか〕2nd day of the month	

二 → 二 → 二 → 二   ¹⟍ ²⟍

3. 三	three	さん	三月〔さんがつ〕March	
		みっ	三つ〔みっつ〕three (general counter)	
			三日〔みっか〕3rd day of the month	

三 → 三 → 三 → 三   ¹⟍ ²⟍ ³⟍

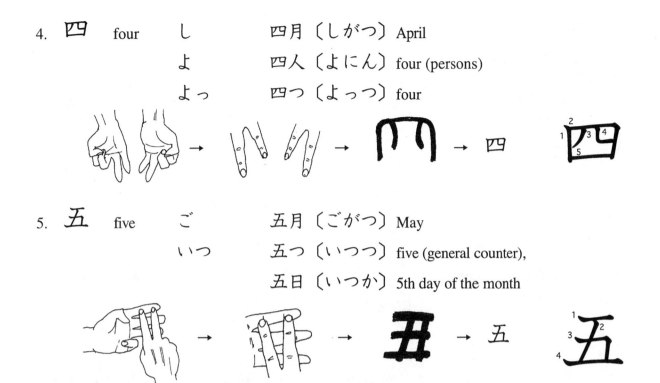

4. 四　four　　し　　　四月〔しがつ〕April

　　　　　　　よ　　　四人〔よにん〕four (persons)

　　　　　　　よっ　　四つ〔よっつ〕four

5. 五　five　　ご　　　五月〔ごがつ〕May

　　　　　　　いつ　　五つ〔いつつ〕five (general counter),

　　　　　　　　　　　五日〔いつか〕5th day of the month

【ぶんぽう : Grammar】

A. Verb TE form ＋ ください。

　The Verb TE form + extender ください is used to express a request: "Please do . . . "

1. 「ゆっくり　はなして　ください。」　　　"Please speak slowly."

　 「はい、わかりました。」　　　　　　　　"Yes, I understand."

2. 「まどを　あけて　ください。」　　　　　"Please open the window."

　 「はい、いま　あけます。」　　　　　　　"Yes, I will open it now."

3. 「すみません。この　シャツを　みせてください。」

　　　　　　　　　　　　　　　　　　　　　"Excuse me. Please show me this shirt."

　 「はい、どうぞ。」　　　　　　　　　　　"Yes, here it is."

【 ● ぶんかノート : Cultural Notes】

How different is the service at Japanese stores and U.S. stores?

　Japanese sales clerks are trained to be extremely polite and formal with their customers, not only in action but also in their language. Department stores in Japan usually hire many more clerks, thus providing more service to their customers. Every morning, customers are met at the door at opening time by a group of employees who welcome them with a greeting and a bow. In the store, elevator and escalator girls greet and guide customers. Purchases are wrapped free of charge at all sales counters. Also department stores often are equipped with playgrounds and nurseries where parents may entertain or rest with youngsters.

13か

【😊😊アクティビティー: Activities】

A. Pair Work

You are hosting a Japanese student at your school. You bring the student to your Japanese class and request him/her to do the following. The Japanese student states that he/she understands you and does as you request.

1. Please wait here.
2. Please stand now.
3. Please introduce （しょうかいします） yourself.
4. Please write your name on the board （こくばん） in Japanese.
5. Please read your name.
6. Please sit down and observe （みます） our class.

B. Pair Work: Simon Says Game

You ask your partner to act upon your request following the rules of "Simon Says." You may use these examples or create your own.

1. Please stand.
2. Please sit down.
3. Please open the door/window/book.
4. Please close the door/window.
5. Please show me your photo/something.
6. Please take out (だします) your money/something.
7. Please say your name loudly.
8. Please write your name on the board (こくばん).
9. Please read this. (You write *kanji*/something on paper.)
10. Please look at (someone in your class). What color is his/her shirt?

C. Let's read! Read the following dates and give the English equivalent.

Ex. 一月一日 　　　（　いちがつ　ついたち　）　[　January 1st　]

1. 二月二日　　　　（　　　　　　　　　　　）　[　　　　　　　　　]

2. 三月三日　　　　（　　　　　　　　　　　）　[　　　　　　　　　]

3. 四月四日　　　　（　　　　　　　　　　　）　[　　　　　　　　　]

4. 五月五日　　　　（　　　　　　　　　　　）　[　　　　　　　　　]

【かいわ: Dialogue 】

＜おみせで＞

ケン　：ぼくは　くろい　とけいか　しろい　とけいを　かいたいです。

エミ　：わたしは　きれいな　とけいが　ほしいです。

ケン　：すみません。このとけいを　みても　いいですか。

みせのひと：はい、どうぞ。

【ぶんけい: Sentence Structure 】

Noun 1 か　Noun 2	Noun 1 or Noun 2
* Question 1 。　（それとも）　Question 2 。	Question 1. Or Question 2.
Verb (TE form) も　いいですか。	May I do ～? [Asking for permission.]
はい、どうぞ。	Yes, please.
いいえ、だめです。	No, it is not all right.
* Noun 1 も　Noun 2 も　すきです。	I like both Noun 1 and Noun 2.
* Noun 1 も　Noun 2 も　すきではありません。	I don't like either Noun 1 or Noun 2.

【たんご: Vocabulary】

1. シャツ
shirt

2. ジャケット
jacket

3. パンツ
pants
[ズボン is used by the older generation.]

4. くつ
shoes

5. とけい
watch, clock

6. スーパー
supermarket

7. ほんや
bookstore

8. はなや
flower shop

9. すしや
sushi shop/bar

10. きっさてん
coffee shop

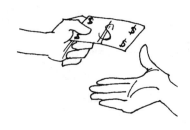

11. かいます[かう/かって]
to buy

【＊オプショナルたんご: Optional Vocabulary】
1.＊コンビニ　　　　　　　　　　　　convenience store

【ぶんぽう: Grammar】

A. Noun 1 か Noun 2	Noun 1 or Noun 2

か is used between two or more nouns. か is <u>not</u> used to conjoin adjectives, verbs or adverbs!

Compare:

＊ Question 1。（それとも）Question 2 。　　Question 1. Or Question 2.

それとも is used to start a new sentence.

1. ジュース<u>か</u>　おみずを　のみます。　　　I will drink juice or water.

2. しろ<u>か</u>　みどりの　くつを　かいます。　　I will buy white or green shoes.

3. スーパーで　かいましょうか。<u>それとも</u>、はなやで　かいましょうか。
Shall we buy it at a supermarket or at a flower shop?

13か

B. Verb (TE form) も　いいですか。　　　May I do such and such?

This structure is used when asking for permission. When granting permission, respond with はい、どうぞ。
When denying permission, say いいえ、だめです。　(いいえ、だめです is a strong response, and should only
be used toward inferiors.)

1. トイレヘ　いっても　いいですか。　　　May I go to the restroom?
2. おみずを　のんでも　いいですか。　　　May I drink (some) water?

C. Summary

い Adjective + X + Noun	あかい　シャツ	red shirt
な Adjective + な + Noun	きれいな　シャツ	pretty shirt
Noun　　+ の + Noun	あかと　しろの　シャツ	red and white shirt

【 ● ぶんかノート: Cultural Notes】

1. What is a きっさてん?

きっさてん is translated into English as "coffee shop" or more accurately, "cafe." The
きっさてん in Japan serves not only as a place to get a cup of coffee, but is a place where one can sit
at leisure to visit with friends, talk business, read, study, or simply rest after a long day of shopping.
There are specialty きっさてん, such as those where only certain types of music (jazz, rock,
classical, etc.) are played. Other cafes are equipped with video games and reading material. One is
never rushed out of a きっさてん and service is good. Though the coffee at きっさてん is
expensive, you are actually paying for the time you spend there. At most きっさてん, you pay for
each cup of coffee you order. Few establishments have a policy of "free refills."

2. パンツ or ズボン?

As is the case with most modern languages, the Japanese language constantly experiences language
shifts, especially in vocabulary. An example is the Japanese word for "trousers" which the older
generation prefers to refer to as ズボン (or ずぼん). The younger generation prefers to use the
word パンツ. This causes a resistance from the older generation, which uses the word パンツ to
refer to underwear. These days, the younger generation uses the words パンティー or ショーツ
for women's underwear and ブリーフ or トランクス for men's undershorts.

【 アクティビティー: Activities】

A. Pair Work

Interview your partner and find out what kind of items he/she wants to buy. Your partner describes
two possible choices of colors he/she would like to buy. Write them down on the chart below.

Ex. Person A: 「どんな　シャツ を　かいたいですか。」
　　Person B: 「そうですねえ... しろ か あか の シャツ を　かいたいです。」
　　Person A: 「そうですか。」

１３か

Purchase	Color
1. シャツ	or
2. ジャケット	or
3. くつ	or
4. パンツ	or
5. とけい	or
6. くるま	or
7. うち	or

B. Pair Work

Your partner wants to do the following things. You are very accommodating and suggest a place where he/she can buy or get what he/she wants. You will accompany him/her to the appropriate place.

Ex.　Person A:　「おすしを　たべたいです。」

　　　Person B:　「じゃ、こんばん　すしやへ　いきましょう。」

　　　Person A:　「いいですねえ。」

1. Wants to buy books
2. Wants to buy milk
3. Wants to drink some good coffee
4. Wants to buy a shirt
5. Wants to buy flowers

C. Pair Work

Your partner is a teacher today. Ask for permission from your teacher to do the following things.

Ex.　せいと　：「トイレへ　いっても　いいですか。」

　　　せんせい：「はい、どうぞ。　or　いいえ、だめです」

1. Go to the locker
2. Drink water
3. Open the windows
4. Turn in today's homework tomorrow

【かいわ: Dialogue 】

ケン：あの　きいろい　シャツは　いくらですか。

エミ：どれですか。

ケン：あの　きいろいのですよ。

エミ：あれは　２８ドル５０セントですよ。

ケン：そうですか。

【ぶんけい: Sentence Structure 】

| きいろいの | yellow one |
| しずか(な)の | quiet one |

【たんご: Vocabulary】

	1. $	2. ¢	3. ¥ (symbol for yen)	4. 100	5. 1,000	6. 10,000
1	いちドル	いっセント	いちえん	ひゃく	＊せん	いちまん
2	にドル	にセント	にえん	にひゃく	にせん	にまん
3	さんドル	さんセント	さんえん	さんびゃく	さんぜん	さんまん
4	よんドル	よんセント	よえん	よんひゃく	よんせん	よんまん
5	ごドル	ごセント	ごえん	ごひゃく	ごせん	ごまん
6	ろくドル	ろくセント	ろくえん	ろっぴゃく	ろくせん	ろくまん
7	ななドル	ななセント	ななえん	ななひゃく	ななせん	ななまん
8	はちドル	はっセント	はちえん	はっぴゃく	はっせん	はちまん
9	きゅうドル	きゅうセント	きゅうえん	きゅうひゃく	きゅうせん	きゅうまん
10	じゅうドル	じっセント じゅっセント	じゅうえん			じゅうまん
?	なんドル	なんセント	なんえん	なんびゃく	なんぜん	なんまん

＊ Usually one says simply せん. いっせん is not usually used.

273

13か

7. (お)いくら　　8. 〜くらい/ぐらい　　9. どれ　　　　　10. どの〜

How much?　　　　　　about 〜　　　　Which one?　　　　　　　Which 〜?

[cost]　　　　　[not used for time]　　(of more than 2)

11. じゅうまん　　　　　100,000 (hundred thousand)
12. ひゃくまん　　　　　1,000,000 (one million)

【*オプショナルたんご: Optional Vocabulary】　　【*オプショナルかんじ: Optional *Kanji*】

1.*ただ　　　　　　　is free (no charge)　　　1. 円　　yen　　えん

【ぶんぽう: Grammar】

A. い Adjective 　　　　　＋の
な Adjective ＋ な ＋ の
の is a noun that means "one," i.e., tall one, good one. In this case, の is not a particle.

1. おおきい<u>の</u>を　ください。　　　　　　Please give me a big one.
2. きれいな<u>の</u>を　ください。　　　　　　Please give me a clean one.

B. Summary

こ一	そ一	あ一	ど一
ここ　here	そこ　there	あそこ　over there	どこ　where?
これ　this one	それ　that one	あれ　that one over there	どれ　which one?
この〜　this 〜	その〜　that 〜	あの〜　that 〜 over there	どの〜　which 〜 ?

【 ● ぶんかノート: Cultural Notes】

Japanese Currency

Japanese currency consists of coins: one yen, five yen, ten yen, fifty yen, a hundred yen and five hundred yen. Unlike the U.S., Japan does not have units of 25. Bills are available in 1,000 yen, 5,000 yen and 10,000 yen denominations. The value of the currency is clearly indicated on the coin or bill. Also, coins and bills graduate in size from small to large according to their value. Japanese bills are difficult to counterfeit. If one holds a Japanese bill to the light, one is able to see an image in the blank portion of the face of the bill. Although Japanese now own credit cards and occasionally use checks, most Japanese still engage primarily in cash transactions. Therefore, it is not uncommon to see Japanese carrying rolls of cash in their pockets. The symbol ￥ is used to indicate yen. It appears before the numerical amount. Japanese also use the *kanji* 円, but it is used after the number, or after numbers which are written in *kanji*. Compare: ￥500 and 五百円.

￥1	￥5	￥10	￥50	￥100	￥500
いちえん	ごえん	じゅうえん	ごじゅうえん	ひゃくえん	ごひゃくえん

いちまんえん

Persons featured on Japanese Currency:

福沢諭吉〔ふくざわゆきち〕 1835—1901

Fukuzawa Yukichi, a famed educator and writer of the Meiji Period, is regarded as one of the major forces who introduced Western thought to Japan in the late 1800's and early 1900's. He is best remembered as the founder of the Keio Gijuku University, now known as Keio University, one of the top private universities in Japan. Born to a low-ranking samurai family in Osaka, Fukuzawa was fascinated by the West and studied Dutch and English. He eventually traveled to the U.S. and Europe as part of the first official missions to the Western world. Profoundly influenced by Western thought, Fukuzawa's prolific works cover a range of subjects from philosophy to women's rights.

13か

ごせんえん

にせんえん

せんえん

ぎんこう bank

新渡戸稲造〔にとべいなぞう〕 1862—1933

Born and raised in Hokkaido, Nitobe Inazou graduated from Sapporo Agricultural College, which later became Hokkaido University. He became a Christian and entered Tokyo University where he continued his study of English literature and economics. He then spent a total of six years in the U.S. and Germany and authored several works in English, German and Japanese. His most famous work is *Bushido: The Soul of Japan*. During his lifetime, *Nitobe* was also a college professor and international diplomat who was widely recognized in Japan and the West. He was married to an American.

紫式部〔むらさきしきぶ〕 978—1014

In the summer of 2000, a new 2000 yen note was issued by the Japanese government to mark the start of the new millenium. The design on the of the new bill features the Shurei no Mon, a historical landmark in Okinawa. The issuance of the bill coincided with a Summit Meeting of the leaders of eight major world powers held in July, 2000 in the city of Nago in Okimawa. On the reverse side of the bill is a depiction of a portion of the world's oldest known novel, the *Genji Monogatari* (Tales of *Genji*) written on a scroll. Alongside of this famous piece of literature is an illustration of its authoress, Murasaki Shikibu. In order to prevent counterfeiting, it is said that the most high-tech form of printing is being used to produce the bills.

夏目漱石〔なつめそうせき〕 1867—1916

Natsume Soseki is one of the most famous modern writers to emerge from Japan's literary world. He suffered through a tragic childhood, but successfully completed his education at Tokyo University where he studied English literature. He was a teacher at schools in Shikoku and Kyushu for about six years, and then traveled to England to further his studies. Upon his return, Natsume became a lecturer at Tokyo University. His writings include poetry, novels and short stories. Many of his works draw from his experiences as a child and young man. Among his most beloved is his earliest novel, *I Am a Cat*, a satire on human society told from the viewpoint of a cat. Numerous works which gained worldwide recognition followed. Although often written as humorous pieces, many of his works were critical of modern society and individualism.

【アクティビティー: Activities】

A. | Pair Work |

Ask about the price of your partner's shoes, bag, shirt, pants, watch, cap/hat, pencil, eraser, etc.
Ask for prices in dollars and yen. Write your partner's answers below. Use the exchange rate of
$1.00 = 100 yen as a guide.

Ex. You:　そのくつは　いくらでしたか。
　　Partner:　５０ドルぐらいでした。
　　You:　　５０ドルは　えんで　いくらですか。
　　Partner:　５せんえんです。

1. くつ	$	¥	5. とけい	$	¥
2. バッグ	$	¥	6. ぼうし	$	¥
3. シャツ	$	¥	7. えんぴつ	$	¥
4. パンツ	$	¥	8. けしゴム	$	¥

B. | Pair Work:　Communication |

Price each item pictured below. Randomly ask your partner for his/her prices for each item and write
them down. Compare your prices to check whether your communication was correct.

Ex. 「 きいろい　シャツ or きいろいの は　いくらですか。」
　　　「 あおと　しろの　シャツ or あおと　しろの は　いくらですか。」
　　　「 しずかな　いぬ or しずかなの は　いくらですか。」

	YELLOW	BLUE + WHITE	RED	BLACK + WHITE
My price				
Partner's price				

	new	old	quiet	noisy
My price				
Partner's price				

【かいわ: Dialogue 】

みせのひと：このチョコレートは　いかがですか。
とても　おいしいですよ。それに、やすいです。
エミ：いくらですか。
みせのひと：３ドルです。
エミ：わあ、やすいですねえ。ひとつ　ください。

【たんご: Vocabulary】

1. たかい [いAdj.]
is expensive

2. やすい [いAdj.]
is cheap

3. おいしい [いAdj.]
is delicious

4. まずい [いAdj.]
is unappetizing

5. すごい [いAdj.]
is terrific, terrible
Describes something extreme.

6. すばらしい [いAdj.]
is wonderful

7. 〜は　いかがですか。
How about 〜?
Polite equivalent of どうですか.

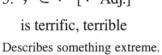

8. わあ！
Wow!

【 ● ぶんかノート: Cultural Notes】

Japanese do not accept praise or compliments easily.

Japanese will almost always deny compliments and will often even add a disparaging remark after denying the compliment.

    Example.   A: What a pretty sweater!

                  B: Oh no! It is quite old and the color does not suit me well.

This occurs not only with compliments about one's possessions, but also about one's self and persons belonging to one's in-group, deeds one has done, or decisions one has made.

【 アクティビティー: Activities】

A. Pair Work

You praise something your partner wears or has, such as his/her accessories, clothing, etc. Your partner is very humble and denies it. You are curious and ask where he/she bought the items. Your partner responds with information such as the store where he/she bought it, the price, etc.

Ex. Person A: Bさんの　とけいは　すばらしいですねえ。

     Person B: どうも　ありがとう。でも、やすかったです。

     Person A: どこで　かいましたか。

     Person B: (Place) で　かいました。(Price)ドルでした。

     Person A: そうですか。

１３か

B. Pair Work

You are a salesperson and want to sell the following items to a customer. Describe each item and try to sell them as expensively as possible. Your partner is a customer and wants to bargain.

Ex. みせのひと (Clerk) ：このチョコレートは　いかがですか。

　　　　　　　　　　　　　とても　おいしいですよ。それに、やすいです。

きゃく (Customer) ：いくらですか。

みせのひと(Clerk) ：２ドルです。

きゃく (Customer) ：それは　たかいですねえ。

みせのひと(Clerk) ：じゃ、１ドル４５セントです。

きゃく (Customer) ：いいです。　ひとつ　ください。

Ex. 　　1. 　　2. 　　3.

4. 　　5. 　　6. 　　7.

 Find the answers by investigating books, by talking to friends, or by using the Internet.

Despite the common belief that the Japanese are incredibly wealthy, most of the country's wealth is concentrated in corporations and a few families. The average Japanese is no richer than the average American. In fact, they face higher costs for everyday goods than most people in the U.S.

1. How much does an adult movie ticket cost in Japan?

2. How much does a music CD cost in Japan?

3. What is the average cost of your family's phone bill?

4. What is the average cost of a phone in Japan?

5. What is the average cost of gasoline where you live?

6. What is the average cost of gasoline in Japan?

7. How much does it cost to get a driver's license where you live?

8. How much does it cost to get a a driver's license in Japan? Circle.
   A. Free   B. Same as in America   C. $100   D. $500   E. $1,000

13 か

おしまい

THE END

This lesson is a traditional folktale. It is written in traditional Japanese storybook form. That is, the story begins from the opposite end of the book (p. 287), the lines in the story are written vertically, and the story is to be read right to left. Go to p. 287 to begin the story.

「おやまあ！
ねずみさんたち
でしたか。」
「おじいさん、
こんにちは。
おむすびを
ありがとう。
こんどは
ぼくたちが
おもちを
つくります。」

14.

ねずみたちは　もちつきを
はじめました。
「ねずみの　もちつき
たんたん　ぺったん
たんたん　ぺったん
たん　ぺたん

やれやれ　ぺたぺた
たんたん　ぺたん
たんたん　ぺたん
たん　ぺたん
もう　ひとつ　ぺたぺた
たんたん　ぺたん
たんたん　ぺたん
たん　ぺたん」

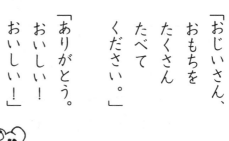

15.

「おじいさん、
おもちを
たくさん
たべて
ください。」
「ありがとう。
おいしい！
おいしい！」

16.

おじいさんは
おもちを
たくさん
たべて、
おばあさんの
おもちを　もって、
うちへ
かえりました。

17.

13か

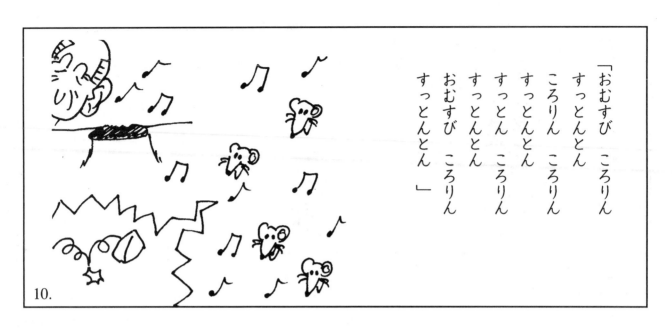

10.

「おむすび　ころりん
すっとんとん
ころりん　ころりん
すっとんとん
すっとんとん
ころりん　ころりん
すっとんとん
おむすび　ころりん
すっとんとん　」

11.

「これは
おもしろい！
これは
おもしろい！　」

12.

おじいさんは
おむすびを
ぜんぶ　おとして、
こんどは
おじいさんが
あなに　おちました。

13.

「じいさま　どっすん
どっすんすん
どっすんすん　どっすん
どっすんすん
じいさま　どっすん
どっすんすん
じいさま　どっすん
どっすんすん　」

「あっ！」
おじいさんは
おむすびを
おとしました。
おむすびは
あなに
おちました。

7.

あなから
うたが
きこえました。
「おむすび　ころりん
すっとんとん
ころりん　ころりん
すっとんとん
すっとん　ころりん
すっとんとん
おむすび　ころりん
すっとんとん」
うつくしい
こえでした。

8.

「これは
おもしろい！
これは
おもしろい！」
おじいさんは
また
おむすびを
ひとつ
おとしました。

9.

2.
おばあさんは
おむすびを
つくって、
おじいさんは
それを
やまで
たべました。

1.
むかし　むかし
おじいさんと
おばあさんが
いました。

4.
きょうも
おじいさんは
やまへ
いきました。

3.
「おじいさん、きょうの
おむすびですよ。
いってらっしゃい。」

「おばあさん、
ありがとう。
いってきます。」

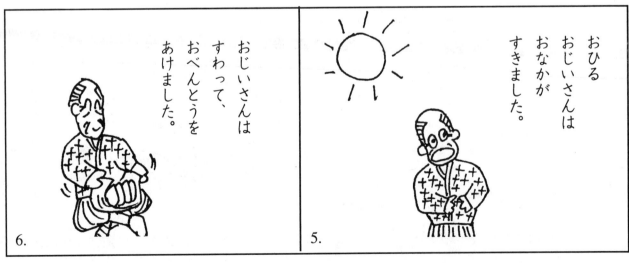

6.
おじいさんは
すわって、
おべんとうを
あけました。

5.
おひる
おじいさんは
おなかが
すきました。

FUN CORNER 9:

日本むかしばなし Japanese Folk Tale
おむすびころりん Rolling Musubi

イラスト：マークベイリー

287

13か

【たんご: Vocabulary】

1. むかし むかし　　　　　once upon a time

2. つくって　　　　　to make [TE form of つくります]

3. いってらっしゃい。　　　[Used by a family member who sends off another family member for the day.]

4. いってきます。　　　　[Used by a family member who leaves home for the day.]

5. おなかが　すきました。　I am hungry. [lit. My stomach got empty.]

6. あっ！　　　　　[expression of surprise]

7. おとしました　　　　dropped [TE form is おとして]

8. あな　　　　　a hole

9. おちました　　　　(something) fell down [TE form is おちて]

10. ころりん　　　　[Onomatopoetic expression for something rolling down]

11. すっとんとん　　　　[Onomatopoetic expression for something rolling down very quickly]

12. ぜんぶ　　　　　everything

13. こんど　　　　　this time

14. じいさま　　　　old man [さま is a polite form of さん]

15. どっすん　　　　[Onomatopoetic expression for something heavy falling down]

16. おや、まあ！　　　　Oh, my goodness!

17. もちつき　　　　mochi pounding

18. たんたん　　　　[Onomatopoetic expression for pounding something hard]

19. ぺったん　　　　[Onomatopoetic expression for pounding something sticky]

20. それやれ！　　　　Go for it!

21. ぺたぺた　　　　[Onomatopoetic expression for pounding something very sticky]

22. もう　ひとつ　　　　one more

23. もって　　　　　hold, carry, have (something) [TE form of もちます]

By the end of this lesson, you will be able to communicate the information below in the given situations.

【 I-１４ タスク１ 】

You are very hungry and ask your friend whether he/she has already eaten lunch. Your partner already had lunch, but is thirsty. You decide to go to the cafeteria together. You start to eat and complain about cafeteria food in general. Your friend is happy drinking his cold delicious juice.

【 I-１４ タスク２ 】

You want to buy lunch at a fast food restaurant. You order two hamburgers, one package of french fries and one large cola. The worker tells you the price of each item and gives you the total. The worker also asks you how many packets of ketchup you want.

【 I-１４ タスク３ 】

You are at the breakfast table with your Japanese host family in Tokyo. You have a Western-style breakfast. You start to eat after saying the traditional pre-meal Japanese expression. Your host mother offers you another cup of coffee, but you have had enough coffee and you are full. You finish your breakfast with the post-meal Japanese expression. Your host mother asks you what time you are coming home tonight. You tell her that you will go to the library and then return home at about 6:00 p.m.

【かいわ: Dialogue 】

ケン：おなかが　ペコペコです。
　　　エミさんは　もう　おひるを　たべましたか。
エミ：いいえ、まだです。
ケン：じゃ、いっしょに　たべませんか。
エミ：ええ、たべましょう。

【ぶんけい: Sentence Structure 】

もう　＋　Affirmative predicate。	already 〜
まだ　＋　Negative predicate。	(not) yet 〜
まだです。	Not yet.

【たんご: Vocabulary】

1. おなかが　すきました。
I got hungry.
おなかが　ペコペコです。
I am hungry.

おなか means "stomach" and すきました means "became empty." ペコペコ is an onomatopoetic expression suggesting emptiness. 「おなかが すいています。」also means "I am hungry."

2. のどが　かわきました。
I got thirsty.
のどが　カラカラです。
I am thirsty.

のど means "throat" and かわきました means "became dry." カラカラ is an onomatopoetic expression suggesting dryness. 「のどが かわいています。」 also means "I am thirsty."

3. もう＋Aff.

already

4. いいえ、まだです。

No, not yet.

5. じゃ、

Well then [informal]

6. では、

Well then [formal]

Kanji	Meaning	Readings	Examples		Stroke Order
1. 六	six	ろく	六月〔ろくがつ〕	June	
		むい	六日〔むいか〕	6th of the month	
		むっ	六つ〔むっつ〕	six	

2. 七	seven	しち	七月〔しちがつ〕	July	
		なな	七つ〔ななつ〕	seven	
		なの	七日〔なのか〕	7th of the month	

5+2

3. 八	eight	はち	八月〔はちがつ〕	August	
		よう	八日〔ようか〕	8th of the month	
		やっ	八つ〔やっつ〕	eight	

4. 九	nine	く	九月〔くがつ〕	September	
		きゅう	九人〔きゅうにん〕	nine (persons)	
		ここの	九つ〔ここのつ〕	nine	
			九日〔ここのか〕	9th of the month	

14か

5. 十　ten　　じゅう　　十月〔じゅうがつ〕October
　　　　　　　とお　　　十〔とお〕ten,　十日〔とおか〕10th of the month

5+5

【ぶんぽう: Grammar】

> A. もう ＋ Affirmative predicate。　　　already
> まだです。　　　　　　　　　　　not yet
>
> When used with an affirmative predicate, もう means "already." A simple negative response to a もう question is まだです.

1. 「もう　おひるごはんを　たべましたか。」　"Did you already eat lunch?"
　「いいえ、まだです。」　　　　　　　　"No, not yet."

2. 「もう　しゅくだいを　だしましたか。」　"Did you already turn in your homework?"
　「いいえ、まだです。」　　　　　　　　"No, not yet."

【 ● ぶんかノート: Cultural Notes】

Fast Food in Japan

Because of the increasingly fast pace of life, fast food is very popular in Japan, especially among young people. Chains such as McDonald's and Kentucky Fried Chicken abound in urban areas and can be found even in remote towns throughout Japan. Other "native" fast food chains, which are designed and operated like their U.S. counterparts, are also very popular. The concept of "fast food, however," has long been a part of Japanese eating habits. Noodle shops near stations are always crowded with men who literally drop in, gobble up a bowl of noodles while standing, and rush off in several minutes. "*Obentoo* (boxed lunches)" bought at stores can also be considered one of the earliest forms of fast food.

【アクティビティー: Activities】

A. Pair Work

Ask your partner whether he/she has already done the following things.

Ex. Question:　　もう　おひるごはんを　たべましたか。
　Yes Answer: はい、もう　たべました。
　No Answers: いいえ、まだです。

1. Eaten lunch	
2. Seen a (movie title)	
3. Read a (book title)	
4. Read today's newspaper	
5. Listened to (CD title)	
6. Traveled to Japan	
7. Finished (project title)	

B. Pair Work

Make the comments given as cues below. Your partner responds with an appropriate suggestion.

Ex. I am hungry.　　You:　　おなかが　すきました。

　　　　　　　　　Partner:　じゃ、おひるごはんを　たべましょうか。

　　　　　　　　　You:　　はい、そう　しましょう。

1. I am thirsty.	
2. I have a headache.	
3. I am tired.	
4. I have lots of homework.	
5. I have a big exam tomorrow.	

C. Let's read!　　Read the dates and provide their English equivalents.

　　Ex. 五月六日　　　　　　（　　ごがつ　むいか　）　　[　May 6th　]
　　1. 八月十日　　　　　　（　　　　　　　　　　）　　[　　　　　]
　　2. 九月四日　　　　　　（　　　　　　　　　　）　　[　　　　　]
　　3. 七月八日　　　　　　（　　　　　　　　　　）　　[　　　　　]
　　4. 十月五日　　　　　　（　　　　　　　　　　）　　[　　　　　]
　　5. 十二月二十五日　　　（　　　　　　　　　　）　　[　　　　　]
　　6. 四月十九日　　　　　（　　　　　　　　　　）　　[　　　　　]
　　7. 十一月三十日　　　　（　　　　　　　　　　）　　[　　　　　]
　　8. 六月七日　　　　　　（　　　　　　　　　　）　　[　　　　　]

14か

【かいわ: Dialogue 】

ケン：ピザを　ふたつと　コーラを　ください。

みせのひと：サイズは　S(エス)と　M(エム)と　L(エル)が　あります。

ケン：M(エム)を　ください。

みせのひと：ピザは　３ドルで、コーラは　７５セントです。

ぜんぶで　３ドル７５セントです。

【ぶんけい: Sentence structure 】

| Noun 1 | は | Noun 2 / な Adjective | で | Sentence 2 。 |

ピザ　は　３ドル　　　　　で　　　コーラは　７５セントです。

Pizza is $3 and cola is 75 cents.

| ふたつ／ぜんぶ | で |

for two / for everything (total)

【たんご: Vocabulary】

1. ピザ

pizza

2. ハンバーガー

hamburger

3. ホットドッグ

hotdog

4. サンドイッチ

sandwich

5. サラダ

salad

6. フライドポテト

French fries

7. (お)べんとう

box lunch

8. (お)むすび
or (お)にぎり

rice ball

9. サイズ

size

10. S(エス)サイズ

small size

11. M(エム)サイズ

medium size

12. L(エル)サイズ

large size

 13. ぜんぶ

everything

 14. ぜんぶで

for all

[で is a totalizing particle.]

15. Noun 1 は   Noun 2/ な Adjective で、 Sentence 2。   Noun 1 is Noun 2/な Adj. and Sentence 2.

☆ Review: General counters are used to order foods and drinks.

1 ひとつ	2 ふたつ	3 みっつ	4 よっつ	5 いつつ
6 むっつ	7 ななつ	8 やっつ	9 ここのつ	10 とお

【*オプショナルたんご: Optional Vocabulary】

1.*ラーメン

Chinese noodles in soup

2.*うどん

Japanese white thick noodles in soup

3.*やきそば

Chinese fried noodles

4.*ぶたまん

Chinese steamed bun stuffed with pork

【ぶんぽう: Grammar】

A. Noun 1 は   Noun 2 / な Adjective で、 Sentence 2。

＝Noun1 は   Noun 2 / な Adjective です。そして、 Sentence 2。

で is the TE form of です and conjoins two sentences. It only can be used when the first sentence ends with a noun or な adjective, but never with a sentence ending with an い adjective or verb.

14か

1. あには　だいがくせい<u>で</u>、いま　サンフランシスコに　います。
    My older brother is a college student and is now in San Francisco.

2. いもうとは　しょうがくせい<u>で</u>、ねこが　だいすきです。
    My younger sister is an elementary school student and loves cats.

3. ははは　テニスが　すき<u>で</u>、ちちは　ゴルフが　すきです。
    My mother likes tennis and my dad likes golf.

4. この　レストランは　きれい<u>で</u>　しずかですね。
    This restaurant is clean and quiet, isn't it?

B. Counter＋で

で totalizes the quantity word it follows and may be translated as "for."

---

1. この　シャツは　２まい<u>で</u>　３０ドルです。　　This shirt is $30 for two.

2. 「いくらですか。」　　　　　　　　　　　　"How much is it?"
   「ぜんぶ<u>で</u>　４ドル　５０セントです。」　　"It is $4.50 for all."

【 ● ぶんかノート: Cultural Notes】

1. What is a typical lunch for Japanese people?

Lunch in Japan varies widely. Lunch may mean eating *(o)bentoo* (home lunches). *(O)bentoo* often consist of rice or riceballs, pickles, cooked vegetables and some form of protein. Lunch may also mean eating at a company or school cafeteria that offers full hot meals and hot noodles. More and more, young Japanese enjoy fast food meals such as hamburgers and pizzas for lunch. Some people return home for lunch. Others may go out to a relaxing lunch at a restaurant. One can find almost any kind of food in the urban areas of Japan. Besides Japanese foods, Chinese, Italian and American foods are popular.

2. U.S. "medium" size equals Japanese "large."

Japanese people are in general smaller than Americans. Thus the size of drinks and clothing are smaller, too. When Japanese people order drinks at fast food stores in the U.S., they often are surprised that they are so large.

【🙂🙂アクティビティー: Activities】

A. Pair Work

First, determine prices for the items below with your partner. Play the role of a customer at a snack bar. Your partner plays a snack bar worker. You order lunch, a snack and a drink. Your partner tells you the price of each item, then gives you the total cost.

メニュー

たべもの		スナック		のみもの	
ピザ	$_____	ポテトチップ	$_____	ミルク	$_____
ハンバーガー	$_____	コーンチップ	$_____	オレンジジュース	$_____
ホットドッグ	$_____	プレッツル	$_____	コーラ	
サンドイッチ	$_____	ケーキ	$_____	ソーダ	
フライドポテト	$_____	ジェロ	$_____	アイスティー	
サラダ	$_____	アイスクリーム	$_____	L	$_____
フルーツサラダ	$_____	チョコレート	$_____	M	$_____
べんとう	$_____	キャンディ	$_____	S	$_____
むすび	$_____	ガム	$_____		

Ex. 2 sandwiches, 1 large cola

Customer: 「サンドイッチを　ふたつと　L（エル）サイズの　コーラを
　　　　　　ひとつ　ください。」

Worker: 「サンドイッチは　ふたつで　$_____で、
　　　　　L（エル）サイズの　コーラは　ひとつ（で）　$_____です。
　　　　　ぜんぶで　$_____です。」

Order the following:

1. 2 slices of pizza, 1 pkg. potato chips, 1 large size cola

2. 1 hotdog, 1 order of French fries, 1 medium soda

3. 1 salad, 2 riceballs, 1 orange juice

4. 1 *bentoo*, 1 jello, 1 small iced tea

5. (Your own choice)

14か

【かいわ: Dialogue 】

ケン：あっ、フォークを　わすれました。

エミさんも　フォークが　いりますか。

エミ：いいえ、けっこうです。

わたしは　おはしで　たべます。

でも、おみずを　いっぱい　おねがいします。

【たんご: Vocabulary】

1. cupful, glassful, bowlful, spoonful	

1	いっぱい
2	にはい
3	さんばい
4	よんはい
5	ごはい
6	ろっぱい
7	ななはい
8	はっぱい
9	きゅうはい
10	じ(ゅ)っぱい
?	なんばい

 2.(お)はし
chopsticks

 3. フォーク
fork

 4. スプーン
spoon

 5. ナイフ
knife

 6. ストロー
straw

 7.(お)さら
a plate, a dish

 8. コップ
cup

 9. ナプキン
napkin

 10. フォークで
with a fork

 11. いいえ、けっこうです。
No, thank you.

12. わすれました
[わすれる/わすれて]
I forgot.

13. 〜が いります
[いる/いって]
need 〜

14. 〜を かしてください。
[かします/かす]
Please lend me 〜.

【*オプショナルたんご: Optional Vocabulary】

1.*(お)さとう	sugar
2.*しお	salt
3.*こしょう	pepper
4.*ケチャップ	ketchup
5.*ドレッシング	dressing

【ぶんぽう: Grammar】

A. Means＋で

This particle で is the same で used after "means of transportation," a particle you learned in an earlier lesson.
It tells <u>how</u>, or the means by which an action is done.

1. この しゅくだいを えんぴつ<u>で</u> かきました。
I wrote this homework with a pencil.

2. 「はし<u>で</u> たべますか。」 "Do you eat with chopsticks?"
「いいえ、フォーク<u>で</u> たべます。」 "No, I eat with a fork."

14か

【 ● ぶんかノート: Cultural Notes】

How to hold chopsticks (はし)

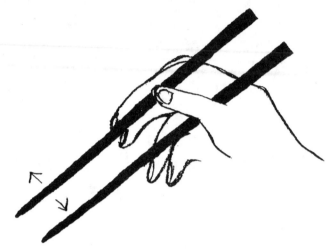

Hold the chopsticks slightly toward the thick end as shown
above. Keeping the lower chopstick steady, move the upper
one with a scissor-like action and pinch the food between the tip
of the upper chopstick and the tip of the lower one.

【 アクティビティー: Activities】

A. Pair Work

Ask your partner how he/she does the following things.

Ex. eat rice.　　You:　　ごはんを　なんで　たべますか。

Partner:　おはしで　たべます。

1. Eat spaghetti （スパゲッティ）	
2. Eat steak （ステーキ）	
3. Eat *obentoo*	
4. Eat stew （シチュー）	
5. Drink milk	
6. Eat *musubi*	
7. Eat salad	

B. Pair Work

You offer the following foods or drinks to your partner. Your partner accepts or declines.

Ex. one rice ball.　You:　「おむすびを　ひとつ　どうぞ。」

Partner:　「どうも　ありがとう。or いいえ、けっこうです。」

1. One cup of tea	
2. One piece of *sushi*	
3. One cup of hot coffee	
4. One piece of chocolate	
5. One sandwich	

C. Pair Work

Make the following comments. Your partner responds appropriately with a helpful suggestion.

Ex. I forgot my money.　You:　「あっ、おかねを　わすれました。」

Partner:　「そうですか。おかねが　いりますか。」

1. I forgot my money.	
2. Please lend me money.	
3. I need a car.	
4. Oh, I forgot my homework.	
5. Please lend me a pencil.	

D. Class Work - Chopstick Race

Bring chopsticks and dry beans to class. See how many beans each person can pick up with chopsticks in one minute.

14か

【かいわ: Dialogue 】

ケン：いただきます。

　　　この　ピザは　つめたくて、あまり　おいしくないです。

エミ：この　おべんとうは　あたたかくて、おいしいですよ。

ケン：ああ、おなかが　いっぱいです。

　　　ごちそうさま。

【ぶんけい: Sentence Structure 】

| Noun 1 | は | いAdj. (-くて) | 、 | Sentence 2 | 。 |

しけんは　ながくて、　　　　むずかしいです。　　The exam is long <u>and</u> difficult.

【たんご: Vocabulary】

1. つめたい [いAdj.]

is cold (to the touch)

2. あたたかい [いAdj.]

is warm

3. もう　（いっぱい）

(one) more (cup)

4. いただきます。

Used before beginning a meal.
Literally means "I will receive."

5. ごちそうさま。

Used upon finishing a meal.
Literally means "It was a feast."

6. おなかが　いっぱいです。

I am full.

Literally means "The stomach is full."

【ぶんぽう: Grammar】

A. い Adjective ＋ くて、 Sentence2。

When conjoining a sentence ending with an い adjective with another sentence, the final -い of the adjective of the first sentence is dropped, replaced by -くて and attached to the next sentence. The tense of the entire sentence is determined by the tense of the sentence ending. The TE form of いい is よくて.

1. にほんごの　じゅぎょうは　おもしろくて、たのしいです。

    Japanese class is interesting and fun.

2. カフェテリアの　たべものは　すこし　まずくて、たかいですね。

    The cafeteria's food is a little unappetizing and expensive, isn't it?

3. きのうの　しけんは　ながくて、むずかしかったです。

    Yesterday's exam was long and difficult.

4. あの　せんせいは　やさしくて、いいです。

    That teacher is kind and (she is) good.

【● ぶんかノート: Cultural Notes】

1. Eating Japanese Noodles

The many varieties of noodles in Japan make them a popular dish. Though noodles are also served fried, most noodles are prepared in soup. When eating noodles, Japanese will often noisily slurp them down. Although Americans consider this bad manners, this behavior is accepted, and even expected, in Japan. Americans who do not slurp are perceived by Japanese as not enjoying the noodles.

2. いただきます and ごちそうさま

Before and after meals, one utters the appropriate いただきます and ごちそうさま expressions. Often, Japanese will also briefly place their hands together as if in prayer and slightly bow their heads as they say いただきます or ごちそうさま.

【アクティビティー: Activities】

A. Pair Work

Ask your partner for his/her opinion of the following. Your partner comments using two descriptive words in one sentence.

Ex. cafeteria food　　You:　　カフェテリアのたべものは　どうですか。

                 Partner:　おいしくて、やすいです。

1. (Famous restaurant's) food	
2. (Fast food restaurant's) food	
3. School cafeteria's spaghetti	
4. (Teacher)	
5. (Class)	
6. (School)	
7. Library	
8. (Someone's) house	
9. Japanese classroom	
10. (Friend)	

B. Pair Work

Role play the following skit with your partner. A U.S. student stays over at his/her Japanese friend's house in Japan. The Japanese student's mother makes a Japanese-style breakfast for the U.S. student and serves it on the table. The Japanese mother speaks only Japanese. Use appropriate body language.

アメリカじん：おはよう　ございます。

おかあさん　　：おはよう。よく　ねましたか。

アメリカじん：はい。 ＜Sits at a table.＞

おかあさん　　：あさごはんを　どうぞ。

アメリカじん：ありがとう　ございます。いただきます。

　　　　　　　　　＜Eats most of the food.＞

おかあさん　　：ごはんを　もう　いっぱい　いかがですか？

アメリカじん：いいえ、けっこうです。もう　おなかが　いっぱいです。
　　　　　　　　　ごちそうさま。

【かいわ: Dialogue 】

ケン : これから　なにが　ありますか。

エミ : １じから　えいごの　じゅぎょうが　あります。

ケン : ぼくは　いま　としょかんへ　いって、しゅくだいを　します。
　　　じゃ、また　あとでね。

エミ : バイバイ。

【ぶんけい: Sentence Structure 】

| Verb（TE form） | 、 | Sentence 2 | 。 |

テレビを　みて、　　ねます。　I will watch TV, and (then) go to bed.

【たんご: Vocabulary】

3. これから

From now on

4. それから

And then

1. じゃ、また　あとで。

Well then, see you later.

「では、また　あとで。」is
a formal equivalent.

2. バイバイ。

Good-bye.

Used informally only.

【ぶんぽう: Grammar】

A. Sentence 1 (Verb TE form)、 Sentence 2。

To conjoin two sentences with "and" when the first of the two sentences ends with a verb, convert the verb in the first sentence into its TE form and attach the second sentence. A sequence of actions may be described using this construction. The first sentence occurs chronologically before the second.

1. あさごはんを　たべて、しんぶんを　よみます。

I eat breakfast and read the newspaper.

2. テレビを　みて、しゅくだいを　して、それから　ねます。

I watch television, do homework and then go to bed.

3. うちへ　かえって、それから　なにを　しますか。

      You go home and then what do you do?

B. Summary

Sentence Endings	Conjoining Sentences
Noun ending	ピザは　２ドル<u>で</u>、べんとうは　５ドルです。 Pizza is $2 and bento is $5.
な Adjective ending	このみせは　きれい<u>で</u>、しずかです。 This store is clean and quiet.
い Adjective ending	この　べんとうは　<u>やすくて</u>、おいしいです。 This box lunch is cheap and delicious.
Verb ending	うちへ　<u>かえって</u>、ねました。 I went home and went to bed.

【 ● ぶんかノート: Cultural Notes】

What is しょうゆ and みそ?

Shoyu or "soy sauce" and *miso* "soy bean paste" are two distinctive Japanese seasonings. *Miso* is made by crushing boiled soybeans, adding salt and malted rice, wheat, barley or beans. The paste is allowed to mature for as long as several years to draw out its flavor. Different kinds of *miso* are produced in the different regions of Japan. *Miso* is most commonly used in the preparation of *miso* soup. *Shoyu* is the most common seasoning used in Japanese cooking. It is made from soy beans also. The soybeans are steamed and mixed with roasted wheat. The mixture is blended with brine and transferred to fermentation tanks for brewing. *Shoyu* is used as a seasoning and dipping sauce.

【アクティビティー: Activities】

A. Pair Work

Interview your partner and ask what he/she has done today since getting up in the morning.
Use 〜て、〜。

You: けさ　おきて、なにを　しましたか。
Partner: けさ　おきて、あさごはんを　たべました。
You: あさごはんを　たべて、　なにを　しましたか。
          、
          、
          、
          、
          、
          、
You: これから、なにを　しますか。
Partner: これから、〜。

307

14か

Ask your partner these questions in Japanese.
Your partner answers in Japanese.

1. Please write your birthdate in *kanji* and read it aloud.

2. [You are participating in a fund raising project.] Please buy one box of chocolate.

3. What kind of shirts do you want to buy?

4. Where do you usually eat hamburgers? [List two places.]

5. What do Japanese people do at coffee shops? [List two things.]

6. Where did you buy your shirt and pants?

7. [Use the pictures below.] How much is the (quiet or noisy) dog?

8. [Use the pictures below.] Which TV is cheap?

9. [Use the pictures below.] Which one do you want to buy?

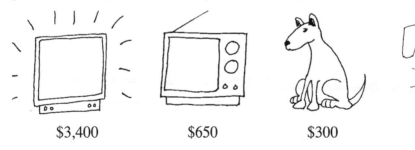

| $3,400 | $650 | $300 | $170 |

10. Compliment your partner on something he/she has.

11. How is the school cafeteria's food? [Use two descriptive words in one sentence.]

12. How is your math class? [Use two descriptive words in one sentence.]

13. Are you hungry? Are you thirsty?

14. Did you already study for tomorrow's Japanese exam?

15. What happened? Do you have a fever?

16. What sports do your father and mother like? [Answer in one sentence.]

17. Please give me two pizzas and one large size cola. [Give the total price.]

18. What do you eat *bento* with?

19. Please have one cookie.

20. Please have a cup of hot coffee.

21. Did you forget your money today?

22. Do we need our Japanese textbook today?

23. How is Japanese class? [Use two descriptive words in one sentence.]

24. How is the school library? [Use two descriptive words in one sentence.]

25. Do you like cola? Why? [Use two descriptive words in one sentence.]

26. What did you do after getting up this morning?

27. Where did you go after you came to school today?

28. What did you do last night after you ate dinner?

29. Where are the paper plates?

30. What (class) do you have after this class?

つる

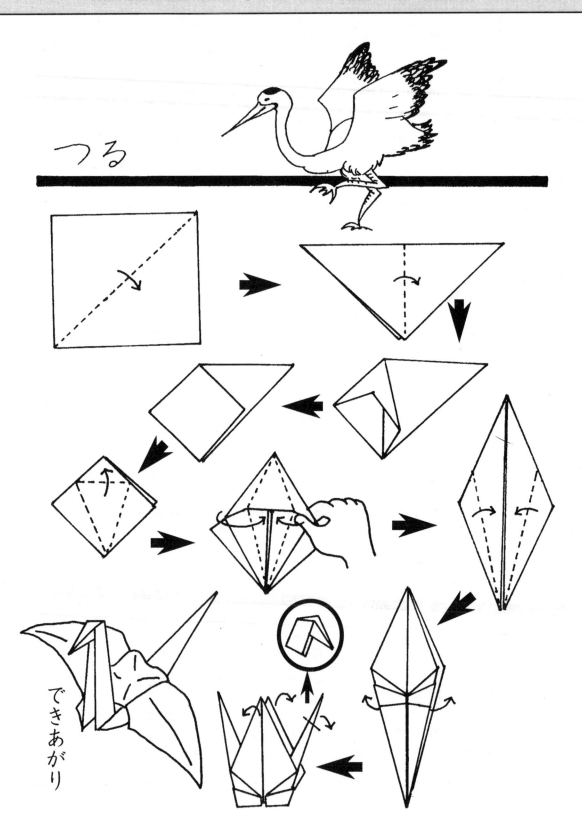

できあがり

Birthday Party

By the end of this lesson, you will be able to communicate the information below in the given situations.

【1-15 タスク1】

Today is your friend's birthday. You made a birthday cake and brought it to class. You congratulate your friend and give him/her a present. You ask how old he/she is and what year he/she was born. Your friend is happy and asks you to take a picture with his/her camera. You tell your friend to smile.

【1-15 タスク2】

Your friend received lots of presents for his/her birthday. You are curious and ask what he/she received. Your friend lists some of the presents. You also ask who some of the presents are from. Your friend tells you who gave the gifts to him/her. Your friend has lots of cake and offers one piece to you. You decline politely.

【1-15 タスク3】

Your friend invites you to a birthday party at his/her house. You ask for the date of the party, the day of the week, the time and ask how many people are coming, etc. You also ask for your friend's address and telephone number. Your friend tells you what they are planning to do at the party (playing games, singing songs, swimming in the pool, etc.) You say you are looking forward to the party.

【 おはなし：Story 】　たんじょうパーティー

　きょうは　５月１日です。ぼくの　１５さいの　たんじょう日です。
ぼくは　がっこうで　ともだちに　たくさんの　プレゼントを
もらいました。はなや　コンサートの　きっぷなど　もらいました。
エミさんは　きれいな　はなを　３ぼんと　かわいい　ふうせんを
ひとつ　くれました。ジョアンさんは　ほんを　いっさつ　くれました。
リサさんは　コンサートの　きっぷを　２まい　くれました。とても
うれしかったです。６じごろ　うちへ　かえりました。ぼくは
ははに　はなを　いっぽん　あげて、いもうとにも　いっぽん
やりました。

１５か

【かいわ: Dialogue 】

エミ　　：ケンさん、たんじょう日〔び〕　おめでとう。プレゼントを　どうぞ。

ケン　　：どうも　ありがとう。

エミ　　：みなさん、たんじょう日〔び〕の　うたを　うたいましょう。

みんな：おたんじょう日〔び〕　おめでとう

　　　　おたんじょう日〔び〕　おめでとう

　　　　おめでとう　ケンさん

　　　　おたんじょう日〔び〕　おめでとう

(Sing to the tune of "Happy Birthday.")

【たんご: Vocabulary 】

1. (お)たんじょう日〔び〕　おめでとう(ございます)。

Happy Birthday!
おめでとう（ございます）。 means "Congratulations."
Using 「ございます」 makes the greeting more formal.

2. うたいます
[うたう/うたって]
to sing

3. みんな
everyone

4. みなさん
everyone
Polite form of みんな. Often
used to address a group of people.

5. プレゼント
a present

【かんじコーナー: *Kanji* Corner 】

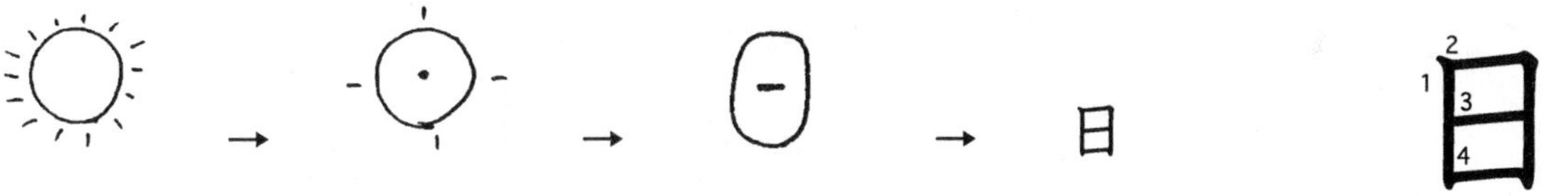

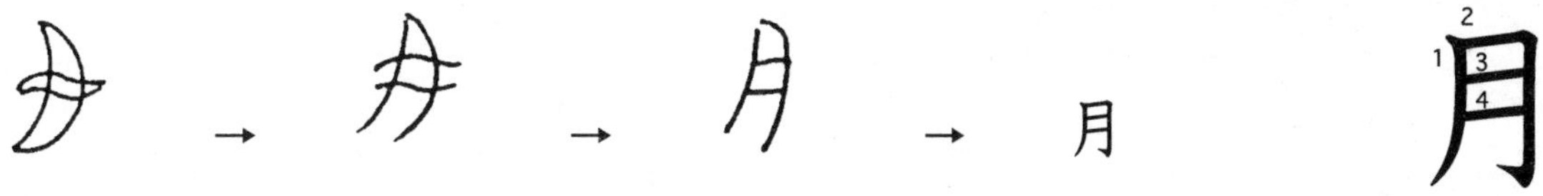

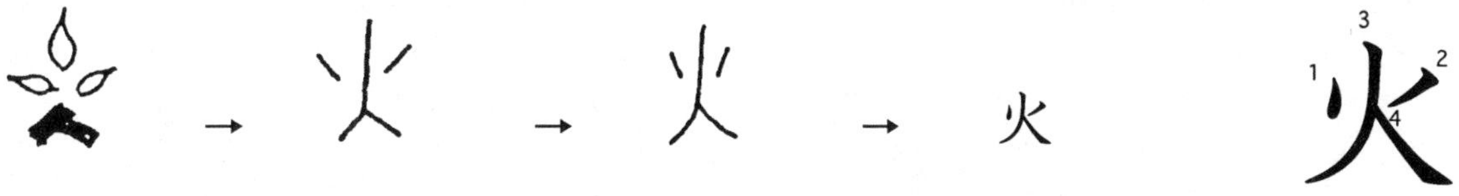

Kanji	Meaning	Readings	Examples	Stroke Order

1. 日　sun, day　にち　三十日〔さんじゅうにち〕30th of the month

日曜日〔にちようび〕Sunday

び　日曜日〔にちようび〕Sunday

か　二日〔ふつか〕2nd day of the month; 2 days

2. 月　moon, month　がつ　一月〔いちがつ〕January

げつ　月曜日〔げつようび〕Monday

今月〔こんげつ〕this month

来月〔らいげつ〕next month

先月〔せんげつ〕last month

3. 火　fire　か　火曜日〔かようび〕Tuesday

4. 水　water　みず　お水〔おみず〕water

すい　水曜日〔すいようび〕Wednesday

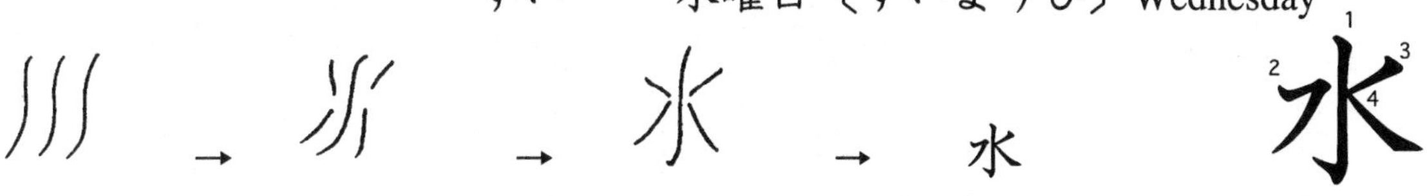

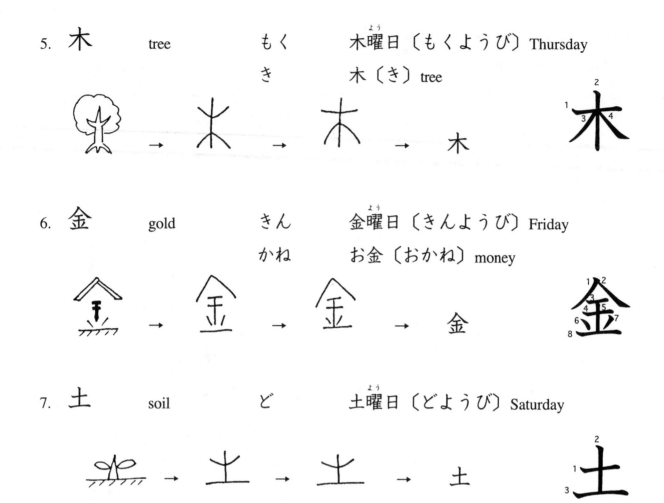

5. 木　　tree　　　　もく　　木曜日〔もくようび〕Thursday
　　　　　　　　　　　き　　　木〔き〕tree

6. 金　　gold　　　　きん　　金曜日〔きんようび〕Friday
　　　　　　　　　　　かね　　お金〔おかね〕money

7. 土　　soil　　　　ど　　　土曜日〔どようび〕Saturday

【 ● ぶんかノート: Cultural Notes】

Japanese and Parties

Japanese do not generally have parties in their own homes. When a large group gathers for a celebration, it is often at a restaurant, tea house or other public location. Parties associated with work, business and even formal family celebrations do not usually include in-laws and children. "Significant others" and friends are not included at such gatherings.

【アクティビティー: Activities】

A. Class Work

Everyone in the class gives their own birthdate in Japanese. Your classmates write the students'
names and their birthdates below. At the end, one student reads the correct answers to the entire
class.

なまえ	たんじょう日	なまえ	たんじょう日

B. Pair Work

Ask your partner when his/her birthday is, how old he/she is now and what kind of presents he/she
wants for his/her next birthday.

1. Birthdate?	
2. How old now?	
3. What kind of presents do you want?	

C. Let's read!

Ex. 十月四日　土曜日　（ じゅうがつ　よっか　どようび　　）[Oct. 4th, Saturday　　]
1. 八月十日　月曜日　（　　　　　　　　　　　　　　）[　　　　　　　　　]
2. 五月七日　水曜日　（　　　　　　　　　　　　　　）[　　　　　　　　　]
3. 九月九日　金曜日　（　　　　　　　　　　　　　　）[　　　　　　　　　]
4. 六月三日　土曜日　（　　　　　　　　　　　　　　）[　　　　　　　　　]
5. 七月一日　火曜日　（　　　　　　　　　　　　　　）[　　　　　　　　　]

317

15か

【かいわ: Dialogue 】

エミ：だれに　ふうせんを　もらいましたか。

ケン：ケリーさんに　もらいました。

エミ：かわいい　ふうせんですねえ。

【ぶんけい: Sentence Structure 】

Giver は	Receiver (Me) に	Something を	くれます。	give (me)
Giver (Outsider) は	Receiver (My family member) に	Something を	くれます。	give
Receiver は	Giver に／から	Something を	もらいます。	receive

【たんご: Vocabulary 】

1.	Bound Objects

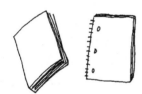

1	いっさつ
2	にさつ
3	さんさつ
4	よんさつ
5	ごさつ
6	ろくさつ
7	ななさつ
8	はっさつ
9	きゅうさつ
1 0	じ（ゅ）っさつ
？	なんさつ

2. コンサート

concert

3. きっぷ

ticket

4. ふうせん

balloon

5. くれます

[くれる/くれて]

give (to me or to my family)

6. もらいます

[もらう/もらって]

receive, get from

7. おじさん

uncle, middle-aged man

8. おばさん

aunt, middle-aged lady

9. いとこ

cousin

10. しんせき

relatives

【*オプショナルたんご: Optional Vocabulary 】

1.*カーネーション　　　　　　carnation

2.*バラ　　　　　　　　　　　rose

3.*らん or オーキッド　　　　　orchid

4.*レイ　　　　　　　　　　　lei

【ぶんぽう: Grammar 】

A. Giver は　Receiver (<u>me</u>) に　Something を　くれます。

　　Giver (<u>Outsider</u>) は　Receiver (<u>my family member</u>) に　Something を　くれます。

The Japanese system of verbs of giving and receiving reflect a society which functions on horizontal and vertical relationships. The verb one selects is dependent on the relative status of the giver and receiver, or whether the giver is an outsider or member of one's own in-group.

くれます means "to give" and is used when someone gives something to the speaker or when an outsider gives something to the speaker's family.

1. ともだちは　わたし<u>に</u>　プレゼントを　くれました。

　　　My friend gave me a present.

2. たなかさんは　いもうと<u>に</u>　コンサートの　きっぷを　くれました。

　　　Mr. Tanaka gave my younger sister concert tickets.

B. Receiver は　Giver に／から　Something を　もらいます。

もらいます means "receive, get." Note that くれます expresses an action of someone giving to the speaker or an outsider giving to the speaker's family member whereas もらいます means that someone has <u>received</u> something from someone else.

1. わたしは　おばあさん<u>に</u>　おかねを　もらいました。

　　　I received some money from my grandmother.

2. ジョンさんは　ともだち<u>から</u>　おむすびを　ひとつ　もらいました。

　　　John received one rice ball from his friend.

【 ● ぶんかノート : Cultural Notes 】

Japanese Culture of Giving

Japanese are perennial gift-givers. Gifts are given at New Year's, on children's festivals, at mid-summer, at the end of the year, at weddings, during illnesses, funerals and other significant celebrations of life. Japanese also give gifts to travelers upon their departure. In turn, travelers buy souvenir gifts for friends and relatives at home. With the introduction of Western holidays, gifts are also given at Christmas, birthdays, Valentine's and Mother's Day. A guest never goes to a Japanese home without a gift. Gifts are tokens of appreciation, which help to cement relationships. Businesses in Japan capitalize on this custom and promote the never-ending practice of exchanging gifts.

【 アクティビティー : Activities 】

A. Class Work

_____さんへ、

The teacher will give everyone a sheet like the one on the left. Write your name in the blank. The teacher will collect the papers and re-distribute them. You should receive a sheet of paper with a classmate's name on it. Draw a sketch of a present you think this classmate would like. The teacher will collect the papers and deliver them to you and your classmates. After you receive your "gift," you will try to find the person who gave you your gift. Ask your classmates. 「～さんは　わたしに　このプレゼントを　くれましたか。」 After everyone has found their senders, each student will tell the whole class what he/she has received. 「わたしは　～さんに／から　～を　もらいました。」 Make a comment about the gift.

【かいわ: Dialogue 】

ケン：おかあさんの　たんじょう日〔び〕に　なにを　あげますか。

エミ：はなや　ケーキを　あげます。

ケン：そうですか。おとうさんには？

エミ：ちちにも　はなや　ケーキを　あげます。

ケン：そうですか。やさしいですねえ。

【ぶんけい: Sentence Structure 】

Giver は　Receiver (Equal) に　Something を　あげます。　give (equal)

Giver は　Receiver (Inferior) に　Something を　やります。　give (inferior)

★ Giver は　Receiver (Me) に　Something を　くれます。　give (me)

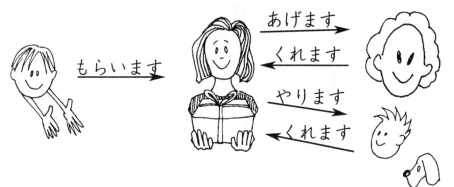

Noun 1 や　Noun 2 など　Noun 1 and Noun 2, etc.

★ Noun 1 と　Noun 2　Noun 1 and Noun 2

Place 1 へ　いきました。Place 2 へも　いきました。

I went to Place 1. I also went to Place 2.

【たんご: Vocabulary】

1. あげます
[あげる/あげて]
to give (to equal)

2. やります
[やる/やって]
to give (to inferior)

3. Noun 1 や Noun 2 （など）

Noun 1 and Noun 2, etc.

など is used with or without other particles.

4. 日 〔ひ〕

day

5. ははの日 〔ひ〕

Mother's Day

6. ちちの日 〔ひ〕

Father's Day

7. もう　すぐ

very soon

【*オプショナルたんご: Optional Vocabulary】
1.*さしあげます [さしあげる/さしあげて]　　　to give (to superior)

【ぶんぽう: Grammar】

A. Giver は　Receiver (equal) に　Something を　あげます。
　 Giver は　Receiver (inferior) に　Something を　やります。

Both あげます and やります mean "give." あげます is used when a giver gives to an equal and やります is used when a giver gives to an inferior. Whether a receiver is an equal or an inferior is determined by the status of the giver.

1. これを　あなたに　あげます。　　　　I will give this to you.

2. ははは　まいにち　いぬに　たべものを　やります。

My mother gives food to the dog everyday.

B. Noun 1 や　(Noun 1 や)　Noun 2 (など)

や is used to conjoin two or more nouns. It means "and" but suggests inclusion of other similar items besides those named. Therefore, the word など "etc." is often used in the same sentence.

*Noun 1 と　Noun 2

と "and" is also used to conjoin nouns. However, と suggests the inclusion of only those nouns mentioned.

Compare: ピザや　ホットドッグを　たべました。I ate pizza, hotdogs (and other such things).
　　　　　 ピザと　ホットドッグを　たべました。I ate pizza and hotdogs.

1. にわに　きや　はなが　たくさん　ありますねえ。
> There are many trees and flowers, etc., in the garden, aren't there?

2. としょかんで　しんぶんや　ざっしなど　(を)　よみました。
> I read newspapers, magazines and the like at the library.

3. たんじょうびに　シャツや　チョコレートなど　(を)　もらいました。
> I received a shirt and chocolates, etc., on my birthday.

C. ～にも

も means "too, also" and replaces を, が and は. も does not replace other particles such as に, へ, で, から, まで, etc., but is attached to them.

1. ははに　あげました。いもうとにも　やりました。
> I gave it to my mother. I gave it to my younger sister, too.

2. ちちは　にほんへ　いきました。ちゅうごくへも　いきました。
> My father went to Japan. He went to China, too.

3. ゆうべ　うちで　べんきょうしましたが、けさ　としょかんでも　べんきょうしました。
> I studied at home last night, but this morning I studied at the library, too.

Review: Usage of も

In general, when the particle も appears after a noun (or a noun and a particle) in a sentence, it follows a related sentence or pre-supposed sentence in which a similar noun has been named. See the example below. It is important that も follows the correct noun. When a speaker states (B), a sentence like (A) is presupposed.

1. A. ちちは　せんげつ　おおさかへ　いきました。　　Dad went to Osaka last month.
　 B. ちちは　せんげつ　とうきょうへも　いきました。　Dad went to Tokyo last month, too.

2. A. ははは　せんげつ　とうきょうへ　いきました。　Mom went to Tokyo last month.
　 B. ちちも　せんげつ　とうきょうへ　いきました。　Dad went to Tokyo last month, too.

3. A. ちちは　こんげつ　とうきょうへ　いきました。　Dad went to Tokyo this month.
　 B. ちちは　せんげつも　とうきょうへ　いきました。　Dad went to Tokyo last month, too.

【 ● ぶんかノート : Cultural Notes】

Why do Japanese have so many words for "to give"?

The system of verbs of giving and receiving is just one of many examples that illustrate how the Japanese language reflects Japanese society. Japanese people make clear hierarchical distinctions in their personal and social lives. Factors such as job position, age and family background all determine how one is treated, and in this case, how one is spoken to or about. They are also very conscious of belonging to an in-group (such as one's own family) or not.

【 アクティビティー : Activities】

A. Pair Work

Ask what Christmas presents or birthday presents your partner received from the following people. Write down your partner's responses.

Ex. 「あなたは おとうさん から なんのプレゼントを もらいましたか。」
「わたしは ちち から 〜を もらいました。」

1. Grandfather	
2. Grandmother	
3. Father	
4. Mother	
5. Sibling	
6. Boyfriend/girlfriend	

*なにも もらいませんでした。 I did not receive anything.

Now, ask what Christmas or birthday presents you gave to the following people.

Ex. 「あなたは おとうさん に なにを あげましたか。」
「わたしは ちち に 〜を あげました。」

1. Grandfather	
2. Grandmother	
3. Father	
4. Mother	
5. Sibling	
6. Boyfriend/girlfriend	

*だれにも あげませんでした。 I did not give anything.

【かいわ: Dialogue 】

ケン：ことしは　うちで　ぼくの　たんじょうパーティーを　します。

エミさんも　きませんか。この　土曜日の　四時からです。

エミ：どうも　ありがとう。うちは　どこですか。

ケン：これは　じゅうしょと　でんわばんごうです。

エミ：じゃ、たのしみにしています。

【たんご: Vocabulary 】

1. きょねん

last year

2. ことし

this year

3. らいねん

next year

4. まいとし / まいねん

every year

5. １９９９年　５月　１日　金曜日
〔せんきゅうひゃくきゅうじゅうきゅうねん
ごがつ　ついたち　きんようび〕

6. １９９０年うまれです。
I was born in 1990.

7. でんわばんごう

telephone number

8. じゅうしょ

address

9. (〜を)たのしみに　しています。

I am looking forward to 〜.

【 ● ぶんかノート : Cultural Notes】

1. Writing Japanese Addresses

Japanese names and addresses are written on envelopes in an opposite order from English. In Japanese, one begins by writing the largest geographical area first, i.e., the prefecture (state), city, district, street and number. The name is written last.

2. Writing Dates in Japanese

Likewise, when one writes dates in Japanese, one starts off with the largest unit which is the year, followed by the character for year (年〔ねん〕), the month (月〔がつ〕), date (日) and day of the week (曜日〔ようび〕).

Ex. ２０１０年〔ねん〕　３月　１０日　木曜日〔もくようび〕

【 アクティビティー : Activities】

A. Class Work

Everyone takes turns announcing his/her birth year. Write each person's name and year of birth. At the end, one person will read each of the answers.

B. Class Work

Some students give their telephone numbers. Write the numbers down. At the end, one student will read the correct answers aloud.

Ex. _____944 — 8705_____   5. _____

1. _____   6. _____

2. _____   7. _____

3. _____   8. _____

4. _____   9. _____

C. Class Work

Some students give their addresses. Write them down. At the end, one student will read the correct answers aloud.

Ex. _1601 King Street_____

1. _____

2. _____

3. _____

4. _____

5. _____

D. Pair Work

Ask your partner these questions. Write your partner's answers.

1. What birthday presents did you receive last year?	
2. What Christmas presents do you want to receive this year?	
3. Do you have a birthday party every year?	
4. Do you want to study Japanese next year, too?	

E. Pair Work

Your friend wants to go to Ken's birthday party, but he lost his invitation. Since you have the same invitation, your friend calls you for the information. Your friend asks the following questions. You answer them according to the information on the invitation below.

1. Date	
2. Day of the week	
3. Time	
4. Address	
5. Telephone number	
6. How many people are coming	

ケンの誕生日パーティー
五月四日 （土曜日）
十二時～三時
住所：３０４５　キングストリート
電話番号：７３２－５０４８

ぜひ来てください。

【かいわ: Dialogue 】

エミ：みんなで　しゃしんを　とりましょう。

ケン：はい、チーズ！　<Ken takes a picture.>

いま　プールで　およぎましょう。

そして、あとで　ゲームを　して、あそびましょう。

ははが　たくさん　たべものを　つくりましたから、

たくさん　たべてください。

【たんご: Vocabulary】

1. あそびます
[あそぶ/あそんで]

to play, amuse

<u>Not</u> used when discussing actions
involving sports or musical instruments.

2. およぎます
[およぐ/およいで]

to swim

3. ゲームを　します
[する/して]

to play a game

4. つくります
[つくる/つくって]

to make, create

5. しゃしんを　とります
[とる/とって]

to take a picture

6. カメラ

camera

7. はい、チーズ！/はい、ピース！

Say cheese!/ Say peace!

【 ● ぶんかノート: Cultural Notes】

Who eats first at a Japanese party?

When invited to a party in Japan, it is not polite to start eating on one's own. Usually, one waits until the guest of honor and others of higher rank have begun. It is also generally considered rude to complete one's meal too much faster than others.

【アクティビティー: Activities】

A. Pair Work

Ask your partner if he/she wants to do the following for or at a birthday party.

1. make a birthday cake （バースデーケーキ）	
2. sing songs	
3. swim in a pool	
4. play a bingo game	
5. dance （ダンスをします）	
6. watch videos	
7. eat Japanese food	
8. take pictures	

B. Pair Work

Look at the pictures on p. 312 and p. 313 and re-tell the story in Japanese.

１５か

Ask your partner these questions in Japanese.
Your partner answers in Japanese.

1. What will/did you give to your mother on Mother's Day?

2. What do you want to receive on your next birthday?

3. What kind of present did your parents give to you on your last birthday?

4. Who feeds (gives) food to your pet (ペット) everyday?

5. When is your birthday?

6. How old are you now?

7. What is your phone number?

8. What is your address? Is your house near school?

9. What year were you born?

10. What is today's date? [include the year, month, date, day of week]

11. Do you have a birthday party every year?

12. What did you do last summer vacation?

13. What are you going to do this summer vacation?

14. Where are you traveling this summer?

15. Do you want to study Japanese next year, too?

16. Please take a picture of everyone with this camera. [Respond appropriately.]

17. What do you want to do at your birthday party?

18. Where do you want to swim this Saturday?

19. May we play Bingo in Japanese class today?

20. Everyone, let's sing a birthday song together!

21. May I play with water balloons at your birthday party?

22. My mother made this cake, so please eat a lot. [Respond to invitation.]

23. What do you buy at the school cafeteria everyday?

24. How many books did you read this year?

25. What kind of presents do you usually give to your friends on their birthdays?

26. Happy Birthday! Here is a present. [Respond appropriately.]

27. What are you looking forward to now?

Find the answers by investigating books, by talking to friends, or by using the Internet.

1. When do people in the U.S. exchange gifts?

2. When do Japanese exchange gifts?

3. What types of gifts do Japanese traditionally give? Circle all those that apply.

   A. personal gifts (gifts to fit the personality and wishes of the receiver)

   B. cash   C. food   D. flowers   E. expensive, impressive gifts

4. What do you usually eat for breakfast?

5. What do most Japanese today eat for breakfast? Circle all those that apply.

   A. cereal   B. fast food   C. rice and miso soup   D. fish   E. toast and salad

6. Write the names of at least five Japanese dishes and a description of each.

7. Why is meat such a small part of the Japanese diet? Why is fish a large part of the Japanese diet?

15か

Try a game of *gomokunarabe*!

Gomokunarabe is a board game that is a popular pastime for children as well as seniors. The game is played by two. Round, shiny black and white stones are used as markers. Each player chooses to play with either the black or white stones. The top of the simple wooden gameboard is designed with a grid of black intersecting vertical and horizontal lines. The two players take turns placing their stones (either black or white) on the intersecting points. The first player who connects a vertical, horizontal or diagonal line of five stones of his/her own color wins.

The original *Go* game first became popular in the 17th century. Today, international tournaments, much like chess tournaments, are held.

15か

Gameboard:

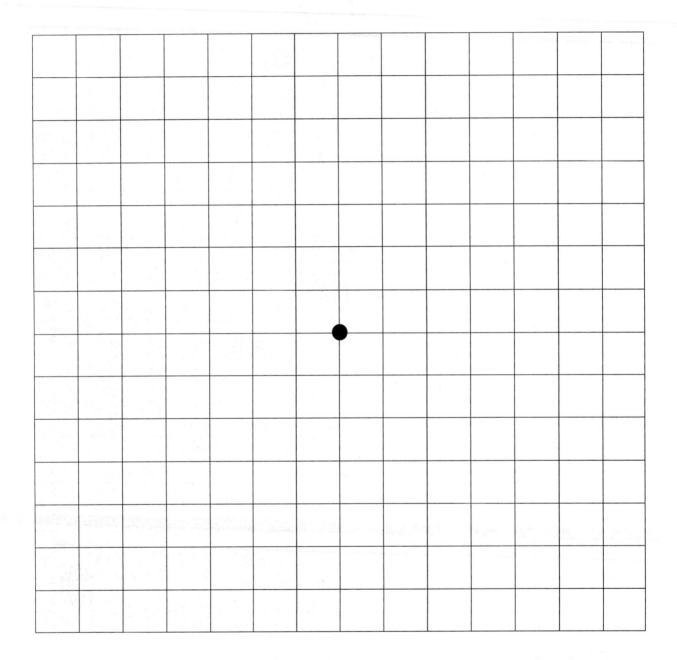

Cut the black or white markers:

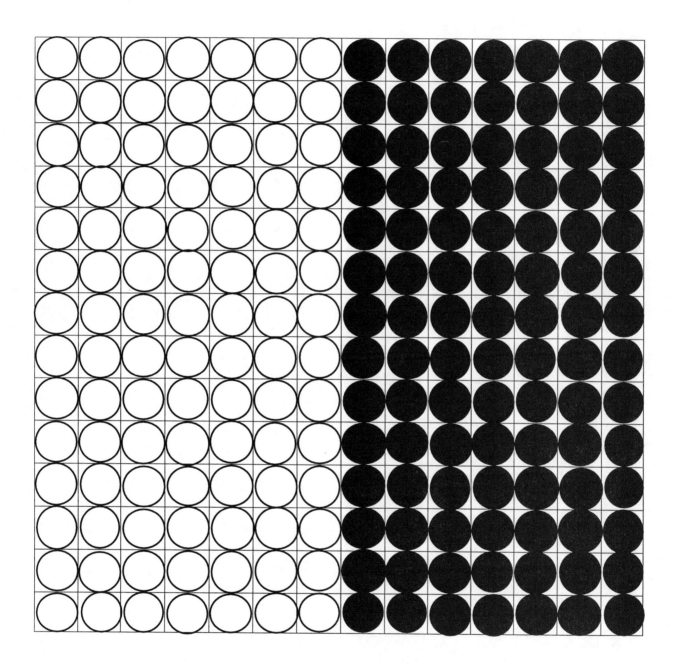

[The number preceding each sentence indicates the lesson in which it was introduced.]

I. Sentence Patterns

Lesson 10

10-1 えんぴつけずりは　あそこに　あります。 — The pencil sharpener is over there.

10-1 ジョンさんは　そとに　います。 — John is outdoors.

10-1 ごみばこは　あそこです。 — The rubbish can is over there.

10-1 ジョンさんは　そとです。 — John is outdoors.

10-2 あそこに　プールが　あります。 — There is a pool over there.

10-2 あそこに　かわいい　おんなの　こが　いますよ。 — There is a cute girl over there.

10-2 いま　おひるごはんを　たべましょうか。 — Shall we eat lunch now?

10-3 あそこに　おおきい　きが　いっぽん　あります。 — There is a big tree over there.

Lesson 11

11-2 あした　しけんが　あります。 — I have an exam tomorrow.

11-2 わたしは　１０じから　１１じまで　えいごの　じゅぎょうが　あります。

I have (my) English class from 10:00 to 11:00.

11-4 きのうの　しけんは　むずかしかったです。 — Yesterday's exam was difficult.

11-4 その　せんせいは　ぜんぜん　きびしくなかったです。 — That teacher was not strict at all.

11-4 にほんごは　おもしろい（です）から、すきです。 — Japanese is interesting, so I like it.

11-4 なぜ　せいせきが　わるかったですか。 — Why was your grade bad?

　　　べんきょうしませんでしたから。 — It is because I did not study.

11-5 いま　おみずが　ほしいです。 — I want water now.

　　　コーヒーは　ほしくないです。 — I don't want coffee.

11-5 すうがくは　しゅくだいが　とても　おおいです。 — There is a lot of math homework.

11-5 おとこの　がくせいは　すくないですね。 — There are few male students, aren't there?

Lesson 12

12-2 いま　テレビを（or が）　みたいです。 — I want to watch T.V. now.

12-2 おちゃは（or を）　のみたくありません。 — I do not want to drink tea.

12-2 ゆうべ　フットボールを　みたかったです。 — I wanted to watch football last night.

12-2 ゆうべ　フットボールは（or を）　みたくなかったです。

I did not want to watch football last night.

12-3 つよい　チームでした。　　　　　　　(They) were a strong team.

12-4 あした　だいじな　しあいが　あります。　I have an important game tomorrow.

12-5 ダンスは　カフェテリアで　あります。　The dance will be at the cafeteria.

Lesson 13

13-2 ゆっくり　はなして　ください。　　Please speak slowly.

13-3 ジュースか　おみずを　のみます。　I will drink juice or water.

13-3 トイレへ　いっても　いいですか。　May I go to the restroom?

13-4 おおきいのを　ください。　　Please give me a big one.

Lesson 14

14-1 もう　おひるごはんを　たべましたか。　Did you already eat lunch?

　　いいえ、まだです。　　　　　　No, not yet.

14-2 ははは　テニスが　すきで、ちちは　ゴルフが　すきです。

My mother likes tennis and my dad likes golf.

14-2 この　シャツは　２まいで　３０ドルです。　This shirt is $30 for two.

14-3 この　しゅくだいを　えんぴつで　かきました。　I wrote this homework with a pencil.

14-4 にほんごは　おもしろくて、たのしいです。　Japanese is interesting and fun.

14-5 あさごはんを　たべて、しんぶんを　よみます。　I eat breakfast and read the newspaper.

Lesson 15

15-2 ともだちは　わたしに　ふうせんを　くれました。My friend gave me balloons.

15-2 わたしは　ともだちに　おかねを　もらいました。I received some money from my friend.

15-3 これを　あなたに　あげます。　I will give this to you.

15-3 ははは　いぬに　たべものを　やります。My mother gives food to the dog.

15-3 しんぶんや　ざっしなど　よみました。I read newspapers, magazines, etc.

15-3 ははに　あげました。いもうとにも　やりました。I gave it to my mother. I gave it to my younger sister, too.

15-3 ちちは　にほんへ　いきました。ちゅうごくへも　いきました。

My father went to Japan. He went to China, too.

１６か

338

II. Verbs, いAdjectives and なAdjectives

[The number preceding each word indicates the lesson in which the word was introduced.]

A. Verbs

1-4 はじめます	begin, start	10-1 います	exist (animate)
1-4 おわります	finish	10-1 あります	exist (inanimate)
2-1 わかります	understand	11-2 あります	have
2-1 しりません	do not know	12-1 しにます	die
2-1 みえます	can see	12-2 やすみます	rest, be absent
2-1 きこえます	can hear	12-2 (くすりを)のみます	take (medicine)
2-1 いいます	say	12-2 つかれています	tired
4-1 はなします	speak, talk	12-3 かちます	win
4-2 たべます	eat	12-3 まけます	lose
4-2 のみます	drink	12-4 がんばります	do one's best
4-4 よみます	read	12-5 あいます	meet
4-4 ききます	listen, hear	12-5 れんしゅう（を）します	practice
4-4 します	do	12-5 はしります	run
4-4 べんきょう（を）します	study	13-2 すわります	sit
4-5 みます	see, watch, look	13-2 たちます	stand
4-5 かきます	write	13-2 だします	turn in
4-5 タイプ（を）します	type	13-2 みせます	show
6-4 ふとっています	is fat	13-2 あけます	open
6-4 やせています	is skinny	13-2 しめます	close
6-4 としを　とっています	is old (age)	13-2 しずかにします	quiet (down)
7-3 いきます	go	13-2 いいます	say
7-3 きます	come	13-2 まちます	wait
7-3 かえります	return (place)	13-2 かいます	buy
7-3 おきます	get up, wake up	14-3 わすれます	forget
7-3 ねます	go to bed, sleep	14-3 (～が)いります	need ～
7-4 あるいて　いきます	go by walking	14-3 かします	lend
7-4 あるいて　きます	come by walking	15-1 うたいます	sing
7-4 あるいて　かえります	return by walking	15-2 くれます	give (me)
7-5 スポーツを　します	play sports	15-2 もらいます	receive, get
7-5 パーティーをします	have a party	15-3 あげます	give (to equal)
7-5 りょこう（を）します	travel	15-3 やります	give (to inferior)
7-5 かいもの（を）します	shop	15-5 あそびます	play (for fun)
7-5 しょくじ（を）します	have a meal, dine	15-5 およぎます	swim
7-5 でんわ（を）します	make a phone call	15-5 ゲームをします	play a game
		15-5 つくります	make
		15-5 (しゃしんを)とります	take (picture)

Verb Conjugation [Formal]

2-1 nonpast	のみます	drink, will drink, is going to drink
2-1 neg. nonpast	のみません	do not drink, will not drink
4-3 past	のみました	drank, have drunk
4-3 neg., past	のみませんでした	did not drink, have not drunk
7-1 volitional	のみましょう	Let's drink. [Suggestion]
7-1 volitional	のみましょうか	Shall we drink? [Suggestion]
7-1 invitational	のみませんか	Would you like to drink? [Invitation]
12-2 want to do	のみたいです	I want to drink.
12-2 do not want to do	のみたくないです	I do not want to drink.
12-2 wanted to do	のみたかったです	I wanted to drink.
12-2 did not want to do	のみたくなかったです	I did not want to drink.
13-2 request	のんでください。	Please drink. [Request]
13-3 permission	のんでも いいですか。	May I drink? [Permission]
14-5 conjoining	のんで、ねます。	I drink (it) and sleep.

B. い Adjectives

[The number preceding each word indicates the lesson in which the word was introduced.]

1-7 あつい	hot		10-4 あたらしい	new
1-7 さむい	cold		10-4 ふるい	old (not for age)
1-7 すずしい	cool		10-4 うつくしい	beautiful
2-1 いい	good		10-5 ひろい	spacious, wide
6-1 たかい	tall, high		10-5 せまい	narrow, small (space)
6-1 ひくい	short (height), low		10-5 ちかい	near
6-2 よい	good		10-5 とおい	far
6-2 わるい	bad		11-3 むずかしい	difficult
6-2 おおきい	big		11-3 やさしい	easy
6-2 ちいさい	small		11-3 たのしい	fun, enjoyable
6-2 ながい	long		11-3 おもしろい	interesting
6-2 みじかい	short (length)		11-3 つまらない	boring, uninteresting
6-3 あかい	red		11-4 ひどい	terrible
6-3 しろい	white		11-4 うれしい	happy
6-3 くろい	black		11-4 かなしい	sad
6-3 あおい	blue		11-5 おおい	many
6-3 きいろい	yellow		11-5 すくない	few, a little
6-3 ちゃいろい	brown		11-5 (〜が)ほしい	want (something)
6-4 わかい	young		12-1 いたい	sore, painful
6-4 きびしい	strict		12-2 ねむい	sleepy
6-4 やさしい	kind, nice		12-3 つよい	strong
6-5 きたない	dirty		12-3 よわい	weak
6-5 かわいい	cute		12-5 たかい	expensive
6-5 うるさい	noisy		12-5 やすい	cheap
7-2 はやい	early		12-5 おいしい	delicious, tasty
7-2 おそい	late		12-5 まずい	unappetizing
7-5 いそがしい	busy		12-5 すごい	terrific, terrible
			12-5 すばらしい	wonderful
			14-4 つめたい	cold (drink)
			14-4 あたたかい	warm

い Adjectives Conjugation [Formal]

6-2	nonpast	あついです	is hot
6-2	neg. nonpast	あつくないです or あつくありません	is not hot
6-2	past	あつかったです	was hot
6-2	neg. past	あつくなかったです or あつくありませんでした	was not hot
12-3	pre-noun	あつい X おちゃ	hot tea
14-4	conjoining	あつくて、おいしいです。	It is hot and tasty.

いい is an irregular い adjective.

6-2	nonpast	いいです	is good
6-2	neg. nonpast	よくないです or よくありません	is not good
6-2	past	よかったです	was good
6-2	neg. past	よくなかったです or よくありませんでした	was not good
12-3	pre-noun	いい X ひと	good person
14-4	conjoining	あたまが よくて、せが たかいです。	He is smart and tall.

C. な Adjectives

[The number preceding each word indicates the lesson in which the word was introduced.]

な Adjectives

1-7	げんき	healthy, fine	10-4	ゆうめい	famous
2-1	だめ	no good	11-5	たいへん	hard
5-2	すき	like	12-1	だいじょうぶ	all right
5-2	だいすき	like very much, love	12-4	だいじ	important
5-2	きらい	dislike			
5-2	だいきらい	dislike a lot, hate			
5-3	じょうず	skillful, be good at			
5-3	へた	unskillful, be poor at			
5-3	とくい	be strong in, can do well			
5-3	にがて	be weak in			
6-5	きれい	pretty, clean, neat			
6-5	しずか	quiet			
6-5	じゃま	is a hindrance, is a nuisance, is in my way			

な Adjectives Conjugation [Formal]

5-2	nonpast	すきです	like
5-2	neg. nonpast	すきではありません or すきじゃありません	do not like
5-2	past	すきでした	liked
5-2	neg. past	すきではありませんでした or すきじゃありませんでした	did not like
12-4	pre-noun	すき な ひと	person I like
14-2	conjoining	すきで、まいにち たべます。	I like it and eat it everyday.

III. Nouns

[The number preceding each word indicates the lesson in which the word was introduced.]

A. People

1-1 わたし	I	3-4 アメリカじん	U.S. citizen
1-1 ぼく	I (Used by male)	3-5 いしゃ	medical doctor
1-3 せんせい	teacher	3-5 おいしゃさん	medical doctor [polite]
2-4 あなた	you	3-5 べんごし	lawyer
3-1 ちち	my father	3-5 かいしゃいん	company employee
3-1 はは	my mother	3-5 しゅふ	housewife
3-1 あに	my older brother	3-5 エンジニア	engineer
3-1 あね	my older sister	4-1 ともだち	friend
3-1 おとうと	my younger brother	10-2 おとこ	male
3-1 いもうと	my younger sister	10-2 おんな	female
3-1 かぞく	family	10-2 ひと	person
3-1 きょうだい	siblings	10-2 こども	child, children
3-3 おとうさん	(someone's) father	10-2 おとこのひと	man
3-3 おかあさん	(someone's) mother	10-2 おんなのひと	woman, lady
3-3 おじいさん	grandfather, elderly man	10-2 おとこのこ	boy
3-3 おばあさん	grandmother, elderly woman	10-2 おんなのこ	girl
3-3 おにいさん	(someone's) older brother	10-2 ～かた	~ person (polite)
3-3 おねえさん	(someone's) older sister	12-3 わたしたち	we
3-3 おとうとさん	(someone's) younger brother	12-3 ぼくたち	we (used by male)
3-3 いもうとさん	(someone's) younger sister	12-5 だいがくせい	college student
3-3 せいと	student (not college)	15-1 みんな	everyone
3-3 がくせい	college student	15-1 みなさん	everyone (polite)
3-3 ちゅうがくせい	intermediate student	15-2 おじさん	uncle, middle-aged man
3-3 こうこうせい	high school student	15-2 おばさん	aunt, middle-aged lady
3-4 こちら	this one (refer to a person)	15-2 いとこ	cousin
3-4 にほんじん	Japanese citizen	15-2 しんせき	relatives

B. Animals

10-1 いぬ	dog
10-1 ねこ	cat
10-3 さかな	fish
10-3 とり	bird
10-5 ごきぶり	cockroach
10-5 ねずみ	mouse
10-5 ぶた	pig

C. Plants

10-3 き	tree
10-3 はな	flower

16 か

344

D. Things　　　　　　　[The number preceding each word indicates the lesson in which the word was introduced.]

1-2 これ	this one		4-4 しんぶん	newspaper
1-6 それ	that one		4-4 ざっし	magazine
1-6 あれ	that one over there		4-4 ウォークマン	walkman
2-3 えんぴつ	pencil		4-4 テープ	tape
2-3 ボールペン	ballpoint pen		4-5 テレビ	TV
2-3 けしごむ	(rubber) eraser		4-5 レポート	report, paper
2-3 ほん	book		4-5 てがみ	letter
2-3 かみ	paper		4-5 ラジオ	radio
2-3 きょうかしょ, テキスト	textbook		4-5 でんわ	telephone
			4-5 コンピューター	computer
2-3 じしょ	dictionary		4-5 ビデオ	video
2-3 ノート	notebook		10-1 ドア, と	door
2-3 おかね	money		10-1 まど	window
2-3 しゃしん	photo		10-1 つくえ	desk
2-3 バッグ	bag		10-1 いす	chair
2-3 ぼうし	cap, hat		10-1 えんぴつけずり	pencil sharpener
2-3 ごみ	rubbish		10-1 ごみばこ	trash can
2-5 ティッシュ	tissue		10-5 ベッド	bed
2-5 しゅくだい	homework		15-1 プレゼント	present
2-5 しけん	exam		15-2 きっぷ	ticket
2-5 しょうテスト	quiz		15-2 ふうせん	balloon
2-5 ワークシート	worksheet		15-4 カメラ	camera

E. Food

2-5 チョコレート	chocolate		5-2 さしみ	raw fish
2-5 あめ	candy		5-2 てんぷら	*tempura*
4-2 ごはん	cooked rice		14-2 ピザ	pizza
4-2 パン	bread		14-2 ハンバーガー	hamburger
4-3 あさごはん	breakfast		14-2 ホットドッグ	hotdog
4-3 ひるごはん	lunch		14-2 サンドイッチ	sandwich
4-3 ばんごはん	dinner, supper		14-2 サラダ	salad
4-3 なにも + Neg.	(not) anything, nothing		14-2 フライドポテト	French fries
5-2 もの	(tangible) things		14-2 （お）べんとう	box lunch
5-2 たべもの	food		14-2 （お）むすび	rice ball
5-2 すし	*sushi*		14-2 （お）にぎり	rice ball

F. Drinks

[The number preceding each word indicates the lesson in which the word was introduced.]

4-2（お）みず	water	4-2 おちゃ	tea
4-2 ジュース	juice	4-2 コーヒー	coffee
4-2 ぎゅうにゅう, ミルク	(cow's) milk	5-2 のみもの	a drink
4-2 コーラ	cola		

G. Places

2-5 ここ	here	10-1 そと	outdoors
2-5 そこ	there	10-2（お）トイレ,（お）てあらい	toilet, bathroom
2-5 あそこ	over there	10-2 プール	pool
3-3 がっこう	school	10-3 いけ	pond
3-3 ちゅうがく	intermediate school	10-4 たてもの	building
3-3 こうこう	high school	10-4 じむしょ	office
3-5 びょういん	hospital	10-4 きょうしつ	classroom
4-1 うち	house, home	10-4 ロッカー	locker
4-4 としょかん	library	10-5 にわ	garden, yard
4-4 カフェテリア	cafeteria	10-5 ガレージ	garage
4-4 スナックバー	snack bar	10-5 へや	room
7-3 かいしゃ	company	10-5 だいがく	college, university
7-5 うみ	beach, ocean, sea	13-2（お）みせ	store
7-5 やま	mountain	13-3 スーパー	supermarket
7-5 かわ	river	13-3 ほんや	bookstore
7-5 レストラン	restaurant	13-3 はなや	flower shop
7-5 デパート	department store	13-3 すしや	sushi shop
7-5 どこへも + Neg.	(not) anywhere	13-3 きっさてん	coffee shop

H. Countries

3-4 にほん	Japan
3-4 アメリカ	U.S.
3-4 ちゅうごく	China
3-4 かんこく	Korea
3-4 フランス	France
3-4 スペイン	Spain
3-4 ドイツ	Germany

I. Languages

4-1 にほんご	Japanese
4-1 えいご	English
4-1 ちゅうごくご	Chinese
4-1 かんこくご	Korean
4-1 フランスご	French
4-1 スペインご	Spanish
4-1 ドイツご	German

J. Time

3-5	いま	now	11-5	せんしゅう	last week
3-5	まえ	before	11-5	こんしゅう	this week
4-2	まいにち	everyday	11-5	らいしゅう	next week
4-3	きのう	yesterday	11-5	まいしゅう	every week
4-3	きょう	today	11-5	しゅうまつ	weekend
4-3	あした	tomorrow	12-2	ゆうべ	last night
4-3	あさ	morning	12-2	けさ	this morning
4-3	（お）ひる	daytime	12-2	こんばん	tonight
4-3	ばん	evening, night	12-4	はる	spring
4-3	よる	night	12-4	なつ	summer
4-3	ゆうがた	late afternoon, early evening	12-4	あき	fall, autumn
7-1	にちようび	Sunday	12-4	ふゆ	winter
7-1	げつようび	Monday	12-4	せんげつ	last month
7-1	かようび	Tuesday	12-4	こんげつ	this month
7-1	すいようび	Wednesday	12-4	らいげつ	next month
7-1	もくようび	Thursday	12-4	まいつき	every month
7-1	きんようび	Friday	12-5	～のまえに	before ～
7-1	どようび	Saturday	12-5	～のあとで	after ～
7-1	（お）やすみ	day off, vacation	15-3	ははのひ	Mother's Day
7-2	こんばん	tonight	15-3	ちちのひ	Father's Day
7-2	ごぜん	a.m.	15-4	きょねん	last year
7-2	ごご	p.m.	15-4	ことし	this year
11-3	つぎ	next	15-4	らいねん	next year
11-4	おととい	the day before yesterday	15-4	まいとし, まいねん	every year
11-4	あさって	the day after tomorrow	15-4	１９９９ねん	the year of 1999

K. Transportation

7-4	くるま	car, vehicle
7-4	じどうしゃ	car, vehicle
7-4	バス	bus
7-4	タクシー	taxi
7-4	じてんしゃ	bicycle
7-4	ちかてつ	subway
7-4	でんしゃ	electric train
7-4	ひこうき	airplane
7-4	ふね	boat, ship

L. Utensils

14-3	（お）はし	chopsticks
14-2	フォーク	fork
14-2	スプーン	spoon
14-2	ナイフ	knife
14-2	ストロー	straw
14-2	（お）さら	dish, plate
14-2	コップ	cup
14-2	ナプキン	napkin

[The number preceding each word indicates the lesson in which the word was introduced.]

M. Sports

5-1	スポーツ	sports
5-1	ジョギング	jogging
5-1	すいえい	swimming
5-3	フットボール	football
5-3	やきゅう	baseball
5-3	バスケット	basketball
5-3	バレーボール	volleyball
5-3	サッカー	soccer
5-3	テニス	tennis
5-3	ゴルフ	golf
12-5	チーム	team

N. Subjects

11-2	かもく	subject(s)
11-2	しゃかい	social studies
11-2	かがく	science
11-2	すうがく	math
11-2	えいご	English
11-2	がいこくご	foreign language
11-2	びじゅつ	art
11-2	おんがく	music
11-2	たいいく	P.E.
11-2	ホームルーム	homeroom
11-2	やすみじかん	break time
11-2	じゅぎょう, クラス	class
11-4	せいせき	grade

O. Activities, Events

5-1	おんがく	music
5-1	ダンス	dance, dancing
5-1	うた	song, singing
5-1	えいが	movie
5-1	テレビゲーム	video game
5-1	トランプ	(playing) cards
5-1	ピアノ	piano
5-1	ギター	guitar
5-1	どくしょ	reading
5-1	え	painting, drawing
5-3	こと	(intangible) thing

7-5	りょこう	trip, traveling
7-5	かいもの	shopping
7-5	しょくじ	meal, dining
7-5	パーティー	party
7-5	ピクニック	picnic
7-5	キャンプ	camping
11-1	たんじょうび	birthday
12-3	しあい	sports game
12-5	れんしゅう	practice
15-2	コンサート	concert

P. Clothing

13-3	シャツ	shirt
13-3	くつ	shoes
13-3	ジャケット	jacket
13-3	パンツ	pants
13-3	とけい	watch, clock

Q. Size

14-2	サイズ	size
14-2	S (エス)サイズ	small size
14-2	M (エム)サイズ	medium size
14-2	L (エル)サイズ	large size

[The number preceding each word indicates the lesson in which the word was introduced.]

R. Colors

5-5 いろ	color	
5-5 あか	red (color)	
5-5 しろ	white (color)	
5-5 くろ	black (color)	
5-5 あお	blue (color)	
5-5 きいろ	yellow (color)	
5-5 ちゃいろ	brown (color)	
5-5 みどり	green (color)	
5-5 むらさき	purple (color)	
5-5 ピンク	pink (color)	
5-5 オレンジ	orange (color)	
5-5 グレイ	grey (color)	
5-5 きんいろ	gold (color)	
5-5 ぎんいろ	silver (color)	

S. Parts of the Body

6-1 あたま	head
6-1 かお	face
6-1 からだ	body
6-1 かみ（のけ）	hair
6-1 みみ	ear(s)
6-1 め	eye(s)
6-1 はな	nose
6-1 くち	mouth
6-1 は	tooth, teeth
6-1 くび	neck
6-1 のど	throat
6-1 ひげ	beard, moustache
6-1 おなか	stomach
6-1 て	hand
6-1 あし	foot, leg
6-1 ゆび	finger, toe
6-1 せ（い）	height
6-1 こころ	heart, spirit
6-1 こえ	voice

T. Illness

12-1 びょうき	illness, sickness
12-1 かぜ	a cold
12-1 ねつ	fever
12-2 くすり	medicine

U. Others

3-1 （お）なまえ	name
3-5 （お）しごと	job
5-1 しゅみ	hobby
15-4 でんわばんごう	phone number
15-4 じゅうしょ	address

[The number preceding each word indicates the lesson in which the word was introduced.]

Copula です Conjugation [Formal]

1-1	nonpast	せいと<u>です</u>	is a student
3-3	neg. nonpast	せいと<u>ではありません</u> or せいと<u>じゃありません</u>	is not a student
3-5	past	せいと<u>でした</u>	was a student
3-5	neg. past	せいと<u>ではありませんでした</u> or せいと<u>じゃありませんでした</u>	was not a student
3-1	possessive	わたし<u>の</u>　ほん	my book
3-1	descriptive	がっこう<u>の</u>　なまえ	school name
14-2	conjoining	ちちは　４０さい<u>で</u>、ははは３８さいです。	My father is 40 and my mother is 38.

IV. Adverbs, Question Words, Sentence Conjunctions, Suffixes and Prefixes

[The number preceding each word indicates the lesson in which the word was introduced.]

A. Adverbs

4-1 よく + Verb	well, often
4-1 すこし	a little
4-1 ちょっと	a little
4-2 ときどき	sometimes
4-2 たいてい	usually
4-2 いつも	always
5-4 とても + Adj.	very
5-4 まあまあ	so so
5-4 あまり + Neg.	(not) very
5-4 ぜんぜん + Neg.	(not) at all
10-1 また	again
10-3 たくさん	a lot, many
10-3 すこし	a few, a little
12-2 はやく	early
12-2 おそく	late
14-1 もう + Positive	already
14-1 まだ + Neg.	(not) yet
14-2 ぜんぶ	everything
14-4 もう(いっぱい)	(one) more (cup)
15-3 もうすぐ	very soon

B. Question Words

1-4 なに, なん	what?
2-5 なんまい	how many (sheets)?
2-5 いくつ	how many (general things)?
3-1 だれ	who?
3-1 なんにん	how many (people)?
3-1 なんさい	how old?
3-1 (お)いくつ	how old?
3-3 なんねんせい	what grade?
3-4 どこ	where?
3-4 なにじん	what nationality?
3-4 なんがつ	what month?
4-1 なにご	what language?
5-2 どんな～	what kind of ～ ?
5-5 なにいろ	what color?
7-1 なんようび	what day of the week?
7-1 いつ	when?
7-2 なんじ	what time?
7-2 なんぷん	how many minutes?
11-4 なぜ, どうして	why?
13-4 (お)いくら	how much?
13-4 どれ	which one?
13-4 どの～	which ～ ?
13-4 いかが	how?

16か

[The number preceding each word indicates the lesson in which the word was introduced.]

C. Sentence Conjunctions

3-2 そして	And
4-1 でも	But
5-3 ～が、～	~ , but ~
6-4 それとも	Q1 or Q2?
7-3 それから	And then
11-4 ～から、～	~ , so ~
11-5 それに	Besides, moreover
14-5 これから	From now (on)
14-5 それから	And then

D. Sentence Interjectives

1-3 はい	Here. [In response to roll call.]
1-6 はい or ええ	Yes
1-6 いいえ	No
2-1 ええと…	Let me see . . .
2-1 あのう	Well . . .
14-1 じゃ、	Well then [informal]
14-1 では、	Well then [formal]

E. Suffixes

1-3 ～せんせい	Mr./Mrs./Ms./Dr.
1-3 ～さん	Mr./Mrs./Ms.
3-4 ～がつうまれ	born in (month)
7-2 ～はん	half past ~
7-2 ～ころ、ごろ	about ~ (time)
7-2 ～まえ	before ~
7-2 ～すぎ	after ~
12-3 ～たち	[plural for animate objects]
13-4 ～くらい、ぐらい	about [not for specific time]
15-4 ～ねんうまれ	born in (year)

F. Prefixes

2-4 この～	this ~
2-4 その～	that ~
2-4 あの～	that ~ over there
3-2 ご～	[polite]
3-2 お～	[polite]

V. Particles

1-1 は	Topic particle
1-4 Sentence + か。	Question-ending particle
1-7 Sentence + ねえ。	Sentence final particle expressing admiration, surprise or exclamation
3-1 の	Possessive and descriptive particle
3-2 と	and [Noun and Noun only]
3-3 も	also, too [replaces を, が, は]
4-1 で	at, in (place) [with action verb]
4-4 と （いっしょに）	(together) with

16か

352

4-5 tool ＋ で	by, with, on, in
6-5 Sentence ＋ ね。	Sentence final particle for seeking agreement or confirmation
6-5 Sentence ＋ よ。	Sentence final particle for emphasis or exclamation
7-1 specific time＋ に	at, on
7-3 place＋ へ／に	to [with direction verb]
7-3 activity ＋ に	to, for (activity)
7-4 transportation ＋ で	by [with direction verb]
10-1 Location ＋ に ＋ Existence Verb	in, at
11-2 ～から～まで	from ~ to ~
14-2 （ふたつ）で	for (two) [totalizing particle]
14-3 （フォーク）で	with, by, by means of
15-3 ～や～（など）	~ and ~, etc.

VI. Expressions

1-1 はじめまして。	How do you do?
1-1 どうぞ　よろしく。	Nice to meet you.
1-3 おはよう。	Good morning.
1-3 おはよう　ございます。	Good morning. [Polite]
1-3 こんにちは。	Hello. Hi.
1-3 さようなら。	Good-bye.
1-4 はじめましょう。	Let's begin.
1-4 きりつ。	Stand. [used at ceremonies]
1-4 れい。	Bow. [used at ceremonies]
1-4 ちゃくせき。	Sit. [used at ceremonies]
1-4 （お）やすみです。	~ is absent.
1-4 ちこくです。	~ is tardy.
1-4 はやく。	Hurry!
1-4 おわりましょう。	Let's finish.
1-5 すみません。もう　いちど　おねがいします。	Excuse me. One more time please.
1-5 すみません。ゆっくり　おねがいします。	Excuse me. Slowly please.
1-5 ちょっと　まってください。	Please wait a minute.

1-5 どうも　ありがとう　ございます。	Thank you very much.
1-5 どういたしまして。	You are welcome.
1-6 はい、そうです。	Yes, it is.
1-6 いいえ、そうではありません。or	No, it is not.
いいえ、そうじゃありません。	
1-7 あついですねえ。	It's hot!
1-7 さむいですねえ。	It's cold!
1-7 すずしいですねえ。	It is cool!
1-7 そうですねえ。	Yes, it is!
1-7 おげんきですか。	How are you?
1-7 はい、げんきです。	Yes, I am fine.
2-1 わかりますか。	Do you understand?
2-1 しりません。	I do not know.
2-1 みえません。	I cannot see.
2-1 きこえません。	I cannot hear.
2-1 Treeは　にほんごで　なんと　いいますか。	How do you say "tree" in Japanese?
2-5 ～を　ください。	Please give me ~.
2-5 はい、どうぞ。	Here, please (take it).
3-1 そうですか。	Is that so?
3-2 ～は？	How about ~?
5-1 そうですねえ…	Let me see . . .
7-2 こんばんは。	Good evening.
11-3 どうですか。	How is it?
11-4 それは　いいですねえ。	How nice! [for a future event]
11-4 それは　よかったですねえ。	How nice! [for a past event]
11-4 それは　ざんねんですねえ。	How disappointing! [for a future event]
11-4 それは　ざんねんでしたねえ。	How disappointing! [for a past event]
12-1 どうしましたか。	What happened?
12-1 かわいそうに。	How pitiful! [to inferior]
12-3 がんばって。	Do your best. Good luck.
13-2 すわってください。	Please sit down.
13-2 たってください。	Please stand up.

13-2 だしてください。	Please turn (it) in.
13-2 みせてください。	Please show (it) to me.
13-2 まどを　あけてください。	Please open the window.
13-2 ドアを　しめてください。	Please close the door.
13-2 しずかにしてください。	Please be quiet.
13-2 もういちど　いってください。	Please say it one more time.
13-2 ちょっと　まってください。	Please wait a minute.
13-2 すみません。	Excuse me. [to get attention]
13-4 いくらですか。	How much is it?
13-5 いかがですか。	How is it? [polite]
13-5 わあ！	Wow!
14-1 おなかが　すきました／ペコペコです。	I am hungry.
14-1 のどが　かわきました／カラカラです。	I am thirsty.
14-1 いいえ、まだです。	No, not yet.
14-3 いいえ、けっこうです。	No, thank you.
14-3 おかねを　かしてください。	Please lend me some money.
14-4 いただきます。	[expression before meal]
14-4 ごちそうさま。	[expression after meal]
14-4 おなかが　いっぱいです。	I am full.
14-5 じゃ、また　あとで。	Well then, see you later.
14-5 バイバイ。	Bye-bye.
15-1 (お)たんじょうび　おめでとう(ございます)。	Happy Birthday!
15-1 おめでとう(ございます)。	Congratulations!
15-4 (〜を)たのしみにしています。	I am looking forward to (something).
15-4 はい、チーズ。	Say "cheese."
15-4 はい、ピース。	Say "peace."

VII. Counters

[The number preceding each at the top indicates the lesson in which the counter was introduced.]

	1-5 1～10	1-6 11～20	1-6 10～100	2-5	2-5	3-1
1	いち	じゅういち	じゅう	いちまい	ひとつ	ひとり
2	に	じゅうに	にじゅう	にまい	ふたつ	ふたり
3	さん	じゅうさん	さんじゅう	さんまい	みっつ	さんにん
4	し, よん	じゅうし	よんじゅう	よんまい	よっつ	よにん
5	ご	じゅうご	ごじゅう	ごまい	いつつ	ごにん
6	ろく	じゅうろく	ろくじゅう	ろくまい	むっつ	ろくにん
7	しち, なな	じゅうしち, じゅうなな	ななじゅう	ななまい	ななつ	ななにん
8	はち	じゅうはち	はちじゅう	はちまい	やっつ	はちにん
9	く, きゅう	じゅうく	きゅうじゅう	きゅうまい	ここのつ	きゅうにん
10	じゅう	にじゅう	ひゃく	じゅうまい	とお	じゅうにん
?				なんまい?	いくつ?	なんにん?

	Age 3-1	Month 3-4	Grade 3-3	Hour 7-2	Minute 7-2
1	いっさい	いちがつ	いちねんせい	いちじ	いっぷん
2	にさい	にがつ	にねんせい	にじ	にふん
3	さんさい	さんがつ	さんねんせい	さんじ	さんぷん
4	よんさい	しがつ	よねんせい	よじ	よんぷん
5	ごさい	ごがつ		ごじ	ごふん
6	ろくさい	ろくがつ		ろくじ	ろっぷん
7	ななさい	しちがつ		しちじ, ななじ	ななふん
8	はっさい	はちがつ		はちじ	はっぷん
9	きゅうさい	くがつ		くじ	きゅうふん
10	じ (ゅ) っさい	じゅうがつ		じゅうじ	じ (ゅ) っぷん
11	じゅういっさい	じゅういちがつ		じゅういちじ	
12	20 はたち	じゅうにがつ		じゅうにじ	
?	なんさい?	なんがつ?	なんねんせい?	なんじ?	なんぷん?

	10-3	10-3	10-3	10-3	14-3	15-2
1	いちだい	いちわ	いっぴき	いっぽん	いっぱい	いっさつ
2	にだい	にわ	にひき	にほん	にはい	にさつ
3	さんだい	さんわ	さんびき	さんぼん	さんばい	さんさつ
4	よんだい	よんわ	よんひき	よんほん	よんはい	よんさつ
5	ごだい	ごわ	ごひき	ごほん	ごはい	ごさつ
6	ろくだい	ろくわ	ろっぴき	ろっぽん	ろっぱい	ろくさつ
7	ななだい	ななわ	ななひき	ななほん	ななはい	ななさつ
8	はちだい	はちわ	はっぴき	はっぽん	はっぱい	はっさつ
9	きゅうだい	きゅうわ	きゅうひき	きゅうほん	きゅうはい	きゅうさつ
10	じゅうだい	じゅうわ	じゅっぴき	じゅっぽん	じゅっぱい	じゅっさつ
?	なんだい?	なんわ?	なんびき?	なんぼん?	なんばい?	なんさつ?

	13-4 $	13-4 ¢	13-4 ¥	13-4 100	13-4 1.000
1	いちドル	いっセント	いちえん	ひゃく	せん
2	にドル	にセント	にえん	にひゃく	にせん
3	さんドル	さんセント	さんえん	さんびゃく	さんぜん
4	よんドル	よんセント	よえん	よんひゃく	よんせん
5	ごドル	ごセント	ごえん	ごひゃく	ごせん
6	ろくドル	ろくセント	ろくえん	ろっぴゃく	ろくせん
7	ななドル	ななセント	ななえん	ななひゃく	ななせん
8	はちドル	はっセンT	はちえん	はっぴゃく	はっせん
9	きゅうドル	きゅうセント	きゅうえん	きゅうひゃく	きゅうせん
10	じゅうドル	じゅっセント	じゅうえん		
?	なんドル?	なんセント?	なんえん?	なんびゃく?	なんぜん?

16か

Days of the Month 10-1

1	ついたち	11	じゅういちにち	21	にじゅういちにち
2	ふつか	12	じゅうににち	22	にじゅうににち
3	みっか	13	じゅうさんにち	23	にじゅうさんにち
4	よっか	14	じゅうよっか	24	にじゅうよっか
5	いつか	15	じゅうごにち	25	にじゅうごにち
6	むいか	16	じゅうろくにち	26	にじゅうろくにち
7	なのか	17	じゅうしちにち	27	にじゅうしちにち
8	ようか	18	じゅうはちにち	28	にじゅうはちにち
9	ここのか	19	じゅうくにち	29	にじゅうくにち
10	とおか	20	はつか	30	さんじゅうにち
?	なんにち?			31	さんじゅういちにち

にほんご１のかんじ

* previously introduced

11-1	月 がつ	日 にち, か					
13-2	一 いち, ひと(つ)	二 に, ふた(つ)	三 さん, みっ(つ)	四 し, よ-, よん, よっ(つ)	五 ご, いつ(つ)		
14-1	六 ろく, むっ(つ)	七 なな, し ち, なな(つ)	八 はち, やっ(つ)	九 く, きゅう, ここの(つ)	十 じゅう, とお		
15-1	日 にち*, か*, び	月 がつ*, げつ	火 か	水 みず, すい	木 もく, き	金 きん, かね	土 ど

16か

358

JAPANESE-ENGLISH & ENGLISH-JAPANESE WORD LIST

Abbreviations of Grammar Term References

A		い Adjective	*atsui, takai, shiroi*
Adv		Adverb	*totemo, amari, sukoshi*
C		Copula	*desu, de, na*
D		Derivative	
	Da	adjectival Derivative	*-tai*
	Dv	verbal Derivative	*masu, mashoo, masen*
N		Noun	
	Na	な Adjective	*kirei, joozu, suki, yuumei*
	Nd	dependent Noun	*-doru, -han*
	Ni	interrogative Noun	*dare, doko, ikura*
	N	Noun	*hana, kuruma, enpitsu*
PN		Pre-Noun	*donna, kono, ano*
P		Particle	*de, e, ni*
Pc		clause Particle	*kara, ga*
SI		Sentence Interjective	*anoo, eeto*
SP		Sentence Particle	*ka, yo, ne, nee*
V		Verb	
	V1	Verb (group) 1	*ikimasu, hanashimasu, nomimasu*
	V2	Verb (group) 2	*tabemasu, nemasu, imasu*
	V3	Verb (group) 3 [irregular verb]	*kimasu, shimasu*

\<A\>

agemasu あげます	15-3	V2	give (to equal)
aimasu あいます＝会います	12-5	V1	meet
aka あか＝赤	5-5	N	red
akai あかい＝赤い	6-3	A	(is) red
akemasu あけます＝開けます	13-2	V2	open
akete kudasai あけてください＝開けて下さい	2-2	Exp	please open.
aki あき＝秋	12-4	N	autumn, (a) fall
amari あまり	5-4	Adv	(not) very
ame あめ＝飴	2-5	N	candy
ame あめ＝雨	1-7	N	rain
amerika アメリカ	3-4	N	America
amerikajin アメリカじん＝アメリカ人	3-4	N	U.S. citizen
anata あなた	2-4	N	you
anatano あなたの＝あなたの	2-4	N	yours
ane あね＝姉	3-1	N	(my) older sister
ani あに＝兄	3-1	N	(my) older brother
ano あの	2-4	PN	that ˜ over there
anoo... あのう...	2-1	SI	let me see . . . , well . . .
ao あお＝青	5-5	N	blue
aoi あおい＝青い	6-3	A	(is) blue
are あれ	1-6	N	that one over there
arigatoo gozaimasu ありがとうございます	1-5	Exp	Thank you very much.
arigatoo ありがとう	1-5	Exp	Thank you.
arimasu あります	10-1	V1	there is (inanimate object)
	11-2	V1	have
aruite \<arukimasu\> あるいて\<あるきます\>＝歩いて\<歩きます\>			
	7-4	V1	walk
asa あさ＝朝	4-3	N	morning
asagohan あさごはん＝朝御飯	4-3	N	breakfast
asatte あさって＝明後日	11-4	N	(the) day after tomorrow
ashi あし＝脚	6-1	N	leg
ashi あし＝足	6-1	N	foot
ashita あした＝明日	4-3	N	tomorrow
asobimasu あそびます＝遊びます	15-5	V1	play, amuse [not used for sports & music]
asoko あそこ	2-5	N	over there
atama あたま＝頭	6-1	N	head
atarashii あたらしい＝新しい	10-4	A	new
atatakai あたたかい＝暖かい	14-4	A	warm
(-no) ato de (-の) あとで＝(-の) 後で	12-5	Pp	after ～

atsui あつい=暑い	1-7	IA	hot [temperature]

\<B\>

baggu バッグ	2-3	N	bag
baibai バイバイ	14-5	Exp	good bye
ban ばん=晩	4-3	N	evening
bangohan ばんごはん=晩御飯	4-3	N	dinner, supper
baree(booru) バレー(ボール)	5-3	N	volleyball
basu バス	7-4	N	bus
basuketto(booru) バスケット(ボール)	5-3	N	basketball
beddo ベッド	10-5	N	bed
bengoshi べんごし=弁護士	3-5	N	lawyer
benkyoo (o) shimasu べんきょう=勉強(を)します	4-4	V3	study
bentoo べんとう=弁当	14-2	N	box lunch
bideo ビデオ	4-5	N	video
bijutsu びじゅつ=美術	11-2	N	art
boku ぼく=僕	1-1	N	I (used by males)
bokutachi ぼくたち=僕達	12-3	N	we [used by males.]
boorupen ボールペン	2-3	N	ballpoint pen
booshi ぼうし=帽子	2-3	N	cap, hat
buta ぶた=豚	10-5	N	pig
byooin びょういん=病院	3-5	N	hospital
byooki びょうき=病気	12-1	N	illness, sickness

\<C\>

chairo ちゃいろ=茶色	5-5	N	brown color
chairoi ちゃいろい=茶色い	6-3	A	(is) brown
chakuseki ちゃくせき=着席	1-4	Exp	Sit.
chichi no hi ちちのひ=父の日	15-3	N	Father's Day
chichi ちち=父	3-1	N	(my) father
chiimu チーム	12-3	N	team
chiisai ちいさい=小さい	6-2	A	small
chikai ちかい=近い	10-5	A	near, close
chikatetsu ちかてつ=地下鉄	7-4	N	subway
chikoku desu ちこくです=遅刻です	1-4	Exp	tardy
chokoreeto チョコレート	2-5	N	chocolate
chotto matte kudasai ちょっとまってください	1-5	Exp	Please wait a minute.
chotto ちょっと	4-1	Adv	a little [more colloquial than すこし]
chuugaku ichinensei ちゅうがくいちねんせい=中学一年生			
	3-3	N	seventh grader
chuugaku ninensei ちゅうがくにねんせい=中学二年生			
	3-3	N	eighth grader
chuugaku sannensei ちゅうがくさんねんせい=中学三年生			
	3-3	N	freshman, ninth grader

chuugaku ちゅうがく=中学	3-3	N	intermediate school
chuugakusei ちゅうがくせい=中学生	3-3	N	intermediate school student
chuugoku ちゅうごく=中国	3-4	N	China
chuugokugo ちゅうごくご=中国語	4-1	N	Chinese language

\<D\>

-dai -だい=-台	10-3	Nd	[counter for mechanized goods]
daigaku だいがく=大学	12-5	N	college, university
daigakusei だいがくせい=大学生	12-5	N	college student
daiji だいじ=大事	12-4	Na	important
daijoobu だいじょうぶ=大丈夫	12-1	Na	all right
daikirai だいきらい=大嫌い	5-2	Na	dislike a lot, hate
daisuki だいすき=大好き	5-2	Na	like very much, love
dame だめ	2-1	Na	no good
dansu ダンス	5-1	N	dance, dancing
dare? だれ=誰	3-1	Ni	who?
dashimasu だします=出します	13-2	V1	turn in
dashite kudasai だしてください=出して下さい	2-2	Exp	please turn in.
[tool] de -で	14-3	P	with [tool]
(place) de で (+ action verb)	4-1	P	at, in (a place)
(too) de で	4-5	P	by, with, on, in [tool particle]
(transportation) de で	7-4	P	by (transportation facility)
(counter) de で	14-2	N	[totalizing particle]
de で	14-2	C	[Te form of copula です]
demo でも	4-1	SI	But [used at the beginning of a sentence.]
densha でんしゃ=電車	7-4	N	electric train
denwa でんわ=電話	4-5	N	telephone
denwabangoo でんわばんごう=電話番号	15-4	N	telephone number
depaato デパート	7-5	N	department store
desu です	1-1	C	am, is, are
dewa では	14-1	Exp	well then [formal]
doa ドア	10-1	N	door
doitsu ドイツ	3-4	N	Germany
doitsugo ドイツご=ドイツ語	4-1	N	German language
doko emo どこへも	7-5	Ni+P	(not to) anywhere
doko どこ	3-4	Ni	where?
dokusho どくしょ=読書	5-1	N	reading
donna～? どんな～	5-2	PN	what kind of ～?
dono-? どの-	13-4	Nd	which ～?
doo desu ka どうですか	11-3	Exp	how is it? [informal]
doo shimashita ka どうしましたか	12-1	Exp	What happened?
dooitashimashite どういたしまして	1-5	Exp	You are welcome.
doomo どうも	1-5	Exp	Thank you.

dooshite? どうして	11-4	Ni	why?
doozo yoroshiku. どうぞ　よろしく。	1-1	N	nice to meet you.
dore? どれ	13-4	Ni	which one?
-doru -ドル	13-4	Nd	dollar(s)
doyoobi どようび＝土曜日	7-1	N	Saturday

\<E\>

e え＝絵	5-1	N	painting, drawing
(place) e へ	7-3	P	to (place)
ee ええ	1-6	SI	no [informal]
eeto... ええと...	2-1	SI	let me see . . . , well . . .
eiga えいが＝映画	5-1	N	movie
eigo えいご＝英語	4-1	N	English
emu-saizu エムサイズ	14-2	N	medium size
-en -えん＝-円	13-4	Nd	yen
enjinia エンジニア	3-5	N	engineer
enpitsu えんぴつ＝鉛筆	2-3	N	pencil
enpitsukezuri えんぴつけずり＝鉛筆削り	10-1	N	pencil sharpener
eru-saizu エルサイズ	14-2	N	large size
esu-saizu エスサイズ	14-2	N	small size

\<F\>

fooku フォーク	14-3	N	fork
futtobooru フットボール	5-3	N	football
-fun -ふん＝-分	7-2	Nd	minute
fune ふね＝船	7-4	N	boat, ship
furaidopoteto フライドポテト	14-2	N	french fries
furansu フランス	3-4	N	France
furansugo フランスご＝フランス語	4-1	N	French language
furui ふるい＝古い	10-4	A	old (not for person's age)
futari ふたり＝二人	3-1	N	two (persons)
futatsu ふたつ＝二つ	2-5	N	two [general counter]
futotte imasu ふとっています＝太っています	6-4	V1	(is) fat
futsuka ふつか＝二日	11-1	N	(the) second day of the month
fuusen ふうせん＝風船	15-2	N	balloon
fuyu ふゆ＝冬	12-4	N	winter

\<G\>

(sentence) ga が	5-3	Pc	but [less formal than でも]
(subject) ga が	7-4	P	[subject particle]
gaikokugo がいこくご＝外国語	11-2	N	foreign language
gakkoo がっこう＝学校	3-3	N	school
gakusei がくせい＝学生	3-3	N	student [college]
ganbarimasu がんばります＝頑張ります	12-4	V1	do one's best
ganbatte がんばって＝頑張って	12-4	V1	Good luck.
gareeji ガレージ	10-5	N	garage

-gatsu umare -がつうまれ=-月生まれ	3-4	Nd	born in (month)
geemu ゲーム	15-5	N	game
geemu(o)shimasu ゲーム(を)します	15-5	V3	play a game
(o)genki (お)げんき=(お)元気	1-7	Na	fine, healthy
(O)genki desu ka. おげんきですか=お元気ですか	1-7	Exp	how are you?
getsuyoobi げつようび=月曜日	7-1	N	Monday
giniro ぎんいろ=銀色	5-5	N	silver color
gitaa ギター	5-1	N	guitar
go ご=五	1-5	N	five
go-juu ごじゅう=五十	1-6	N	fifty
gochisoosama ごちそうさま	14-4	Exp	[after a meal]
gogatsu ごがつ=五月	3-4	N	May
gogo ごご=午後	7-2	N	p.m.
gohan ごはん=ご飯	4-2	N	(cooked) rice
gokiburi ごきぶり	10-5	N	cockroach
gomi ごみ	2-3	N	rubbish
gomibako ごみばこ=ごみ箱	10-1	N	trash can
-goro -ごろ	7-2	Nd	about (time)
gorufu ゴルフ	5-3	N	golf
gozen ごぜん=午前	7-2	N	a.m.
-gurai -ぐらい	13-4	Nd	about ˜ [Not used for time.]
gurei グレイ	5-5	N	grey
gyuunyuu ぎゅうにゅう=牛乳	4-2	N	(cow's) milk

\<H\>

ha は=歯	6-1	N	tooth
hachi はち=八	1-5	N	eight
hachi-juu はちじゅう=八十	1-6	N	eighty
hachigatsu はちがつ=八月	3-4	N	August
haha no hi ははのひ=母の日	15-3	N	Mother's Day
haha はは=母	3-1	N	(my) mother
hai doozo. はい、どうぞ	2-5	Exp	Here, you are.
hai はい	1-3	Exp	yes
	1-6	SI	yes
hai, chiizu はい、チーズ	15-5	Exp	Say "cheese."
hai, piisu はい、ピース	15-5	Exp	Say "peace."
hajimemashite. はじめまして。	1-1	Exp	How do you do?
hajimemashoo はじめましょう=始めましょう	1-4	Exp	Let's begin.
hajimemasu はじめます=始めます	1-4	V	begin
-han -はん=-半	7-2	Nd	half
hana はな=花	10-3	N	flower
hana はな=鼻	6-1	N	nose
hanashimasu はなします=話します	4-1	V1	speak, talk
hanaya はなや=花屋	13-3	N	flower shop

hanbaagaa ハンバーガー	14-2	N	hamburger
haru はる=春	12-4	N	spring
(o) hashi (お)はし=(お)箸	14-3	N	chopsticks
hashirimasu はしります=走ります	12-5	V1	run
hatachi はたち=二十歳	3-1	N	twenty years old
hatsuka はつか=二十日	11-1	N	(the) twentith day of the month
hayai はやい=早い	7-2	A	early
hayaku はやく	1-4	Exp	hurry!
hayaku はやく=早く	12-2	Adv	early [used with a verb]
heta へた=下手	5-3	Na	unskillful, (be) poor at
heya へや=部屋	10-5	N	room
hi ひ=日	15-3	N	day
hidoi ひどい=酷い	11-4	A	terrible
hige ひげ=髭	6-1	N	beard, moustache
-hiki -ひき=-匹	10-3	Nd	[counter for small animals]
hikooki ひこうき=飛行機	7-4	N	airplane
hikui ひくい=低い	6-1	A	short (height)
hiroi ひろい=広い	10-5	A	wide, spacious
(o)hiru (お)ひる=(お)昼	4-3	N	daytime
hirugohan ひるごはん=昼御飯	4-3	N	lunch
hito ひと=人	10-2	N	person
hitori ひとり=一人	3-1	N	one (person)
hitotsu ひとつ=一つ	2-5	N	one [general counter]
hon ほん=本	2-3	N	book
hontoo ほんとう=本当	3-1	N	true
honya ほんや=本屋	13-3	N	bookstore
hoomuruumu ホームルーム	11-2	N	homeroom
hoshii ほしい=欲しい	11-5	A	want (something)
hottodoggu ホットドッグ	14-2	N	hotdog
hyaku ひゃく=百	1-6	N	hundred
hyaku-man ひゃくまん=百万	13-4	N	(one) million

‹I›

ichi いち=一	1-5	N	one
ichigatsu いちがつ=一月	3-4	N	January
ii desu nee いいですねえ	11-4	Exp	How nice! [on the future event]
ii いい	2-1	IA	good
iie いいえ	1-6	SI	no [formal]
iie, kekkoo desu いいえ、けっこうです	14-3	Exp	No, thank you.
iimasu いいます=言います	13-2	V1	say
ikaga desu ka? いかがですか=如何ですか	13-5	Ni	how about ˜? [Polite exp. of どうですか.]
ike いけ=池	10-3	N	pond
ikimasu いきます=行きます	7-3	V1	go

(o)ikura? (お)いくら	13-4	Ni	how much?
ikutsu いくつ	2-5	Ni	how many? [general counter]
(o)ikutsu? (お)いくつ	3-1	Ni	how old?
ima いま=今	3-5	N	now
imasu います	10-1	V2	there is (animate object)
imooto いもうと=妹	3-1	N	(my) younger sister
imootosan いもうとさん=妹さん	3-2	N	(someone's) younger sister
inu いぬ=犬	10-1	N	dog
irimasu いります=要ります	14-3	V1	need
iro いろ=色	5-5	N	color
isha いしゃ=医者	3-5	N	(medical) doctor [informal]
isogashii いそがしい=忙しい	7-5	A	busy
issho ni いっしょに=一緒に	4-4	Adv	together
isu いす=椅子	10-1	N	chair
itadakimasu いただきます	14-4	Exp	[before a meal]
itai いたい=痛い	12-1	A	painful, sore
itoko いとこ	15-2	N	cousin
itsu? いつ	7-1	Ni	when?
itsuka いつか=五日	11-1	N	(the) fifth day of the month
itsumo いつも	4-2	Adv	always
itsutsu いつつ=五つ	2-5	N	five [general counter]
<J>			
ja じゃ	14-1	Exp	well then [informal]
jaketto ジャケット	13-3	N	jacket
jama じゃま=邪魔	6-5	Na	hindrance, nuisance, is in the way
-ji -じ=-時	7-2	Nd	o'clock
jidoosha じどうしゃ=自動車	7-4	N	car, vehicle
jimusho じむしょ=事務所	10-4	N	office
jisho じしょ=辞書	2-3	N	dictionary
jitensha じてんしゃ=自転車	7-4	N	bicycle
jogingu ジョギング	5-1	N	jogging
joozu じょうず=上手	5-3	Na	skillful, (be) good at
jugyoo じゅぎょう=授業	11-2	N	class, instruction
juu じゅう=十	1-5	N	ten
juu-go じゅうご=十五	1-6	N	fifteen
juu-hachi じゅうはち=十八	1-6	N	eighteen
juu-ichi じゅういち=十一	1-6	N	eleven
juu-ku じゅうく=十九	1-6	N	nineteen
juu-kyuu じゅうきゅう=十九	1-6	N	nineteen
juu-man じゅうまん=十万	13-4	N	hundred thousand
juu-nana じゅうなな=十七	1-6	N	seventeen
juu-ni じゅうに=十二	1-6	N	twelve

juu-roku じゅうろく＝十六	1-6	N	sixteen
juu-san じゅうさん＝十三	1-6	N	thirteen
juu-shi じゅうし＝十四	1-6	N	fourteen
juu-shichi じゅうしち＝十七	1-6	N	seventeen
juu-yokka じゅうよっか＝十四日	11-1	N	(the) fourteenth day of the month
juu-yon じゅうよん ＝十四	1-6	N	fourteen
juugatsu じゅうがつ＝十月	3-4	N	October
juuichigatsu じゅういちがつ＝十一月	3-4	N	November
juunigatsu じゅうにがつ＝十二月	3-4	N	December
juusho じゅうしょ＝住所	15-4	N	address
juusu ジュース	4-2	N	juice

＜K＞

ka か	1-4	SP	[question particle]
kachimasu かちます＝勝ちます	12-3	V1	win
kaerimasu かえります＝帰ります	7-3	V1	return (place)
kafeteria カフェテリア	4-4	N	cafeteria
kagaku かがく＝科学	11-2	N	science
kaimasu かいます＝買います	13-3	V1	buy
kaimono かいもの＝買い物	7-5	N	shopping
kaimono(o)shimasu かいもの（を）します＝買い物（を）します			
	7-5	V3	shop
kaisha かいしゃ＝会社	7-3	N	company
kaishain かいしゃいん＝会社員	3-5	N	company employee
kaite kudasai かいてください＝書いて下さい	2-2	Exp	Please write.
kakimasu かきます＝書きます	4-5	V1	write
kamera カメラ	15-5	N	camera
kami かみ＝紙	2-3	N	paper
kami(no ke) かみ（のけ）＝髪(の毛)	6-1	N	hair
kamoku かもく＝科目	11-2	N	subject
kanashii かなしい＝悲しい	11-4	A	sad
(o)kane （お）かね＝(お)金	2-3	N	money
kankoku かんこく＝韓国	3-4	N	Korea
kankokugo かんこくご＝韓国語	4-1	N	Korean language
kao かお＝顔	6-1	N	face
-kara -から	11-2	P	from～
(sentence) kara から	11-4	Pc	because～, since～, ～so
karada からだ＝体	6-1	N	body
kashite kudasai かしてください＝貸して下さい	14-3	V1	(please) lend me.
-kata -かた＝-方	10-2	Nd	person [polite form of ひと]
kawa かわ＝川	7-5	N	river
kawaii かわいい＝可愛い	6-5	A	cute
kawaisoo ni かわいそうに＝可愛そうに	12-1	Exp	How pitiful.
kayoobi かようび＝火曜日	7-1	N	Tuesday

kaze かぜ＝風邪	12-1	N	(a) cold
kazoku かぞく＝家族	3-1	N	(my) family
(go)kazoku （ご）かぞく＝（御）家族	3-2	N	(someone's) family
kesa けさ＝今朝	12-2	N	this morning
keshigomu けしごむ＝消しゴム	2-3	N	eraser [rubber]
ki き＝木	10-3	N	tree
kibishii きびしい＝厳しい	6-4	A	strict
kiiro きいろ＝黄色	5-5	N	yellow color
kiiroi きいろい＝黄色い	6-3	A	(is) yellow
kiite kudasai きいてください＝聞いて下さい	2-2	Exp	Please listen.
kikimasu ききます＝聞きます	4-4	V1	listen, hear
kikoemasen きこえません＝聞こえません	2-1	V2	cannot hear
kikoemasu きこえます＝聞こえます	2-1	V2	can hear
kimasu きます＝来ます	7-3	V3	come
kiniro きんいろ＝金色	5-5	N	gold color
kinoo きのう＝昨日	4-3	N	yesterday
kinyoobi きんようび＝金曜日	7-1	N	Friday
kippu きっぷ＝切符	15-2	N	ticket
kirai きらい＝嫌い	5-2	Na	dislike
kirei きれい	6-5	Na	pretty, clean, neat, nice
kiritsu きりつ＝起立	1-4	Exp	Stand
kissaten きっさてん＝喫茶店	13-3	N	coffee shop
kitanai きたない	6-5	A	dirty, messy
kochira こちら	3-4	N	this one [polite form of これ]
kodomo こども＝子供	10-2	N	child
koe こえ＝声	6-1	N	voice
koko ここ	2-5	N	here
kokonoka ここのか＝九日	11-1	N	(the) ninth day of the month
kokonotsu ここのつ＝九つ	2-5	N	nine [general counter]
kokoro こころ＝心	6-1	N	heart
konban wa こんばんは＝今晩は	7-2	Exp	Good evening.
konban こんばん＝今晩	7-2	N	tonight
kongetsu こんげつ＝今月	12-4	N	this month
konnichi wa.こんにちは。	1-3	Exp	Hello. Hi.
kono この	2-4	PN	this
konpyuutaa コンピューター	4-5	N	computer
konsaato コンサート	15-2	N	concert
konshuu こんしゅう＝今週	11-5	N	this week
koohii コーヒー	4-2	N	coffee
kookoo ichinensei こうこういちねんせい＝高校一年生	3-3	N	sophomore, tenth grader
kookoo ninensei こうこうにねんせい＝高校二年生	3-3	N	junior, eleventh grader
kookoo sannensei こうこうさんねんせい＝高校三年生	3-3	N	senior, twelfth grader

kookoo こうこう＝高校	3-3	N	high school
kookoosei こうこうせい＝高校生	3-3	N	high school student
koora コーラ	4-2	N	cola
koppu コップ	14-3	N	cup
kore これ	1-2	N	this one
korekara これから	14-5	SI	from now on
-koro -ころ	7-2	Nd	about (time)
koto こと＝事	5-3	N	thing [intangible]
kotoshi ことし＝今年	15-4	N	this year
ku く＝九	1-5	N	nine
kubi くび＝首	6-1	N	neck
kuchi くち＝口	6-1	N	mouth
(-o)kudasai （-を）ください	2-5	Exp	please give me ～.
kugatsu くがつ＝九月	3-4	N	September
-kurai -くらい	13-4	Nd	about ～ [Not used for time.]
kurasu クラス	11-2	N	class, instruction
kuremasu くれます	15-2	V2	give (to me or to my family)
kuro くろ＝黒	5-5	N	black
kuroi くろい＝黒い	6-3	A	(is) black
kuruma くるま＝車	7-4	N	car, vehicle
kusuri くすり＝薬	12-2	N	medicine
kutsu くつ＝靴	13-3	N	shoes
kyandii キャンディ	2-5	N	candy
kyanpu キャンプ	7-5	N	camp
kyonen きょねん＝去年	15-4	N	last year
kyoo きょう＝今日	4-3	N	today
kyoodai きょうだい＝兄弟	3-1	N	(my) sibling(s)
kyookasho きょうかしょ＝教科書	2-3	N	textbook
kyooshitsu きょうしつ＝教室	10-4	N	classroom
kyuu きゅう＝九	1-5	N	nine
kyuu-juu きゅうじゅう＝九十	1-6	N	ninety

\<M\>

maamaa まあまあ	5-4	Adv	"so, so"
machimasu まちます＝待ちます	13-2	V1	wait
mada desu (+neg.)まだです	14-1	Exp	not yet
-made -まで	11-2	P	to～; until ～
mado まど＝窓	10-1	N	window
-mae -まえ＝-前	7-2	Nd	before ～
(-no) mae ni （-の）まえに＝（-の）前に	12-5	Pp	before ～
mae まえ＝前	3-5	N	before
-mai -まい＝-枚	2-5	Nd	[counter for flat objects]
mainen まいねん＝毎年	15-4	N	every year
mainichi まいにち＝毎日	4-2	N	everyday

maishuu まいしゅう=毎週	11-5	N	every week
maitoshi まいとし=毎年	15-4	N	every year
maitsuki まいつき=毎月	12-4	N	every month
makemasu まけます=負けます	12-3	V2	lose
(ichi)man (いち)まん=(一)万	13-4	N	ten thousand
-masen ka -ませんか	7-1	Dv	won't you do 〜? [invitation]
-mashoo -ましょう	7-1	Dv	let's do 〜. [suggestion]
(ja) mata ato de (じゃ)またあとで	14-5	Exp	(Well,) see you later.
mata また=又	10-1	Adv	again
mazui まずい	13-5	A	unappetizing
me め=目	6-1	N	eye
midori みどり=緑	5-5	N	green
miemasen みえません=見えません	2-1	V2	cannot see
miemasu みえます=見えます	2-1	V2	can see
mijikai みじかい=短い	6-2	A	short [not for height]
mikka みっか=三日	11-1	N	(the) third day of the month
mimasu みます=見ます	4-5	V2	watch, look, see
mimi みみ=耳	6-1	N	ear
minasan みなさん=皆さん	15-1	N	everyone [polite]
minna みんな=皆	15-1	N	everyone
miruku ミルク	4-2	N	(cow's) milk
(o)mise (お)みせ=(お)店	13-2	N	store
misemasu みせます=見せます	13-2	V2	show
misete kudasai みせてください=見せて下さい	2-2	Exp	Please show.
mite kudasai みてください=見て下さい	2-2	Exp	Please look.
mittsu みっつ=三つ	2-5	N	three [general counter]
(o)mizu (お)みず=(お)水	4-2	N	water
mokuyoobi もくようび=木曜日	7-1	N	Thursday
mono もの=物	5-2	N	thing [tangible]
moo (+aff.) もう	14-1	Exp	already
moo sugu もうすぐ	15-3	Adv	very soon
moo (ippai) もう(いっぱい)=もう(一杯)	14-4	Adv	(one) more (cup)
mooichido もういちど=もう一度	1-5	Adv	one more time
moraimasu もらいます	15-2	V1	receive, get from
muika むいか=六日	11-1	N	(the) sixth day of the month
murasaki むらさき=紫	5-5	N	purple
mushiatsui むしあつい=蒸し暑い	1-7	IA	hot and humid
(o)musubi (お)むすび	14-2	N	riceball
muttsu むっつ=六つ	2-5	N	six [general counter]
muzukashii むずかしい=難しい	11-3	A	difficult

<N>

nado など	15-3	Nd	etc.
nagai ながい=長い	6-2	A	long

naifu ナイフ	14-3	N	knife
namae なまえ=名前	3-1	N	name
(o) namae おなまえ=御名前	3-2	N	(someone's) name
nan なん=何	1-4	Ni	what?
nan-bai? なんばい=何杯	14-3	Ni	how many cups?
nan-gatsu? なんがつ=何月	3-4	Ni	what month?
nan-nensei? なんねんせい=何年生	3-3	N	what grade?
nan-nichi? なんにち=何日	11-1	Ni	(the) what day of the month?
nan-nin? なんにん=何人	3-1	Ni	how many people?
nan-sai? なんさい=何歳, 何才	3-1	Ni	how old?
nan-satsu? なんさつ=何冊	15-2	Ni	how many [bound objects]?
nan-yoobi? なんようび=何曜日	7-1	Ni	what day of the week?
nana なな=七	1-5	N	seven
nana-juu ななじゅう=七十	1-6	N	seventy
nanatsu ななつ=七つ	2-5	N	seven [general counter]
nanbiki? なんびき=何匹	10-3	Ni	how many [small animals]?
nanbon? なんぼん=何本	10-3	Ni	how many [long cylindrical objects]?
nandai? なんだい=何台	10-3	Ni	how many [mechanized goods]?
nani なに=何	1-4	Ni	what?
nani-jin? なにじん=何人	3-4	Ni	what nationality?
nanigo? なにご=何語	4-1	Ni	what language?
naniiro? なにいろ=何色	5-5	N	what color?
nanimo (+ Neg.) なにも(+ Neg.) =何も(+ Neg.)	4-3	Ni+P	(not) anything
nanji? なんじ=何時	7-2	Ni	what time?
nanoka なのか=七日	11-1	N	(the) seventh day of the month
nanwa? なんわ=何羽	10-3	Ni	how many [birds]?
napukin ナプキン	14-3	N	napkin
natsu なつ=夏	12-4	N	summer
naze? なぜ	11-4	Ni	why?
ne ね	6-5	SP	isn't it? [sentence ending particle]
neko ねこ=猫	10-1	N	cat
nemasu ねます=寝ます	7-3	V2	sleep, go to bed
nemui ねむい=眠い	12-2	A	sleepy
-nen -ねん=-年	15-4	Nd	-year
netsu ねつ=熱	12-1	N	fever
nezumi ねずみ=鼠	10-5	N	mouse
(specific time) ni に	7-1	P	at (specific time)
(activity) ni に	7-3	P	for (activity)
(place) ni に (+ existance verb)	10-1	P	in, at (place)
(place) ni に (+ direction verb)	7-3	P	to (place)
ni に=二	1-5	N	two
ni-juu にじゅう=二十	1-6	N	twenty

-nichi -にち=-日	11-1	Nd	day of the month
nichiyoobi にちようび=日曜日	7-1	N	Sunday
nigate にがて=苦手	5-3	Na	(be) weak in
nigatsu にがつ=二月	3-4	N	February
(o)nigiri (お)にぎり	14-2	N	riceball
nihon にほん=日本	3-4	N	Japan
(-wa) nihongo de nan to iimasu ka -はにほんごでなんといいますか =-は日本語で何と言いますか	2-1	Exp	how do you say ˜ in Japanese?
nihongo にほんご=日本語	4-1	N	Japanese language
nihonjin にほんじん=日本人	3-4	N	Japanese citizen
nijuu-yokka にじゅうよっか=二十四日	11-1	N	(the) twenty fourth day of the month
-nin -にん=-人	3-1	Nd	[counter for people]
niwa にわ=庭	10-5	N	garden, yard
no の	3-1	P	[possessive and descriptive particle]
nodo のど=喉	6-1	N	throat
nodo ga karakara desu のどがカラカラです=喉がカラカラです	14-1	Exp	I am thirsty.
nodo ga kawakimashita のどがかわきました=喉が渇きました	14-1	Exp	I got thirsty.
nomimasu のみます=飲みます	4-2	V2	drink
	12-2	V1	take (medicine)
nomimono のみもの=飲み物	5-2	N	(a) drink
nooto ノート	2-3	N	notebook

<O>

obaasan おばあさん	3-2	N	grandmother, elderly woman
obasan おばさん	15-2	N	aunt, middle aged woman
ocha おちゃ=お茶	4-2	N	tea
ohayoo gozaimasu.おはようございます。	1-3	Exp	good morning. (Formal)
ohayoo. おはよう。	1-3	Exp	good morning. (Informal)
oishasan おいしゃさん=御医者さん	3-5	N	(medical) doctor [polite form of いしゃ]
oishii おいしい=美味しい	13-5	A	delicious
ojiisan おじいさん	3-2	N	grandfather, elderly man
ojisan おじさん	15-2	N	uncle, middle aged man
okaasan おかあさん=お母さん	3-2	N	(someone's) mother
okimasu おきます=起きます	7-3	V2	wake up, get up
omedetoo gozaimasu おめでとうございます	15-1	Exp	Congratulations.
omoshiroi おもしろい=面白い	11-3	A	interesting
onaka おなか=お腹	6-1	N	stomach
onaka ga ippai desu おなかがいっぱいです=お腹が一杯です	14-4	Exp	(I am) full.
onaka ga pekopeko desu おなかがペコペコです=お腹がペコペコです	14-1	Exp	I am hungry.

onaka ga sukimashita おなかがすきました=お腹が空きました	14-1	Exp	I got hungry.
oneesan おねえさん=お姉さん	3-2	N	(someone's) older sister
onegaishimasu おねがいします=御願いします	1-5	Exp	please [request]
ongaku おんがく=音楽	5-1	N	music
oniisan おにいさん=お兄さん	3-2	N	(someone's) older brother
onna no hito おんなのひと=女の人	10-2	N	woman, lady
onna no ko おんなのこ=女の子	10-2	N	girl
onna おんな=女	10-2	N	female
ooi おおい=多い	11-5	A	many, much
ookii おおきい=大きい	6-2	A	big
orenji(iro) オレンジいろ=オレンジ色	5-5	N	orange (color)
osoi おそい=遅い	7-2	A	late
osoku おそく=遅く	12-2	Adv	late [used with a verb]
otoko おとこ=男	10-2	N	male
otoko no hito おとこのひと=男の人	10-2	N	man
otoko no ko おとこのこ=男の子	10-2	N	boy
otoosan おとうさん=お父さん	3-2	N	(someone's) father
otooto おとうと=弟	3-1	N	(my) younger brother
otootosan おとうとさん=弟さん	3-2	N	(someone's) younger brother
ototoi おととい=一昨日	11-4	N	(the) day before yesterday
owarimashoo おわりましょう=終わりましょう	1-4	Exp	Let's finish.
owarimasu おわります=終わります	1-4	V	finish
oyogimasu およぎます=泳ぎます	15-5	V1	swim

<P>

paatii パーティー	7-5	N	party
-pai -ぱい=-杯	14-3	Nd	cupful, glassful, bowlful, spoonful
pan パン	4-2	N	bread
pantsu パンツ	13-3	N	pants
piano ピアノ	5-1	N	piano
pikunikku ピクニック	7-5	N	picnic
pinku ピンク	5-5	N	pink
piza ピザ	14-2	N	pizza
-pon -ぽん=-本	10-3	Nd	[counter for long cylindrical objects]
purezento プレゼント	15-1	N	present
puuru プール	10-2	N	pool

<R>

raigetsu らいげつ=来月	12-4	N	next month
rainen らいねん=来年	15-4	N	next year
raishuu らいしゅう=来週	11-5	N	next week
rajio ラジオ	4-5	N	radio

rei れい=礼	1-4	Exp	bow
renshuu(o)shimasu れんしゅう(を)します=練習(を)します			
	12-5	V3	practice
repooto レポート	4-5	N	report, paper
resutoran レストラン	7-5	N	restaurant
rokkaa ロッカー	10-4	N	locker
roku ろく=六	1-5	N	six
roku-juu ろくじゅう=六十	1-6	N	sixty
rokugatsu ろくがつ=六月	3-4	N	June
ryokoo りょこう=旅行	7-5	N	trip, traveling
ryokoo(o)shimasu りょこう(を)します=旅行(を)します			
	7-5	V3	travel

\<S\>

-sai -さい=-才, -歳	3-1	Nd	[counter for age]
saizu サイズ	14-2	N	size
sakana さかな=魚	10-3	N	fish
sakkaa サッカー	5-3	N	soccer
samui さむい=寒い	1-7	IA	cold
-san -さん	1-3	Nd	Mr./Mrs./Ms.
san さん=三	1-5	N	three
san-juu さんじゅう=三十	1-6	N	thirty
sandoitchi サンドイッチ	14-2	N	sandwich
sangatsu さんがつ=三月	3-4	N	March
(o)sara おさら=お皿	14-3	N	plate, dish
sarada サラダ	14-2	N	salad
-satsu -さつ=-冊	15-2	Nd	[counter for bound objects]
sayoonara.さようなら。	1-3	Exp	Good-bye.
se(i) せ(い)=背	6-1	N	height
seiseki せいせき=成績	11-4	N	grade
seito せいと=生徒	3-3	N	student [non-college]
semai せまい=狭い	10-5	A	narrow, small (room)
sen せん=千	13-4	N	thousand
sengetsu せんげつ=先月	12-4	N	last month
sensei せんせい=先生	1-3	N	teacher, Mr./Mrs./Ms./Dr.
senshuu せんしゅう=先週	11-5	N	last week
-sento -セント	13-4	Nd	cent(s)
shakai しゃかい=社会	11-2	N	social studies
shashin しゃしん=写真	2-3	N	photo
shatsu シャツ	13-3	N	shirt
shi し=四	1-5	N	four
shiai しあい=試合	12-3	N	(sports) game
shichiしち=七	1-5	N	seven
shichi-juu しちじゅう=七十	1-6	N	seventy

shichigatsu しちがつ=七月	3-4	N	July
shigatsu しがつ=四月	3-4	N	April
(o)shigoto (お)しごと=(お)仕事	3-5	N	job
shiken しけん=試験	2-5	N	exam
shimasu します	4-4	V3	do
shimemasu しめます=閉めます	13-2	V2	close
shimete kudasai しめてください=閉めて下さい	2-2	Exp	Please close.
shinbun しんぶん=新聞	4-4	N	newspaper
shinimasu しにます=死にます	12-1	V1	die
shinseki しんせき=親戚	15-2	N	relatives
shirimasen しりません=知りません	2-1	V1	do not know
shiro しろ=白	5-5	N	white color
shiroi しろい=白い	6-3	A	(is) white
shizuka ni shimasu しずかにします=静かにします			
	13-2	V3	quiet down
shizuka しずか=静か	6-5	Na	quiet
shizukani shite kudasai しずかにしてください=静かにして下さい			
	2-2	Exp	Please be quiet.
shokuji しょくじ=食事	7-5	N	meal, dining
shokuji(o)shimasu しょくじ（を）します=食事（を）します			
	7-5	V3	dine, have a meal
shootesuto しょうテスト=小テスト	2-5	N	quiz
shufu しゅふ=主婦	3-5	N	housewife
shukudai しゅくだい=宿題	2-5	N	homework
shumi しゅみ=趣味	5-1	N	hobby
shuumatsu しゅうまつ=週末	11-5	N	weekend
soko そこ	2-5	N	there
sono その	2-4	PN	that ~
soo desu nee... そうですねえ...	5-1	Exp	Let me see . . .
soo desu そうです	1-6	Exp	it is
soo desuka そうですか	3-1	Exp	Is that so?
soo dewa arimasen そうではありません	1-6	Exp	It is not so. [formal]
soo ja arimasen そうじゃありません	1-6	Exp	It is not so. [informal]
sore それ	1-6	N	that one
Sorekara それから	7-3	SI	And then
soreni それに	11-5	SI	Moreover, Besides
Soretomo それとも	6-4	SI	Or
soshite そして	3-2	SI	and
soto そと=外	10-1	N	outside
subarashii すばらしい=素晴らしい	13-5	A	wonderful
-sugi -すぎ=-過ぎ	7-2	Nd	after ~
sugoi すごい=凄い	13-5	A	terrible, terrific
suiei すいえい=水泳	5-1	N	swimming

suiyoobi すいようび=水曜日	7-1	N	Wednesday
suki すき=好き	5-2	Na	like
sukoshi すこし=少し	4-1	Adv	a little [formal]
	10-3	Adv	a few, a little
sukunai すくない=少ない	11-5	A	is few, little
sumimasen すみません	1-5	Exp	Excuse me.
	13-2	Exp	Excuse me. (to get attention)
sunakkubaa スナックバー	4-4	N	snack bar
supein スペイン	3-4	N	Spain
supeingo スペインご=スペイン語	4-1	N	Spanish language
supootsu スポーツ	5-1	N	sports
supuun スプーン	14-3	N	spoon
sushiya すしや=寿司屋	13-3	N	sushi shop/bar
sutoroo ストロー	14-3	N	straw
suugaku すうがく=数学	11-2	N	math
suupaa スーパー	13-3	N	super market
suwarimasu すわります=座ります	13-2	V1	sit
suwatte kudasai すわってください=座って下さい	2-2	Exp	please sit.
suzushii すずしい=涼しい	1-7	IA	cool [temperature]

<T>

tabemasu たべます=食べます	4-2	V2	eat
tabemono たべもの=食べ物	5-2	N	food
-tachi -たち=-達	12-3	Nd	[suffix for animate plurals.]
tachimasu たちます=立ちます	13-2	V1	stand
-tai -たい	12-2	Da	want (to do)
taihen たいへん=大変	11-5	Na	hard, difficult
taiiku たいいく=体育	11-2	N	P.E.
taipu(o)shimasu タイプ(を)します	4-5	V3	type
taitei たいてい=大抵	4-2	Adv	usually
takai たかい=高い	6-1	A	tall
	13-5	A	expensive
takusan たくさん=沢山	10-3	Adv	a lot, many
takushii タクシー	7-4	N	taxi
(o)tanjoobi (お)たんじょうび=(お)誕生日	11-1	N	birthday
tanoshii たのしい=楽しい	11-3	A	fun, enjoyable
(-o)tanoshimi ni shite imasu (-を)たのしみにしています=(-を)楽しみにしています			
	15-4	Exp.	I am looking forward to (something).
tatemono たてもの=建物	10-4	N	building
tatte kudasai たってください=立って下さい	2-2	Exp	Please stand.
te て=手	6-1	N	hand
(o)tearai (お)てあらい=(お)手洗い	10-2	N	bathroom, restroom
teepu テープ	4-4	N	tape

tegami てがみ=手紙	4-5	N	letter
tekisuto テキスト	2-3	N	textbook
tenisu テニス	5-3	N	tennis
(o)tenki (お)てんき=(お)天気	1-7	N	weather
terebi テレビ	4-5	N	TV
terebigeemu テレビゲーム	5-1	N	video game
tisshu ティッシュ	2-5	N	tissue
to (issho ni) と(いっしょに)	4-4	P	with (person)
to と	3-2	P	and [used between two nouns]
to と=戸	10-1	N	door
(o)toire (お)トイレ	10-2	N	bathroom, restroom
tokei とけい=時計	13-3	N	watch, clock
tokidoki ときどき=時々	4-2	Adv	sometimes
tokui とくい=得意	5-3	Na	(be) strong in, can do well
tomodachi ともだち=友達	4-1	N	friend
too とお=十	2-5	N	ten [general counter]
tooi とおい=遠い	10-5	A	far
tooka とおか=十日	11-1	N	(the) tenth day of the month
toranpu トランプ	5-1	N	(playing) cards
tori とり=鳥	10-3	N	bird
torimasu とります=取ります	15-5	V1	take
toshi o totteimasu としをとっています=年を取っています			
	6-4	V1	(is) old (age)
toshokan としょかん=図書館	4-4	N	library
totemo とても	5-4	Adv	very
tsugi つぎ=次	11-3	N	next
tsuitachi ついたち=一日	11-1	N	(the) first day of the month
tsukaremashita つかれました=疲れました	12-2	V2	(got) tired
tsukarete imasu つかれています=疲れています	12-2	V2	tired
tsukue つくえ=机	10-1	N	desk
tsukurimasu つくります=作ります	15-5	V1	make
tsumaranai つまらない	11-3	A	boring, uninteresting
tsumetai つめたい=冷たい	14-4	A	cold (to the touch)
tsuyoi つよい=強い	12-3	A	strong
<U>			
uchi うち=家	4-1	N	house
umi うみ=海	7-5	N	beach, ocean, sea
ureshii うれしい=嬉しい	11-4	A	glad, happy
urusai うるさい	6-5	A	noisy
uta うた=歌	5-1	N	song, singing
utaimasu うたいます=歌います	15-1	V1	sing
utsukushii うつくしい=美しい	10-4	A	beautiful

\<W\>

-wa -わ=-羽	10-3	Nd	[counter for birds]
wa は	1-1	P	[particle marking the topic of the sentence]
waa わあ	13-5	SI	Wow!
waakushiito ワークシート	2-5	N	worksheet
wakai わかい=若い	6-4	A	young
wakarimasen わかりません=分かりません	2-1	V1	do not understand
wakarimasu わかります=分かります	2-1	V1	understand
warui わるい=悪い	6-2	A	bad
wasuremasu わすれます=忘れます	14-3	V2	forget
watashi わたし=私	1-1	N	I (used by anyone informally)
watashino わたしの=私の	2-4	N	mine
watashitachi わたしたち=私達	12-3	N	we
wookuman ウォークマン	4-4	N	walkman

\<Y\>

(N1) ya (N2)　(N1) や (N2)	15-3	P	(Noun1) and (Noun2), etc.
yakyuu やきゅう=野球	5-3	N	baseball
yama やま=山	7-5	N	mountain
yarimasu やります	15-3	V2	give (to inferior)
yasashii やさしい=易しい	11-3	A	easy
yasashii やさしい=優しい	6-4	A	nice, kind
yasete imasu やせています=痩せています	6-4	V2	thin
yasui やすい=安い	13-5	A	cheap
(o)yasumi (お)やすみ=(お)休み	7-1	N	day off, vacation
(o)yasumi desu (お)やすみです=(お)休みです	1-4	Exp	absent
yasumijikan やすみじかん=休み時間	11-2	N	(a) break
yasumimasu やすみます=休みます	12-2	V2	rest
(-o) yasumimasu (-を)やすみます=(-を)休みます	12-2	V2	(be) absent (from ~)
yattsu やっつ=八つ	2-5	N	eight [general counter]
(sentence) yo よ	6-5	SP	you know [sentence ending particle]
yoi よい=良い	6-2	A	good
yokatta desu nee よかったですねえ=良かったですねえ	11-4	Exp	How nice! [on a past event]
yokka よっか=四日	11-1	N	(the) fourth day of the month
yoku dekimashita よくできました=良く出来ました	2-2	Exp	Well done.
yoku よく	4-1	Adv	well, often
yomimasu よみます=読みます	4-4	V1	read
yon よん=四	1-5	N	four
yon-juu じょんじゅう=四十	1-6	N	forty
yonde kudasai よんでください=読んで下さい	2-2	Exp	Please read.

yooka ようか＝八日   11-1   N   (the) eighth day of the month
yoru よる＝夜   4-3   N   night
yottsu よっつ＝四つ   2-5   N   four [general counter]
yowai よわい＝弱い   12-3   A   weak
yubi ゆび＝指   6-1   N   finger, toe
yukkuri ゆっくり   1-5   Adv slowly
yuube ゆうべ＝夕べ   12-2   N   last night
yuugata ゆうがた＝夕方   4-3   N   late afternoon, early evening
yuumei ゆうめい＝有名   10-4   Na   famous

<Z>

zannen deshita nee ざんねんでしたねえ＝残念でしたねえ
                                           11-4   Exp How disappointing! [on a past
                                                        event]
zannen desu nee ざんねんですねえ＝残念ですねえ
                                           11-4   Exp How disappointing! [on a
                                                        future event]
zasshi ざっし＝雑誌   4-4   N   magazine
zenbu ぜんぶ＝全部   14-2   N   everything
zenbude ぜんぶ＝全部で   14-2   N   for everything
zenzen (= Neg.) ぜんぜん(= Neg.) ＝全然(= Neg.) 5-4 Adv (not) at all

\<A\>

a.m.	7-2	N	gozen ごぜん=午前
about (time)	7-2	Nd	-koro -ころ, -goro -ごろ
about ～ [Not used for time.]	13-4	Nd	-kurai -くらい, -gurai -ぐらい
absent	1-4	Exp	(o)yasumi (お)やすみです=(お)休みです
(be) absent (from ～)	12-2	V2	(-o) yasumimasu (-を)やすみます=(-を)休みます
address	15-4	N	juusho じゅうしょ=住所
after (time)	7-2	Nd	-sugi -すぎ=-過ぎ
after (an event)	12-5	Pp	(-no) ato de -のあとで=-の後で
again	10-1	Adv	mata また=又
airplane	7-4	N	hikooki ひこうき=飛行機
all right	12-1	Na	daijoobu だいじょうぶ=大丈夫
already	14-1	Exp	moo (+aff.) もう
always	4-2	Adv	itsumo いつも
am	1-1	C	desu です
America	3-4	N	amerika アメリカ
amuse [not used for sports & music]	15-5	V1	asobimasu あそびます=遊びます
and [used between two nouns]	3-2	P	to と
And [used only at the beginning of a sentence]	3-2	SI	Soshite そして
(Noun1) and (Noun2), etc.	15-3	P	(N1) ya (N2) (N1) や (N2) など
And then	7-3	SI	Sorekara それから
(not) anything	4-3	Ni+P	nanimo+Neg. なにも=何も+Neg.
(not to) anywhere	7-5	Ni+P	dokoemo+Neg. どこへも+Neg.
April	3-4	N	shigatsu しがつ=四月
are	1-1	C	desu です
art	11-2	N	bijutsu びじゅつ=美術
at (place) [with action verb]	4-1	P	de で [with action verb]
at (specific time)	7-1	P	(specific time) ni に
at (location) [with existence verb]	10-1	P	ni に[with existence verb]
(not) at all	5-4	Adv	zenzen+Neg. ぜんぜん=全然+Neg.
August	3-4	N	hachigatsu はちがつ=八月
aunt	15-2	N	obasan おばさん
autumn	12-4	N	aki あき=秋

\<B\>

bad	6-2	A	warui わるい=悪い
bag	2-3	N	baggu バッグ
ballpoint pen	2-3	N	boorupen ボールペン
balloon	15-2	N	fuusen ふうせん=風船
baseball	5-3	N	yakyuu やきゅう

basketball	5-3	N	basuketto(booru) バスケット(ボール)
bathroom	10-2	N	(o)toire (お)トイレ, (o)tearai (お)てあらい =(お)手洗い
beach	7-5	N	umi うみ=海
beard	6-1	N	hige ひげ=髭
beautiful	10-4	A	utsukushii うつくしい=美しい
because	11-4	Pc	(reason) kara (reason) から
bed	10-5	N	beddo ベッド
before	3-5	N	mae まえ=前
before (time)	7-2	Nd	-mae -まえ=-前
before (not time)	12-5	Pp	(-no) mae ni -のまえに=-の前に
begin	1-4	V	hajimemasu はじめます=始めます
Besides [used at the beginning of a sentence]			
	11-5	SI	Soreni それに
bicycle	7-4	N	jitensha じてんしゃ=自転車
big	6-2	A	ookii おおきい=大きい
bird	10-3	N	tori とり=鳥
birthday	11-1	N	(o)tanjoobi (お)たんじょうび=(お)誕生日
black color	5-5	N	kuro くろ=黒
(is) black	6-3	A	kuroi くろい=黒い
blue color	5-5	N	ao あお=青
(is) blue	6-3	A	aoi あおい=青い
boat	7-4	N	fune ふね=船
body	6-1	N	karada からだ=体
book	2-3	N	hon ほん=本
bookstore	13-3	N	honya ほんや=本屋
boring	11-3	A	tsumaranai つまらない
born in (month)	3-4	Nd	-gatsu umare -がつうまれ=-月生まれ
bow	1-4	Exp	rei れい=礼
bowlful	14-3	Nd	-pai -ぱい=-杯
box lunch	14-2	N	bentoo べんとう=弁当
boy	10-2	N	otoko no ko おとこのこ=男の子
bread	4-2	N	pan パン
(a) break	11-2	N	yasumijikan やすみじかん=休み時間
breakfast	4-3	N	asagohan あさごはん=朝御飯
brown color	5-5	N	chairo ちゃいろ=茶色
(is) brown	6-3	A	chairoi ちゃいろい=茶色い
building	10-4	N	tatemono たてもの=建物
bus	7-4	N	basu バス
busy	7-5	A	isogashii いそがしい=忙しい
But [used at the beginning of the sentence.]			
	4-1	SI	Demo でも
but [less formal than でも]	5-3	Pc	(sentence 1) ga が, (sentence 2)

381

buy	13-3 V1	kaimasu かいます=買います
by (tool)	4-5 P	(tool) de で
by (transportation facility)	7-4 P	(transportation) de で

<C>

cafeteria	4-4 N	kafeteria カフェテリア
camera	15-5 N	kamera カメラ
camp	7-5 N	kyanpu キャンプ
can do well	5-3 Na	tokui とくい=得意
can hear	2-1 V2	kikoemasu きこえます=聞こえます
can see	2-1 V2	miemasu みえます=見えます
candy	2-5 N	ame あめ=飴, kyandii キャンディ
cannot hear	2-1 V2	kikoemasen きこえません=聞こえません
cannot see	2-1 V2	miemasen みえません=見えません
cap	2-3 N	booshi ぼうし=帽子
car	7-4 N	kuruma くるま=車, jidoosha じどうしゃ =自動車
(playing) cards	5-1 N	toranpu トランプ
cat	10-1 N	neko ねこ=猫
cent(s)	13-4 Nd	-sento -セント
chair	10-1 N	isu いす=椅子
cheap	13-5 A	yasui やすい=安い
child	10-2 N	kodomo こども=子供
China	3-4 N	chuugoku ちゅうごく=中国
Chinese language	4-1 N	chuugokugo ちゅうごくご=中国語
chocolate	2-5 N	chokoreeto チョコレート
chopsticks	14-3 N	(o) hashi (お)はし=(お)箸
class	11-2 N	jugyoo じゅぎょう=授業, kurasu クラス
classroom	10-4 N	kyooshitsu きょうしつ=教室
clean	6-5 Na	kirei きれい
clock	13-3 N	tokei とけい=時計
close, near	10-5 A	chikai ちかい=近い
(to) close	13-2 V2	shimemasu しめます=閉めます
(Please) close.	2-2 Exp	shimete kudasai しめてください =閉めて下さい
cockroach	10-5 N	gokiburi ごきぶり
coffee	4-2 N	koohii コーヒー
coffee shop	13-3 N	kissaten きっさてん=喫茶店
cola	4-2 N	koora コーラ
(a) cold	12-1 N	kaze かぜ=風邪
(is) cold	1-7 IA	samui さむい=寒い
(is) cold (to the touch)	14-4 A	tsumetai つめたい=冷たい
college	12-5 N	daigaku だいがく=大学
college student	12-5 N	daigakusei だいがくせい=大学生

E-J 382

color	5-5	N	iro いろ=色
come	7-3	V3	kimasu きます=来ます
company	7-3	N	kaisha かいしゃ=会社
company employee	3-5	N	kaishain かいしゃいん=会社員
computer	4-5	N	konpyuutaa コンピューター
concert	15-2	N	konsaato コンサート
Congratulations.	15-1	Exp	omedetoo gozaimasu. おめでとうございます。
cool [temperature]	1-7	IA	suzushii すずしい=涼しい
cousin	15-2	N	itoko いとこ
cup	14-3	N	koppu コップ
cupful	14-3	Nd	-pai -ぱい=-杯
cute	6-5	A	kawaii かわいい=可愛い

<D>

dance	5-1	N	dansu ダンス
dancing	5-1	N	dansu ダンス
day	15-3	N	hi ひ=日
(the) day after tomorrow	11-4	N	asatte あさって=明後日
(the) day before yesterday	11-4	N	ototoi おととい=一昨日
day of the month	11-1	Nd	-nichi -にち=-日
day off	7-1	N	(o)yasumi (お)やすみ=(お)休み
daytime	4-3	N	(o)hiru (お)ひる=(お)昼
December	3-4	N	juunigatsu じゅうにがつ=十二月
delicious	13-5	A	oishii おいしい=美味しい
department store	7-5	N	depaato デパート
desk	10-1	N	tsukue つくえ=机
dictionary	2-3	N	jisho じしょ=辞書
die	12-1	V1	shinimasu しにます=死にます
difficult	11-3	A	muzukashii むずかしい=難しい
difficult, hard	11-5	Na	taihen たいへん=大変
dine, have a meal	7-5	V3	shokuji(o)shimasu しょくじをします =食事をします
dining	7-5	N	shokuji しょくじ=食事
dinner	4-3	N	bangohan ばんごはん=晩御飯
dirty	6-5	A	kitanai きたない
dish	14-3	N	(o)sara おさら=お皿
dislike	5-2	Na	kirai きらい=嫌い
dislike a lot	5-2	Na	daikirai だいきらい=大嫌い
do	4-4	V3	shimasu します
do one's best	12-4	V1	ganbarimasu がんばります=頑張ります
(medical) doctor	3-5	N	isha いしゃ=医者
(medical) doctor [polite form of いしゃ]	3-5	N	oishasan おいしゃさん=御医者さん
dog	10-1	N	inu いぬ=犬

dollar(s)	13-4	Nd	-doru -ドル
door	10-1	N	doa ドア, to と＝戸
drawing	5-1	N	e え＝絵
(a) drink	5-2	N	nomimono のみもの＝飲み物
(to) drink	4-2	V2	nomimasu のみます＝飲みます

<E>

ear	6-1	N	mimi みみ＝耳
(is) early	7-2	A	hayai はやい＝早い
early [used with a verb]	12-2	Adv	hayaku はやく＝早く
early evening	4-3	N	yuugata ゆうがた＝夕方
easy	11-3	A	yasashii やさしい＝易しい
eat	4-2	V2	tabemasu たべます＝食べます
eight	1-5	N	hachi はち＝八
eight [general counter]	2-5	N	yattsu やっつ＝八つ
eighteen	1-6	N	juu-hachi じゅうはち＝十八
(the) eighth day of the month	11-1	N	yooka ようか＝八日
eighth grader	3-3	N	chuugaku ninensei ちゅうがくにねんせい ＝中学二年生
eighty	1-6	N	hachi-juu はちじゅう＝八十
elderly woman	3-2	N	obaasan おばあさん
elderly man	3-2	N	ojiisan おじいさん
electric train	7-4	N	densha でんしゃ＝電車
eleven	1-6	N	juu-ichi じゅういち＝十一
eleventh grader	3-3	N	kookoo ninensei こうこうにねんせい ＝高校二年生
engineer	3-5	N	enjinia エンジニア
English language	4-1	N	eigo えいご＝英語
enjoyable	11-3	A	tanoshii たのしい＝楽しい
eraser [rubber]	2-3	N	keshigomu けしごむ＝消しゴム
(N1 and N2) etc.	15-3	Nd	(N1) ya (N2) nado (N1) や (N2) などnado
evening	4-3	N	ban ばん＝晩
every month	12-4	N	maitsuki まいつき＝毎月
every week	11-5	N	maishuu まいしゅう＝毎週
every year	15-4	N	maitoshi まいとし＝毎年, mainen まいねん ＝毎年
everyday	4-2	N	mainichi まいにち＝毎日
everyone	15-1	N	minna みんな＝皆
everyone [polite]	15-1	N	minasan みなさん＝皆さん
everything	14-2	N	zenbu ぜんぶ＝全部
exam	2-5	N	shiken しけん＝試験
Excuse me. (aplogy)	1-5	Exp	sumimasen すみません
Excuse me. (to get attention)	13-2	Exp	sumimasen すみません
expensive	13-5	A	takai たかい＝高い

eye	6-1	N	me め=目

\<F\>

face	6-1	N	kao かお=顔
fall (season)	12-4	N	aki あき=秋
(my) family	3-1	N	kazoku かぞく=家族
(someone's) family	3-2	N	gokazoku ごかぞく=御家族
famous	10-4	Na	yuumei ゆうめい=有名
far	10-5	A	tooi とおい=遠い
(is) fat	6-4	V1	futotte imasu ふとっています =太っています
(my) father	3-1	N	chichi ちち=父
(someone's) father	3-2	N	otoosan おとうさん=お父さん
Father's Day	15-3	N	chichi no hi ちちのひ=父の日
February	3-4	N	nigatsu にがつ=二月
female	10-2	N	onna おんな=女
fever	12-1	N	netsu ねつ=熱
few	11-5	A	sukunai すくない=少ない
(a) few	10-3	Adv	sukoshi すこし=少し
fifteen	1-6	N	juu-go じゅうご=十五
(the) fifth day of the month	11-1	N	itsuka いつか=五日
fifty	1-6	N	go-juu ごじゅう=五十
fine, healthy	1-7	Na	(o)genki (お)げんき=(お)元気
finger	6-1	N	yubi ゆび=指
(to) finish	1-4	V	owarimasu おわります=終わります
(the) first day of the month	11-1	N	tsuitachi ついたち=一日
fish	10-3	N	sakana さかな=魚
five	1-5	N	go ご=五
five [general counter]	2-5	N	itsutsu いつつ=五つ
flower	10-3	N	hana はな=花
flower shop	13-3	N	hanaya はなや=花屋
food	5-2	N	tabemono たべもの=食べ物
foot	6-1	N	ashi あし=足
football	5-3	N	futtobooru フットボール
for (activity)	7-3	P	(activity) ni に
for everything	14-2	N	zenbude ぜんぶで=全部で
foreign language	11-2	N	gaikokugo がいこくご=外国語
forget	14-3	V2	wasuremasu わすれます=忘れます
fork	14-3	N	fooku フォーク
forty	1-6	N	yon-juu じょんじゅう=四十
four	1-5	N	shi し=四, yon よん=四
four [general counter]	2-5	N	yottsu よっつ=四つ
fourteen	1-6	N	juu-shi じゅうし=十四, juu-yon じゅうよん =十四

(the) fourteenth day of the month	11-1	N	juu-yokka じゅうよっか＝十四日
(the) fourth day of the month	11-1	N	yokka よっか＝四日
France	3-4	N	furansu フランス
french fries	14-2	N	furaidopoteto フライドポテト
French language	4-1	N	furansugo フランスご＝フランス語
freshman, 9th grader	3-3	N	chuugaku sannensei ちゅうがく さんねんせい＝中学三年生
Friday	7-1	N	kinyoobi きんようび＝金曜日
friend	4-1	N	tomodachi ともだち＝友達
from now on	14-5	SI	korekara これから
from ～	11-2	P	-kara -から
(I am) full.	14-4	Exp	onaka ga ippai desu おなかがいっぱいです ＝お腹が一杯です
fun	11-3	A	tanoshii たのしい＝楽しい

<G>

(sports) game	12-3	N	shiai しあい＝試合
game	15-5	N	geemu ゲーム
garage	10-5	N	gareeji ガレージ
garden	10-5	N	niwa にわ＝庭
German language	4-1	N	doitsugo ドイツご＝ドイツ語
Germany	3-4	N	doitsu ドイツ
get/receive from ～	15-2	V1	～kara/ni moraimasu ～から/に　もらいます
get up	7-3	V2	okimasu おきます＝起きます
girl	10-2	N	onna no ko おんなのこ＝女の子
give (to speaker or to speaker's family)	15-2	V2	kuremasu くれます
give (to equal)	15-3	V2	agemasu あげます
give (to inferior)	15-3	V2	yarimasu やります
glad	11-4	A	ureshii うれしい＝嬉しい
glassful	14-3	Nd	-pai -ぱい＝-杯
go	7-3	V1	ikimasu いきます＝行きます
go to bed	7-3	V2	nemasu ねます＝寝ます
gold color	5-5	N	kiniro きんいろ＝金色
golf	5-3	N	gorufu ゴルフ
good	2-1	IA	ii いい, yoi よい＝良い
(be) good at	5-3	Na	joozu じょうず＝上手
Good evening.	7-2	Exp	konban wa こんばんは＝今晩は
Good luck.	12-4	V1	ganbatte がんばって＝頑張って
Good morning. (Informal)	1-3	Exp	ohayoo. おはよう。
Good morning. (Formal)	1-3	Exp	ohayoo gozaimasu.おはようございます。
Good-bye. (Formal)	1-3	Exp	sayoonara.さようなら。
Good-bye. (Informal)	14-5	Exp	baibai バイバイ
grade	11-4	N	seiseki せいせき＝成績

grandfather	3-2	N	ojiisan おじいさん
grandmother	3-2	N	obaasan おばあさん
green	5-5	N	midori みどり=緑
grey	5-5	N	gurei グレイ
guitar	5-1	N	gitaa ギター

\<H\>

hair	6-1	N	kami(no ke) かみ(のけ)=髪(の毛)
half	7-2	Nd	-han -はん=-半
hamburger	14-2	N	hanbaagaa ハンバーガー
hand	6-1	N	te て=手
happy	11-4	A	ureshii うれしい=嬉しい
hard (difficult)	11-5	Na	taihen たいへん=大変
hat	2-3	N	booshi ぼうし=帽子
hate	5-2	Na	daikirai だいきらい=大嫌い
have	11-2	V1	arimasu あります
head	6-1	N	atama あたま=頭
healthy	1-7	Na	(o)genki (お)げんき=(お)元気
hear	4-4	V1	kikimasu ききます=聞きます
heart	6-1	N	kokoro こころ=心
height	6-1	N	se(i) せ(い)=背
Hello. Hi.	1-3	Exp	konnichi wa.こんにちは。
here	2-5	N	koko ここ
Here.	1-3	Exp	hai はい
Here, please (take it).	2-5	Exp	hai doozo. はい、どうぞ。
high school	3-3	N	kookoo こうこう=高校
high school student	3-3	N	kookoosei こうこうせい=高校生
hindrance	6-5	Na	jama じゃま=邪魔
hobby	5-1	N	shumi しゅみ=趣味
homeroom	11-2	N	hoomuruumu ホームルーム
homework	2-5	N	shukudai しゅくだい=宿題
hospital	3-5	N	byooin びょういん=病院
hot [temperature]	1-7	IA	atsui あつい=暑い
hot and humid	1-7	IA	mushiatsui むしあつい=蒸し暑い
hotdog	14-2	N	hottodoggu ホットドッグ
house	4-1	N	uchi うち=家
housewife	3-5	N	shufu しゅふ=主婦
how about 〜? [Polite exp. of どうですか.]			
	13-5	Ni	Ikaga desu ka? いかがですか=如何ですか
How are you?	1-7	Exp	Ogenki desu ka. おげんきですか。
How disappointing! [on the future event]	11-4	Exp	zannen desu nee ざんねんですねえ =残念ですねえ
How disappointing! [on the past event]	11-4	Exp	zannen deshita nee ざんねんでした ねえ=残念でしたねえ

How do you do?	1-1	Exp	hajimemashite. はじめまして。
How do you say ～ in Japanese?	2-1	Exp	(-wa) nihongo de nan to iimasu ka
			-はにほんごでなんといいますか
			=～は日本語で何と言いますか。
How is it? [informal]	11-3	Exp	doo desu ka どうですか
how many [mechanized goods]?	10-3	Ni	nandai? なんだい=何台
how many [birds]?	10-3	Ni	nanwa? なんわ=何羽
how many [small animals]?	10-3	Ni	nanbiki? なんびき=何匹
how many [long cylindrical objects]?	10-3	Ni	nanbon? なんぼん=何本
how many [bound objects]?	15-2	Ni	nan-satsu? なんさつ=何冊
how many cups?	14-3	Ni	nan-bai? なんばい=何杯
how many people?	3-1	Ni	nan-nin? なんにん=何人
how many? [general counter]	2-5	Ni	ikutsu いくつ
how much? [price]	13-4	Ni	(o)ikura? おいくら
How nice! [on a future event]	11-4	Exp	ii desu nee いいですねえ
How nice! [on a past event]	11-4	Exp	yokatta desu nee よかったですねえ
how old?	3-1	Ni	nan-sai? なんさい=何歳, 何才,
			(o)ikutsu? (お)いくつ
How pitiful.	12-1	Exp	kawaisoo ni かわいそうに=可愛そうに
hundred	1-6	N	hyaku ひゃく=百
hundred thousand	13-4	N	juu-man じゅうまん=十万
(I am) hungry.	14-1	Exp	onaka ga pekopeko desu
			おなかがペコペコです
			=お腹がペコペコです
(I got) hungry.	14-1	Exp	onaka ga sukimashita おなかがすきました
			=お腹が空きました
Hurry!	1-4	Exp	hayaku はやく

<I>

I (used by anyone informally)	1-1	N	watashi わたし=私
I (used by males)	1-1	N	boku ぼく=僕
illness	12-1	N	byooki びょうき=病気
important	12-4	Na	daiji だいじ=大事
in (location)	10-1	P	(location) ni に
in [tool particle]	4-5	P	(tool) de で
in (place) [with action verb]	4-1	P	(place) de で [with action verb]
instruction	11-2	N	jugyoo じゅぎょう=授業, kurasu クラス
interesting	11-3	A	omoshiroi おもしろい=面白い
intermediate school	3-3	N	chuugaku ちゅうがく=中学
intermediate school student	3-3	N	chuugakusei ちゅうがくせい=中学生
(is) in the way	6-5	Na	jama じゃま=邪魔
is (noun)	1-1	C	(noun) desu です
(It) is not so. [formal]	1-6	Exp	soo dewa arimasen そうではありません
(It) is not so. [informal]	1-6	Exp	soo ja arimasen そうじゃありません

English	Lesson	Type	Japanese
isn't it? [sentence ending particle]	6-5	SP	ne ね
(Yes,) it is.	1-6	Exp	soo desu そうです

<J>

English	Lesson	Type	Japanese
jacket	13-3	N	jaketto ジャケット
January	3-4	N	ichigatsu いちがつ=一月
Japan	3-4	N	nihon にほん=日本
Japanese citizen	3-4	N	nihonjin にほんじん=日本人
Japanese language	4-1	N	nihongo にほんご=日本語
job	3-5	N	(o)shigoto (お)しごと=(お)仕事
jogging	5-1	N	jogingu ジョギング
juice	4-2	N	juusu ジュース
July	3-4	N	shichigatsu しちがつ=七月
June	3-4	N	rokugatsu ろくがつ=六月
junior	3-3	N	kookoo ninensei こうこうにねんせい=高校二年生

<K>

English	Lesson	Type	Japanese
kind	6-4	A	yasashii やさしい=優しい
knife	14-3	N	naifu ナイフ
Korea	3-4	N	kankoku かんこく=韓国
Korean language	4-1	N	kankokugo かんこくご=韓国語
(do not) know	2-1	V1	shirimasen しりません=知りません

<L>

English	Lesson	Type	Japanese
lady	10-2	N	onna no hito おんなのひと=女の人
large size	14-2	N	eru-saizu エルサイズ
last month	12-4	N	sengetsu せんげつ=先月
last night	12-2	N	yuube ゆうべ=夕べ
last week	11-5	N	senshuu せんしゅう=先週
last year	15-4	N	kyonen きょねん=去年
(is) late	7-2	A	osoi おそい=遅い
late [used with a verb]	12-2	Adv	osoku おそく=遅く
late afternoon	4-3	N	yuugata ゆうがた=夕方
lawyer	3-5	N	bengoshi べんごし=弁護士
leg	6-1	N	ashi あし=脚
(Please) lend me.	14-3	V1	kashite kudasai かしてください=貸して下さい
Let me see . . .	2-1	SI	eeto... ええと..., anoo... あのう.., soo desu nee... そうですねえ...
Let's begin.	1-4	Exp	hajimemashoo はじめましょう=始めましょう
let's do 〜. [suggestion]	7-1	Dv	-mashoo -ましょう
Let's finish.	1-4	Exp	owarimashoo おわりましょう=終わりましょう
letter	4-5	N	tegami てがみ=手紙

library	4-4	N	toshokan としょかん=図書館
like	5-2	Na	suki すき=好き
like very much	5-2	Na	daisuki だいすき=大好き
listen	4-4	V1	kikimasu ききます=聞きます
(Please) listen.	2-2	Exp	kiite kudasai きいてください =聞いて下さい
(a) little [formal]	4-1	Adv	sukoshi すこし=少し
(a) little [more colloquial than すこし]	4-1	Adv	chotto ちょっと
(is) little	11-5	A	sukunai すくない=少ない
locker	10-4	N	rokkaa ロッカー
long	6-2	A	nagai ながい=長い
look	4-5	V2	mimasu みます=見ます
(Please) look.	2-2	Exp	mite kudasai みてください=見て下さい
(I am) looking forward to 〜.	15-4	Exp	(-o) tanoshimi ni shite imasu (-を)たのしみにしています =(-を)楽しみにしています
(to) lose	12-3	V2	makemasu まけます=負けます
(a) lot	10-3	Adv	takusan たくさん=沢山
love	5-2	Na	daisuki だいすき=大好き
lunch	4-3	N	hirugohan ひるごはん=昼御飯

\<M\>

magazine	4-4	N	zasshi ざっし=雑誌
make	15-5	V1	tsukurimasu つくります=作ります
male	10-2	N	otoko おとこ=男
man	10-2	N	otoko no hito おとこのひと=男の人
many (with a verb)	10-3	Adv	takusan たくさん=沢山
(are) many	11-5	A	ooi おおい=多い
March	3-4	N	sangatsu さんがつ=三月
math	11-2	N	suugaku すうがく=数学
May	3-4	N	gogatsu ごがつ=五月
meal	7-5	N	shokuji しょくじ=食事
(have a) meal	7-5	V3	shokuji(o)shimasu しょくじをします =食事をします
medicine	12-2	N	kusuri くすり=薬
medium size	14-2	N	emu-saizu エムサイズ
meet	12-5	V1	aimasu あいます=会います
messy	6-5	A	kitanai きたない
middle aged woman	15-2	N	obasan おばさん
middle aged man	15-2	N	ojisan おじさん
(cow's) milk	4-2	N	gyuunyuu ぎゅうにゅう=牛乳, miruku ミルク
(one) million	13-4	N	hyaku-man ひゃくまん=百万
mine	2-4	N	watashino わたしの=私の

-minute	7-2	Nd	-fun -ふん=-分
Monday	7-1	N	getsuyoobi げつようび=月曜日
money	2-3	N	(o)kane (お)かね=(お)金
(one) more (cup)	14-4	Adv	moo (ippai)もう(いっぱい)=もう(一杯)
Moreover	11-5	SI	Soreni それに
morning	4-3	N	asa あさ=朝
(my) mother	3-1	N	haha はは=母
(someone's) mother	3-2	N	okaasan おかあさん=お母さん
Mother's Day	15-3	N	haha no hi ははのひ=母の日
mountain	7-5	N	yama やま=山
mouse	10-5	N	nezumi ねずみ=鼠
moustache	6-1	N	hige ひげ=髭
mouth	6-1	N	kuchi くち=口
movie	5-1	N	eiga えいが=映画
Mr./Mrs./Ms.	1-3	Nd	-san -さん
Mr./Mrs./Ms./Dr. (teacher, doctor, statesman)			
	1-3	N	sensei せんせい=先生
(are) much	11-5	A	ooi おおい=多い
music	5-1	N	ongaku おんがく=音楽

<N>

name	3-1	N	namae なまえ=名前
(someone's) name	3-2	N	(o) namae おなまえ=御名前
napkin	14-3	N	napukin ナプキン
narrow	10-5	A	semai せまい=狭い
near	10-5	A	chikai ちかい=近い
neat	6-5	Na	kirei きれい
neck	6-1	N	kubi くび=首
need 〜	14-3	V1	(〜ga) irimasu (〜が)いります=要ります
new	10-4	A	atarashii あたらしい=新しい
newspaper	4-4	N	shinbun しんぶん=新聞
next	11-3	N	tsugi つぎ=次
next month	12-4	N	raigetsu らいげつ=来月
next week	11-5	N	raishuu らいしゅう=来週
next year	15-4	N	rainen らいねん=来年
nice	6-4	A	yasashii やさしい=優しい
nice	6-5	Na	kirei きれい
Nice to meet you.	1-1	N	doozo yoroshiku. どうぞよろしく。
night	4-3	N	yoru よる=夜
nine	1-5	N	ku く=九
nine	1-5	N	kyuu きゅう=九
nine [general counter]	2-5	N	kokonotsu ここのつ=九つ
nineteen	1-6	N	juu-ku じゅうく=十九,
			juu-kyuu じゅうきゅう=十九

(the) ninth day of the month	11-1	N	kokonoka ここのか＝九日
ninth grader	3-3	N	chuugaku sannensei
			ちゅうがくさんねんせい＝中学三年生
ninety	1-6	N	kyuu-juu きゅうじゅう＝九十
no [informal]	1-6	SI	ee ええ
no [formal]	1-6	SI	iie いいえ
no good	2-1	Na	dame だめ
No, thank you.	14-3	Exp	Iie, kekkoo desu いいえ、けっこうです
noisy	6-5	A	urusai うるさい
nose	6-1	N	hana はな＝鼻
not yet	14-1	Exp	mada desu (+neg.) まだです
notebook	2-3	N	nooto ノート
November	3-4	N	juuichigatsu じゅういちがつ＝十一月
now	3-5	N	ima いま＝今
nuisance	6-5	Na	jama じゃま＝邪魔

\<O\>

-o'clock	7-2	Nd	-ji -じ＝-時
ocean	7-5	N	umi うみ＝海
October	3-4	N	juugatsu じゅうがつ＝十月
office	10-4	N	jimusho じむしょ＝事務所
often	4-1	Adv	yoku よく
(is) old (age)	6-4	V1	toshi o totteimasu としをとっています
			＝年を取っています
old (not for person's age)	10-4	A	furui ふるい＝古い
(my) older brother	3-1	N	ani あに＝兄
(someone's) older brother	3-2	N	oniisan おにいさん＝お兄さん
(my) older sister	3-1	N	ane あね＝姉
(someone's) older sister	3-2	N	oneesan おねえさん＝お姉さん
one	1-5	N	ichi いち＝一
one [general counter]	2-5	N	hitotsu ひとつ＝一つ
one (person)	3-1	N	hitori ひとり＝一人
one more time	1-5	Adv	mooichido もういちど＝もう一度
open	13-2	V2	akemasu あけます＝開けます
(Please) open.	2-2	Exp	Akete kudasai あけてください
			＝開けて下さい
Or	6-4	SI	Soretomo それとも
orange (color)	5-5	N	orenji(iro) オレンジいろ＝オレンジ色
outside	10-1	N	soto そと＝外
over there	2-5	N	asoko あそこ

\<P\>

P.E.	11-2	N	taiiku たいいく＝体育
p.m.	7-2	N	gogo ごご＝午後
painful	12-1	A	itai いたい＝痛い

painting	5-1	N	e え=絵
pants	13-3	N	pantsu パンツ
paper	2-3	N	kami かみ=紙
paper (report)	4-5	N	repooto レポート
party	7-5	N	paatii パーティー
pencil	2-3	N	enpitsu えんぴつ=鉛筆
pencil sharpener	10-1	N	enpitsukezuri えんぴつけずり=鉛筆削り
person	10-2	N	hito ひと=人
person [polite form of ひと]	10-2	Nd	-kata -かた=-方
photo	2-3	N	shashin しゃしん=写真
piano	5-1	N	piano ピアノ
picnic	7-5	N	pikunikku ピクニック
pig	10-5	N	buta ぶた=豚
pink	5-5	N	pinku ピンク
pizza	14-2	N	piza ピザ
plate	14-3	N	(o)sara おさら=お皿
play (for fun)	15-5	V1	asobimasu あそびます=遊びます
play a game	15-5	V3	geemu(o)shimasu ゲーム(を)します
play (sports)	15-5	V3	shimasu します
Please. [request]	1-5	Exp	onegaishimasu おねがいします =御願いします
Please give me ～.	2-5	Exp	(-o)kudasai -をください
(Here) please (take it).	2-5	Exp	hai doozo. はい、どうぞ
pond	10-3	N	ike いけ=池
pool	10-2	N	puuru プール
(be) poor at	5-3	Na	heta へた=下手
(to) practice	12-5	V3	renshuu(o)shimasu れんしゅう(を)します =練習(を)します
(a) present	15-1	N	purezento プレゼント
pretty	6-5	Na	kirei きれい
purple	5-5	N	murasaki むらさき=紫
<Q>			
quiet	6-5	Na	shizuka しずか=静か
(to) quiet down	13-2	V3	shizuka ni shimasu しずかにします =静かにします
(Please be) quiet.	2-2	Exp	shizukani shite kudasai しずかにしてください=静かにして下さい
quiz	2-5	N	shootesuto しょうテスト=小テスト
<R>			
radio	4-5	N	rajio ラジオ
rain	1-7	N	ame あめ=雨
read	4-4	V1	yomimasu よみます=読みます
(Please) read.	2-2	Exp	yonde kudasai よんでください=読んで下さい

reading	5-1	N	dokusho どくしょ=読書
receive	15-2	V1	moraimasu もらいます
red color	5-5	N	aka あか=赤
(is) red	6-3	A	akai あかい=赤い
relatives	15-2	N	shinseki しんせき=親戚
report	4-5	N	repooto レポート
(to) rest	12-2	V2	yasumimasu やすみます=休みます
restaurant	7-5	N	resutoran レストラン
restroom	10-2	N	(o)toire (お)トイレ, (o)tearai (お)てあらい =(お)手洗い
return (place)	7-3	V1	kaerimasu かえります=帰ります
(cooked) rice	4-2	N	gohan ごはん=ご飯
riceball	14-2	N	(o)musubi おむすび, (o)nigiri おにぎり
river	7-5	N	kawa かわ=川
room	10-5	N	heya へや=部屋
rubbish	2-3	N	gomi ごみ
(to) run	12-5	V1	hashirimasu はしります=走ります

<S>

sad	11-4	A	kanashii かなしい=悲しい
salad	14-2	N	sarada サラダ
sandwich	14-2	N	sandoitchi サンドイッチ
Saturday	7-1	N	doyoobi どようび=土曜日
say	13-2	V1	iimasu いいます=言います
Say "cheese".	15-5	Exp	hai, chiizu はい、チーズ
Say "peace".	15-5	Exp	hai, piisu はい、ピース
school	3-3	N	gakkoo がっこう=学校
science	11-2	N	kagaku かがく=科学
sea	7-5	N	umi うみ=海
(the) second day of the month	11-1	N	futsuka ふつか=二日
see	4-5	V2	mimasu みます=見ます
(Well then,) see you later.	14-5	Exp	(ja) mata ato de (じゃ)またあとで
(high school) senior	3-3	N	kookoo sannensei こうこうさんねんせい =高校三年生
September	3-4	N	kugatsu くがつ=九月
seven	1-5	N	shichi しち=七, nana なな=七
seven [general counter]	2-5	N	nanatsu ななつ=七つ
seventeen	1-6	N	juu-shichi じゅうしち, juu-nana じゅうなな=十七
(the) seventh day of the month	11-1	N	nanoka なのか=七日
seventh grader	3-3	N	chuugaku ichinensei ちゅうがくいちねんせい=中学一年生
seventy	1-6	N	nana-juu ななじゅう, shichi-juu しちじゅう=七十

English	Lesson	Type	Japanese
ship	7-4	N	fune ふね=船
shirt	13-3	N	shatsu シャツ
shoes	13-3	N	kutsu くつ=靴
shop	7-5	V3	kaimono(o)shimasu かいものをします =買い物をします
shopping	7-5	N	kaimono かいもの=買い物
short (height)	6-1	A	hikui ひくい=低い
short [not for height]	6-2	A	mijikai みじかい=短い
(to) show	13-2	V2	misemasu みせます=見せます
(Please) show.	2-2	Exp	misete kudasai みせてください =見せて下さい
(my) sibling(s)	3-1	N	kyoodai きょうだい=兄弟
sickness	12-1	N	byooki びょうき=病気
silver color	5-5	N	giniro ぎんいろ=銀色
since (reason)	11-4	Pc	(reason) kara, (reason) から
sing	15-1	V1	utaimasu うたいます=歌います
singing	5-1	N	uta うた=歌
sit	13-2	V1	suwarimasu すわります=座ります
(Please) sit.	2-2	Exp	suwatte kudasai すわってください =座って下さい
Sit. [ceremony]	1-4	Exp	chakuseki ちゃくせき=着席
six	1-5	N	roku ろく=六
six [general counter]	2-5	N	muttsu むっつ=六つ
sixteen	1-6	N	juu-roku じゅうろく=十六
(the) sixth day of the month	11-1	N	muika むいか=六日
sixty	1-6	N	roku-juu ろくじゅう=六十
size	14-2	N	saizu サイズ
skillful	5-3	Na	joozu じょうず=上手
sleep	7-3	V2	nemasu ねます=寝ます
sleepy	12-2	A	nemui ねむい=眠い
slowly	1-5	Adv	yukkuri ゆっくり
small	6-2	A	chiisai ちいさい=小さい
small (room)	10-5	A	semai せまい=狭い
small size	14-2	N	esu-saizu エスサイズ
snack bar	4-4	N	sunakkubaa スナックバー
so, so	5-4	Adv	maamaa まあまあ
(sentence 1,) so (sentence 2).	11-4	Pc	(reason) kara から, (result)
soccer	5-3	N	sakkaa サッカー
social studies	11-2	N	shakai しゃかい=社会
sometimes	4-2	Adv	tokidoki ときどき=時々
song	5-1	N	uta うた=歌
sophomore, 10th grader	3-3	N	kookoo ichinensei こうこういちねんせい =高校一年生

sore	12-1 A	itai いたい=痛い
(Is that) so?	3-1 Exp	soo desuka そうですか
so, so	5-4 Adv	maamaa まあまあ
spacious	10-5 A	hiroi ひろい=広い
Spain	3-4 N	supein スペイン
Spanish language	4-1 N	supeingo スペインご=スペイン語
speak	4-1 V1	hanashimasu はなします=話します
spoon	14-3 N	supuun スプーン
spoonful	14-3 Nd	-pai -ぱい=-杯
sports	5-1 N	supootsu スポーツ
spring	12-4 N	haru はる=春
Stand. [ceremony]	1-4 Exp	kiritsu きりつ=起立
(to) stand	13-2 V1	tachimasu たちます=立ちます
(Please) stand.	2-2 Exp	tatte kudasai たってください=立って下さい
stomach	6-1 N	onaka おなか=お腹
store	13-2 N	(o)mise (お)みせ=(お)店
straw	14-3 N	sutoroo ストロー
strict	6-4 A	kibishii きびしい=厳しい
strong	12-3 A	tsuyoi つよい=強い
(be) strong in	5-3 Na	tokui とくい=得意
student [non-college]	3-3 N	seito せいと=生徒
student [college]	3-3 N	gakusei がくせい=学生
(to) study	4-4 V3	benkyoo (o) shimasu べんきょう=勉強(を)します
subject	11-2 N	kamoku かもく=科目
subway	7-4 N	chikatetsu ちかてつ=地下鉄
summer	12-4 N	natsu なつ=夏
Sunday	7-1 N	nichiyoobi にちようび=日曜日
supermarket	13-3 N	suupaa スーパー
supper	4-3 N	bangohan ばんごはん=晩御飯
sushi shop/bar	13-3 N	sushiya すしや=寿司屋
swim	15-5 V1	oyogimasu およぎます=泳ぎます
swimming	5-1 N	suiei すいえい=水泳

\<T\>

TV	4-5 N	terebi テレビ
take	15-5 V1	torimasu とります=取ります
take (medicine)	12-2 V1	nomimasu のみます=飲みます
talk	4-1 V1	hanashimasu はなします=話します
tall	6-1 A	takai たかい=高い
tape	4-4 N	teepu テープ
tardy	1-4 Exp	chikoku desu ちこくです=遅刻です
taxi	7-4 N	takushii タクシー
tea	4-2 N	ocha おちゃ=お茶

teacher	1-3	N	sensei せんせい=先生
team	12-3	N	chiimu チーム
telephone	4-5	N	denwa でんわ=電話
telephone number	15-4	N	denwabangoo でんわばんごう=電話番号
ten	1-5	N	juu じゅう=十
ten [general counter]	2-5	N	too とお=十
ten thousand	13-4	N	(ichi)man (いち)まん=(一)万
tennis	5-3	N	tenisu テニス
(the) tenth day of the month	11-1	N	tooka とおか=十日
tenth grader	3-3	N	kookoo ichinensei こうこういちねんせい =高校一年生
terrible	11-4	A	hidoi ひどい=酷い
terrific	13-5	A	sugoi すごい=凄い
textbook	2-3	N	kyookasho きょうかしょ=教科書, tekisuto テキスト
Thank you very much.	1-5	Exp	arigatoo gozaimasu ありがとうございます
Thank you.	1-5	Exp	Doomo どうも, Arigatoo ありがとう
that one	1-6	N	sore それ
that one over there	1-6	N	are あれ
that ～	2-4	PN	sono ～その～
that ～ over there	2-4	PN	ano～ あの～
there	2-5	N	soko そこ
there is (animate object)	10-1	V2	imasu います
there is (inanimate object)	10-1	V1	arimasu あります
thin	6-4	V2	yasete imasu やせています=痩せています
thing [tangible]	5-2	N	mono もの=物
thing [intangible]	5-3	N	koto こと=事
(the) third day of the month	11-1	N	mikka みっか=三日
(I am) thirsty.	14-1	Exp	nodo ga karakara desu のどがカラカラです =喉がカラカラです
(I got) thirsty.	14-1	Exp	nodo ga kawakimashita のどがかわきました =喉が渇きました
thirteen	1-6	N	juu-san じゅうさん=十三
thirty	1-6	N	san-juu さんじゅう=三十
this month	12-4	N	kongetsu こんげつ=今月
this morning	12-2	N	kesa けさ=今朝
this one	1-2	N	kore これ
this one [polite form of これ]	3-4	N	kochira こちら
this week	11-5	N	konshuu こんしゅう=今週
this year	15-4	N	kotoshi ことし=今年
this ～	2-4	PN	kono ～この～
thousand	13-4	N	sen せん=千
three	1-5	N	san さん=三

three [general counter]	2-5	N	mittsu みっつ=三つ
throat	6-1	N	nodo のど=喉
Thursday	7-1	N	mokuyoobi もくようび=木曜日
ticket	15-2	N	kippu きっぷ=切符
(be) tired	12-2	V2	tsukarete imasu つかれています =疲れています
(got) tired	12-2	V2	tsukaremashita つかれました=疲れました
tissue	2-5	N	tisshu ティッシュ
to (place)	7-3	P	(place) e へ, (place) ni に
today	4-3	N	kyoo きょう=今日
toe	6-1	N	yubi ゆび=指
together	4-4	Adv	issho ni いっしょに=一緒に
tomorrow	4-3	N	ashita あした=明日
tonight	7-2	N	konban こんばん=今晩
tooth	6-1	N	ha は=歯
(from～) to～	11-2	P	(～kara) -made (～から)-まで
trash can	10-1	N	gomibako ごみばこ=ごみ箱
(to) travel	7-5	V3	ryokoo(o)shimasu りょこうをします =旅行をします
traveling	7-5	N	ryokoo りょこう=旅行
tree	10-3	N	ki き=木
trip	7-5	N	ryokoo りょこう=旅行
true	3-1	N	hontoo ほんとう=本当
Tuesday	7-1	N	kayoobi かようび=火曜日
turn in	13-2	V1	dashimasu だします=出します
(Please) turn in.	2-2	Exp	dashite kudasai だしてください =出して下さい
twelve	1-6	N	juu-ni じゅうに=十二
twelvth grader	3-3	N	kookoo sannensei こうこうさんねんせい =高校三年生
twenty	1-6	N	ni-juu にじゅう=二十
(the) twenty fourth day of the month	11-1	N	nijuu-yokka にじゅうよっか=二十四日
twenty years old	3-1	N	hatachi はたち=二十歳
(the) twentith day of the month	11-1	N	hatsuka はつか=二十日
two	1-5	N	ni に=二
two [general counter]	2-5	N	futatsu ふたつ=二つ
two (persons)	3-1	N	futari ふたり=二人
type	4-5	V3	taipu(o)shimasu タイプ(を)します

<U>

U.S. citizen	3-4	N	amerikajin アメリカじん=アメリカ人
unappetizing	13-5	A	mazui まずい
uncle	15-2	N	ojisan おじさん
understand	2-1	V1	wakarimasu わかります=分かります

(do not) understand	2-1	V1	wakarimasen わかりません＝分かりません
uninteresting	11-3	A	tsumaranai つまらない
university	12-5	N	daigaku だいがく＝大学
unskillful	5-3	Na	heta へた＝下手
untasty	13-5	A	mazui まずい
usually	4-2	Adv	taitei たいてい＝大抵
<V>			
vacation	7-1	N	(o)yasumi (お)やすみ＝(お)休み
vehicle	7-4	N	kuruma くるま＝車, jidoosha じどうしゃ ＝自動車
very	5-4	Adv	totemo とても
(not) very	5-4	Adv	amari あまり
very soon	15-3	Adv	moo sugu もうすぐ
video	4-5	N	bideo ビデオ
video game	5-1	N	terebigeemu テレビゲーム
voice	6-1	N	koe こえ＝声
volleyball	5-3	N	baree(booru) バレー(ボール)
<W>			
wait	13-2	V1	machimasu まちます＝待ちます
(Please) wait a minute.	1-5	Exp	chotto matte kudasai ちょっとまってください ＝ちょっと待って下さい
wake up	7-3	V2	okimasu おきます＝起きます
walk	7-4	V1	aruite <arukimasu> あるいて＝歩いて
walkman	4-4	N	wookuman ウォークマン
want (something)	11-5	A	(something が) hoshii ほしい＝欲しい
want (to do)	12-2	Da	(verb stem form)-tai -たい
warm	14-4	A	atatakai あたたかい＝暖かい
(to) watch	4-5	V2	mimasu みます＝見ます
(a) watch	13-3	N	tokei とけい＝時計
water	4-2	N	(o)mizu (お)みず＝(お)水
we	12-3	N	watashitachi わたしたち＝私達
we [Used by males.]	12-3	N	bokutachi ぼくたち＝僕達
weak	12-3	A	yowai よわい＝弱い
(be) weak in	5-3	Na	nigate にがて＝苦手
weather	1-7	N	(o)tenki (お)てんき＝(お)天気
Wednesday	7-1	N	suiyoobi すいようび＝水曜日
weekend	11-5	N	shuumatsu しゅうまつ＝週末
well	4-1	Adv	yoku よく
Well done.	2-2	Exp	yoku dekimashita よくできました ＝良く出来ました
Well then [informal]	14-1	Exp	ja じゃ
Well then [formal]	14-1	Exp	dewa では

English	Ref	Type	Japanese
Well . . .	2-1	SI	eeto... ええと..., anoo... あのう...
(You are) welcome.	1-5	Exp	dooitashimashite どういたしまして
what color?	5-5	N	naniiro? なにいろ=何色
(the) what day of the month?	11-1	Ni	nan-nichi? なんにち=何日
what day of the week?	7-1	Ni	nan-yoobi? なんようび=何曜日
what grade?	3-3	N	nan-nensei? なんねんせい=何年生
What happened?	12-1	Exp	doo shimashita ka どうしましたか
what kind of 〜?	5-2	PN	donna〜? どんな〜
what language?	4-1	Ni	nanigo? なにご=何語
what month?	3-4	Ni	nan-gatsu? なんがつ=何月
what nationality?	3-4	Ni	nani-jin? なにじん=何人
what time?	7-2	Ni	nanji? なんじ=何時
what?	1-4	Ni	nani なに=何, nan なん=何
when?	7-1	Ni	itsu? いつ
where?	3-4	Ni	doko どこ
which one?	13-4	Ni	dore? どれ
which 〜?	13-4	Nd	dono-? どの-
white color	5-5	N	shiro しろ=白
(is) white	6-3	A	shiroi しろい=白い
who?	3-1	Ni	dare? だれ=誰
why?	11-4	Ni	naze? なぜ, dooshite? どうして
wide	10-5	A	hiroi ひろい=広い
win	12-3	V1	kachimasu かちます=勝ちます
window	10-1	N	mado まど=窓
winter	12-4	N	fuyu ふゆ=冬
with (tool)	4-5	P	(tool) de で
with (person)	4-4	P	to (issho ni) と(いっしょに)
woman	10-2	N	onna no hito おんなのひと=女の人
won't you do 〜? [invitation]	7-1	Dv	-masen ka -ませんか
wonderful	13-5	A	subarashii すばらしい=素晴らしい
worksheet	2-5	N	waakushiito ワークシート
Wow!	13-5	SI	waa わあ
write	4-5	V1	kakimasu かきます=書きます
(Please) write.	2-2	Exp	kaite kudasai かいてください =書いて下さい

<y>

English	Ref	Type	Japanese
(a) yard	10-5	N	niwa にわ=庭
-year	15-4	Nd	-nen -ねん=-年
yellow color	5-5	N	kiiro きいろ=黄色
(is) yellow	6-3	A	kiiroi きいろい=黄色い
yen	13-4	Nd	-en -えん=-円
Yes	1-6	SI	hai はい
yesterday	4-3	N	kinoo きのう=昨日

you	2-4	N	anata あなた
You are welcome.	1-5	Exp	dooitashimashite どういたしまして
you know [sentence ending particle]	6-5	SP	yo よ
young	6-4	A	wakai わかい＝若い
(my) younger brother	3-1	N	otooto おとうと＝弟
(someone's) younger brother	3-2	N	otootosan おとうとさん＝弟さん
(my) younger sister	3-1	N	imooto いもうと＝妹
(someone's) younger sister	3-2	N	imootosan いもうとさん＝妹さん
yours	2-4	N	anatano あなたの＝あなたの

HIRAGANA

W	R	Y	M	H	N	T	S	K	
ん n	わ	ら	や	ま	は	な	た	さ	か	あ	A
		り		み	ひ	に	ち chi	し shi	き	い	I
		る	ゆ	む	ふ	ぬ	つ tsu	す	く	う	U
		れ		め	へ	ね	て	せ	け	え	E
	を o	ろ	よ	も	ほ	の	と	そ	こ	お	O

(particle)

P	B	D	Z	G	
ぱ	ば	だ	ざ	が	A
ぴ	び	ぢ ji	じ ji	ぎ	I
ぷ	ぶ	づ zu	ず zu	ぐ	U
ぺ	べ	で	ぜ	げ	E
ぽ	ぼ	ど	ぞ	ご	O

KATAKANA

	W	R	Y	M	H	N	T	S	K		
ン n	ワ	ラ	ヤ	マ	ハ	ナ	タ	サ	カ	ア	A
		リ		ミ	ヒ	ニ	チ chi	シ shi	キ	イ	I
		ル	ユ	ム	フ	ヌ	ツ tsu	ス	ク	ウ	U
		レ		メ	ヘ	ネ	テ	セ	ケ	エ	E
	ヲ o	ロ	ヨ	モ	ホ	ノ	ト	ソ	コ	オ	O

(particle)

P	B	D	Z	G	
パ	バ	ダ	ザ	ガ	A
ピ	ビ	ヂ ji	ジ ji	ギ	I
プ	ブ	ヅ zu	ズ zu	グ	U
ペ	ベ	デ	ゼ	ゲ	E
ポ	ボ	ド	ゾ	ゴ	O

403

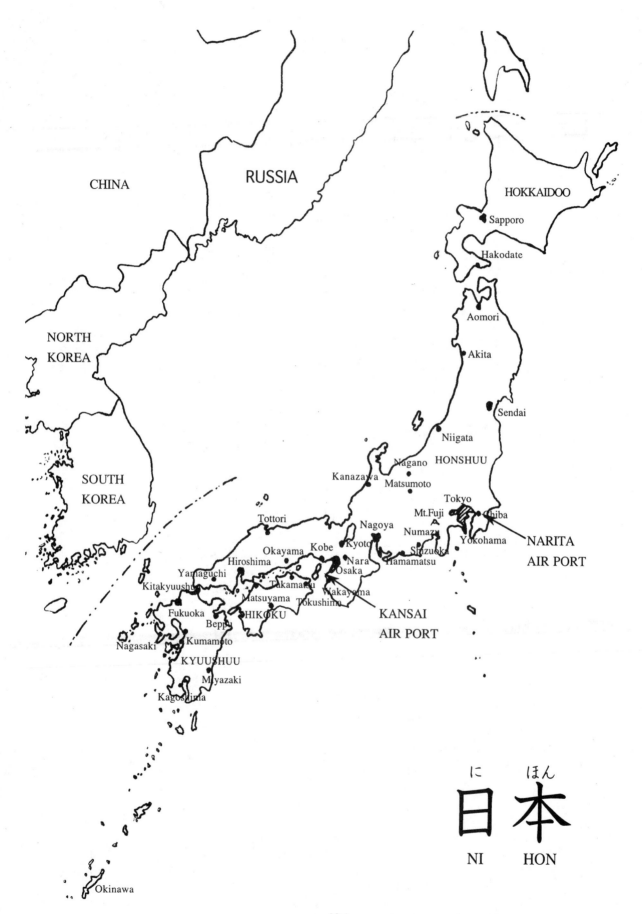

CHINA

RUSSIA

HOKKAIDOO

Sapporo

Hakodate

NORTH
KOREA

Aomori

Akita

Sendai

Niigata

Nagano

HONSHUU

SOUTH
KOREA

Kanazawa

Matsumoto

Tokyo

Tottori

Nagoya

Mt.Fuji

Chiba

Numazu

Yokohama

NARITA
AIR PORT

Okayama

Kobe

Kyoto

Hiroshima

Nara

Shizuoka

Yamaguchi

Osaka

Hamamatsu

Kitakyuushuu

Takamatsu

Wakayama

Matsuyama

Tokushima

KANSAI
AIR PORT

Fukuoka

SHIKOKU

Beppu

Nagasaki

Kumamoto

KYUUSHUU

Miyazaki

Kagoshima

に　　　　ほん
日本
NI　HON

Okinawa

404